IMAGES
of Rail

SOUTHERN RAILWAY'S HISTORIC SPENCER SHOPS

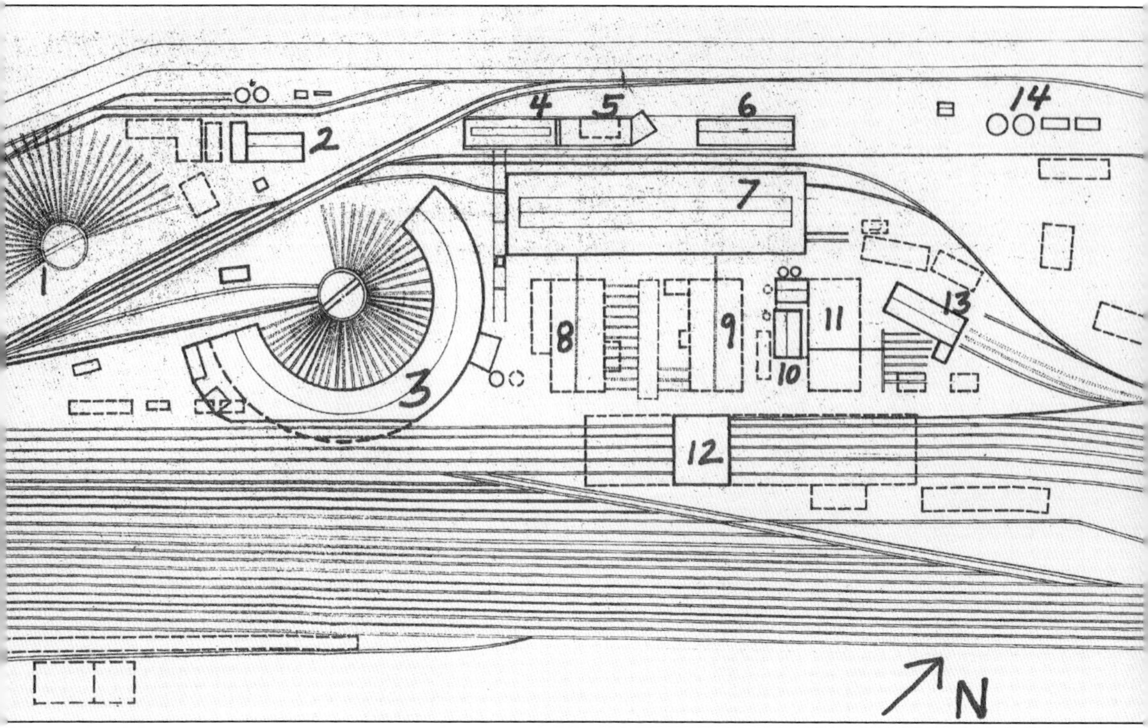

The following buildings belonged to the Spencer Shops: 1. the additional turntable; 2. oil house; 3. 1924 roundhouse and turntable; 4. flue shop; 5. warehouse No. 3; 6. master mechanic's office; 7. back shop; 8. machine shop and transfer table; 9. boiler shop; 10. powerhouse; 11. woodworking shop; 12. car repair shed; 13. tender repair shop, later rebuilt as a paint shop; and 14. fire suppression water tanks. The buildings with the dotted lines were razed during the 1960s. (Historic American Engineering Record, National Park Service, delineated by Michele Lewis and Patti Stammer, 1977. North Carolina Transportation Museum Collection.)

On the Cover: Here is one of the early locomotive types serviced at Spencer Shops. In 1907, Baldwin Locomotive Works manufactured Ps-class 4-6-2 Pacific No. 1211, which was used to pull passenger trains between Washington, DC, and Atlanta. These larger locomotives required the Southern to continue improving and updating Spencer Shops to meet the demands of modern steam power. (North Carolina Division of Archives and History.)

IMAGES
of Rail

SOUTHERN RAILWAY'S HISTORIC SPENCER SHOPS

Larry K. Neal Jr.
Foreword by Jim Wrinn

ARCADIA
PUBLISHING

Copyright © 2011 by the North Carolina Transportation Museum Foundation
ISBN 978-0-7385-8780-6

Published by Arcadia Publishing
Charleston, South Carolina

Printed in the United States of America

Library of Congress Control Number: 2011923575

For all general information, please contact Arcadia Publishing:
Telephone 843-853-2070
Fax 843-853-0044
E-mail sales@arcadiapublishing.com
For customer service and orders:
Toll-Free 1-888-313-2665

Visit us on the Internet at www.arcadiapublishing.com

Contents

FOREWORD

Work history often goes neglected. Employers traditionally go to great lengths to make sure that labor under dangerous or dirty conditions is hidden from view. Toil amidst sweat and grime is rarely documented for the sake of history. But jobs such as these are often among the most fascinating subjects because of the difficult conditions under which they take place. These are the crucibles of commerce where the most basic components of our daily lives are forged, hammered, and riveted into the objects that make up our world. Transportation is chief among them.

The public has lauded the work of American railroaders for almost two centuries. The sights, sounds, and scents of a steam locomotive can breed excitement in the heart and soul of anyone who understands what an amazingly human machine this is. So does the excitement of travel, of exploration, of seeing what's around the next bend. Because of this fascination with railroading, every child knows the story of the brave engineer, Casey Jones, who died trying to save his passengers from an unavoidable crash. Every adult knows the appearance of the dainty 19th-century locomotives that joined the nation with the completion of first transcontinental railroad. To this day, the colorful red, black, and yellow Santa Fe Railway logo is still among one of the most recognizable business trademarks in the land.

Behind the shiny locomotives, the sleek passenger trains, or the manly freights that the public saw were thousands of unsung workers in places like the Southern Railway's Spencer Shops. They welded, scraped, machined, polished, riveted, and performed a thousand and one other messy, difficult, physical tasks that it took to overhaul and run engines. In oily coveralls, they went to work every day to put together hundreds of steam locomotives that moved the majority of the region's freight and passengers in the age before good roads or jet planes. By helping the region's goods to reach distant markets, they gave people of the Southeast the ability to earn a wage and improve their lives. They prepared giant coal-burning steam locomotives that pulled passenger trains that sent families on vacations, soldiers off to war, and businessmen off to conduct trade. Trains ran because people demanded good, efficient transportation.

Spencer workers exercised precision and care to rebuild these instruments of power. They did so with the knowledge that once a locomotive left the shop, it had to be ready to go hundreds of miles away—from Washington, DC, to Atlanta. It had to be right when it left. To break down on the road meant losses or an accident. In the age before the term "failure is not an option," they practiced this belief.

They did it because it was good work, even in the Great Depression of the 1930s. It paid better than mill jobs, and fathers often brought their sons to join them in the railroad business. Sons fired locomotives for their fathers, and brothers worked in the roundhouse together. You could count on the railroad. It would always be there. The famous bard of everyman, Studs Turkel, said it best, "Work is about a search for daily meaning as well as daily bread, for recognition as well as cash, for astonishment rather than torpor; in short, for a sort of life rather than a Monday through Friday sort of dying."

The Spencer Shops was not unique in America. Rather, the complex was representative of other shops, other shop towns, and shop workers everywhere. You could find them across North Carolina (Hamlet on the Seaboard Air Line and Rocky Mount on the Atlantic Coast Line railways were also major locomotive shops on their respective railroads), throughout the region (Roanoke, Virginia, on the Norfolk & Western; Erwin on the Clinchfield Railroad; and Knoxville, Tennessee, and Atlanta, also on the Southern Railway), and nationwide (Altoona, Pennsylvania, on the Pennsylvania Railroad main line being the largest of all).

Like those other steam shops, Spencer came to a sad day in the 20th century when its usefulness ended. The unrelenting forces of technology and change swept it away. Diesel locomotives replaced steam locomotives. The work changed from rivets and boiler tubes to electrical wiring and power assemblies. Worse, it required fewer workers, and because of that, the railroad took the step to consolidate the work elsewhere. With the task and the people gone, that should have been the end of the story of Spencer Shops and even the town of Spencer.

Thankfully, when that time came, the Southern Railway's enlightened management saw the importance of saving the shops as a historical landmark, and the people of North Carolina saw value in reusing them as the state transportation museum. The magnificent buildings where thousands once labored have been saved and made into a place for fun, adventure, and education. Workers—volunteers now mostly, who keep the flame of history burning bright—still repair locomotives and cars in the buildings to preserve them and also to allow a new generation to experience the joy and fascination that is a moving train. All that is missing are the people who made the history.

In these pages are preserved the faces, the names, and the people who made history at Spencer Shops. You will see them at their place of work in the days of steam, when Spencer Shops workers moved the region. You will meet people like beloved shop foreman Bob Julian, for whom the Spencer roundhouse was named. These photographs tell the story of the trains that helped make a region an economic player on a national scale. Those days are gone but not forgotten.

Years after the shop complex had closed, I began to spend my volunteer time there, and the retired railroad workers I came in contact with provided a living link to the shops' past. In the voice of engineer H.S. "Hot Shot" Williams, I came to know a brave engineer. In foreman Jim Mesimore, I saw the skill and devotion of a railroad mechanic. And in dozens of men, I came to understand why they loved this place like a second home—because of the workers and their dedication to the goal of making things move.

—Jim Wrinn

Acknowledgments

While working on this book, I was reassured that photographs of Spencer Shops were plentiful. I would like to thank those who visited Spencer during the 1940s and 1950s and recorded the transition from steam to diesel. The photographers include David P. Driscoll, C.K. Marsh, and David Patton. A thank you also goes to J. Marvin Black for looking through his extensive collection on the Southern Railway and graciously contributing Spencer Shops images. While working for the Southern, he collected and preserved information pertaining to steam and diesel locomotives, a treasure trove of information for researchers. Marvin Rogers, an engineer for Norfolk Southern, supplied photographs he took of Spencer Shops during the final years of operation in the 1970s, as well as images of steam locomotives collected through the years. Kim Cumber of the North Carolina State Archives was a great help in locating images relating to Spencer Shops, which furnished the majority of photographs for the book. Vernon Lane contributed an image of the Shriner locomotive from 1928. Patsy McBride, Bill Rabon, and June Pryor all contributed images of relatives who worked at Spencer.

In addition to the photographers and collectors mentioned above, the resources of the North Carolina Transportation Museum were invaluable. Duane Galloway's research on the buildings and operation of Spencer Shops provided information for many captions used in the book. Museum historian Walter Turner and Jim Wrinn provided editorial support and feedback, keeping me on track through this fun and interesting project. Jim, the editor of *Trains* magazine, wrote the back page summary and an introduction on the unique role of unsung railroad workers. At the North Carolina Transportation Museum, Elizabeth Smith rearranged my schedule to accommodate a writing schedule, while Kelly Alexander and the North Carolina Transportation Museum Foundation provided initial funding. Lindsay Carter of Arcadia Publishing guided me through the guidelines and opportunities of becoming an Arcadia author. Finally, a big thank you goes to my wife, Traci, for her understanding and support of my lifelong interest in railroad history and preservation, and to my daughter Kerstin, who is just starting to follow in her father's footsteps.

One

Creation of Spencer Shops and the Town of Spencer

The Southern Railway formed in 1894 from the merger of several railroads, including the Richmond & Danville, which had leased the North Carolina Railroad since 1871. Company Shops (later Burlington) became the main locomotive and repair facility in North Carolina. This 1850s facility performed services to locomotives of the North Carolina Railroad but became outdated with the newer steam locomotives operating through the state.

Samuel Spencer, the first president of the Southern Railway, wanted a new shop built on the main line halfway between Washington, DC, and Atlanta, Georgia. Rowan County, North Carolina, became the target location for these new facilities, which interested John Steele Henderson, a former state senator and US congressman. He learned of the railroad plans for the area and began secretly buying land between Salisbury and the Yadkin River. One of the largest tracts was 101.8 acres from Robert Partee, an African American farmer. Henderson acquired over 162 acres of land and then sold 141 acres to the Southern for the shop complex and the rest to the families who would eventually work at the shops and develop the town of Spencer. Construction for the shops began on March 23, 1896, and the town of Spencer was incorporated in 1905.

Samuel Spencer grew up on a cotton farm near Columbus, Georgia. At the age of 17, he joined a Confederate cavalry unit for the last year of the Civil War. He was educated at the University of Georgia and then studied engineering at the University of Virginia. He was briefly president of the Baltimore & Ohio Railroad, worked as a railroad advisor for a financial company with J.P. Morgan, and served as first president of the Southern Railway from 1894 until his death in a railroad wreck in 1906. The town of Spencer was named for him. (North Carolina Division of Archives and History.)

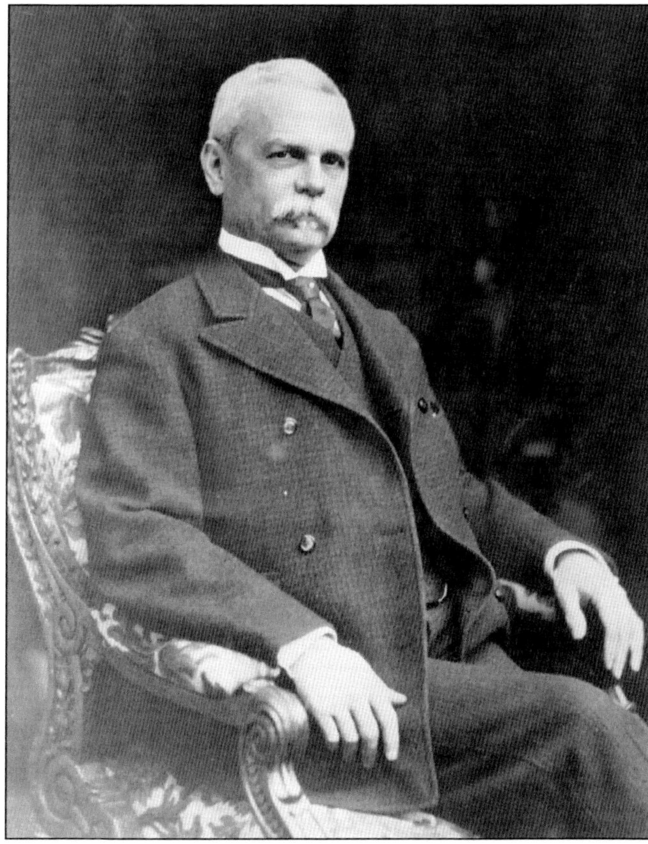

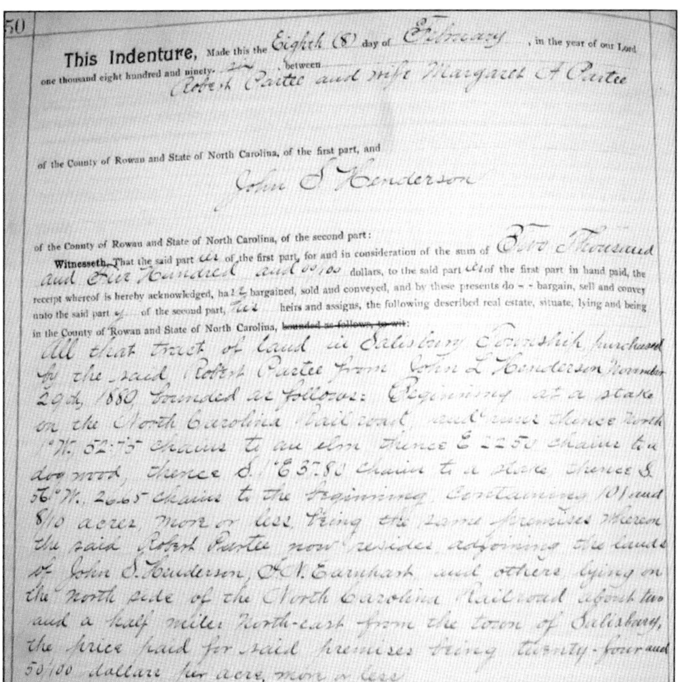

50

This Indenture, Made this the Eighth (8) day of February, in the year of our Lord one thousand eight hundred and ninety-five between Robert Partee and wife Margaret A Partee

of the County of Rowan and State of North Carolina, of the first part, and

John S Henderson

of the County of Rowan and State of North Carolina, of the second part:

Witnesseth, That the said parties of the first part, for and in consideration of the sum of Two Thousand and Five Hundred and 00/100 dollars, to the said parties of the first part in hand paid, the receipt whereof is hereby acknowledged, have bargained, sold and conveyed, and by these presents do - - bargain, sell and convey unto the said party of the second part, his heirs and assigns, the following described real estate, situate, lying and being in the County of Rowan and State of North Carolina, ~~bounded as follows, to wit~~:

All that tract of land in Salisbury Township purchased by the said Robert Partee from John L Henderson November 29th, 1880 bounded as follows: Beginning at a stake on the North Carolina Railroad [illegible] thence North 1° W. 52.75 chains to an elm thence E 22.50 chains to a dogwood, thence S. 1° E 37.80 chains to a stake thence S. 56° W. 26.65 chains to the beginning, containing 101 and 8/10 acres, more or less being the same premises whereon the said Robert Partee now resides adjoining the lands of John S. Henderson, A.N. Earnhart and others lying on the North side of the North Carolina Railroad about two and a half miles North-east from the town of Salisbury, the price paid for said premises being twenty-four and 50/100 dollars per acre, more or less

On February 8, 1895, farmer Robert Partee and his wife, Margaret A., sold their home and 101 acres to John Henderson for $2,500. The business deal furnished the largest track of land purchased for Spencer Shops. The deed also reveals that the surveyor, as was customary for the times, measured the amount of acreage by trees (an elm and dogwood), as well as a stake, and that the land was located 2.5 miles northeast of Salisbury. The next week, Henderson bought 40 more acres from Isaac Earnhart. (Rowan County Register of Deeds.)

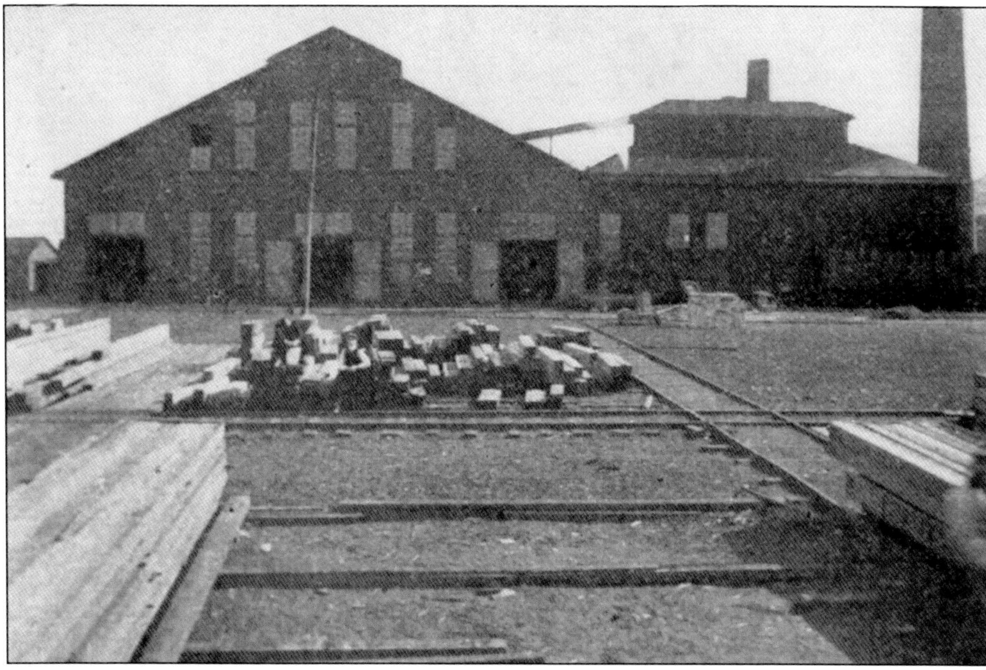

One of the earliest photographs of construction at Spencer Shops shows the woodworking shop on the left and the powerhouse on the right. The woodworking shop provided cut lumber for repair of early wooden passenger and freight cars. The powerhouse originally supplied electricity to the shops and the town of Spencer. (North Carolina State Archives.)

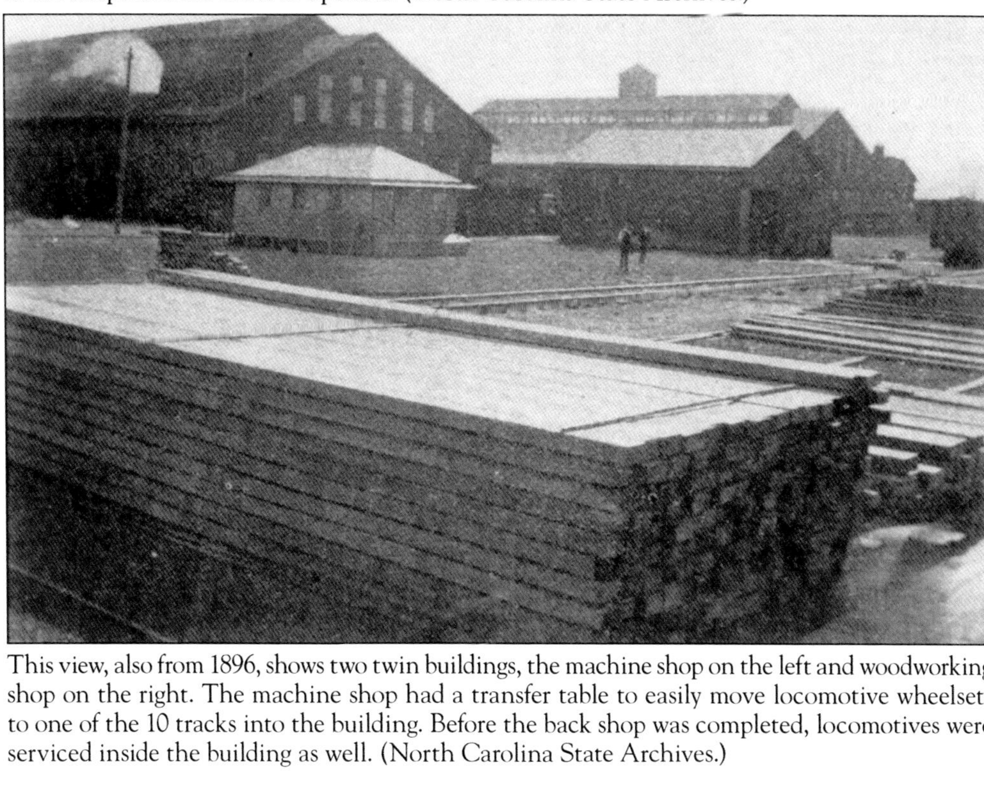

This view, also from 1896, shows two twin buildings, the machine shop on the left and woodworking shop on the right. The machine shop had a transfer table to easily move locomotive wheelsets to one of the 10 tracks into the building. Before the back shop was completed, locomotives were serviced inside the building as well. (North Carolina State Archives.)

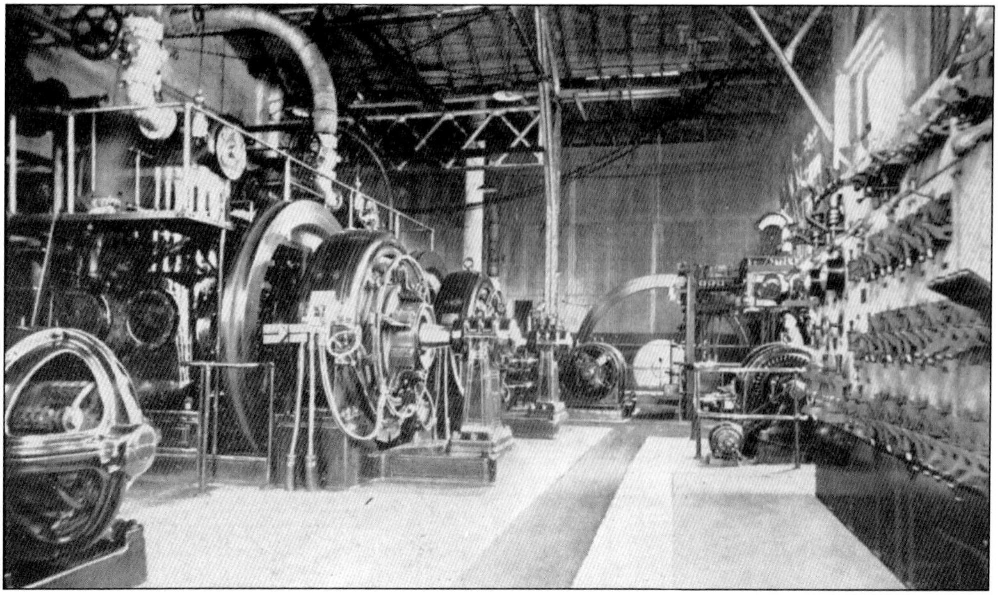

Here is an interior view of the powerhouse showing the turbines and other equipment to generate electricity. The state-of-the-art powerhouse included four 100-horsepower boilers supplying steam to the generators and the adjacent buildings. New additions were made in 1904, 1913, and 1926. (North Carolina State Archives.)

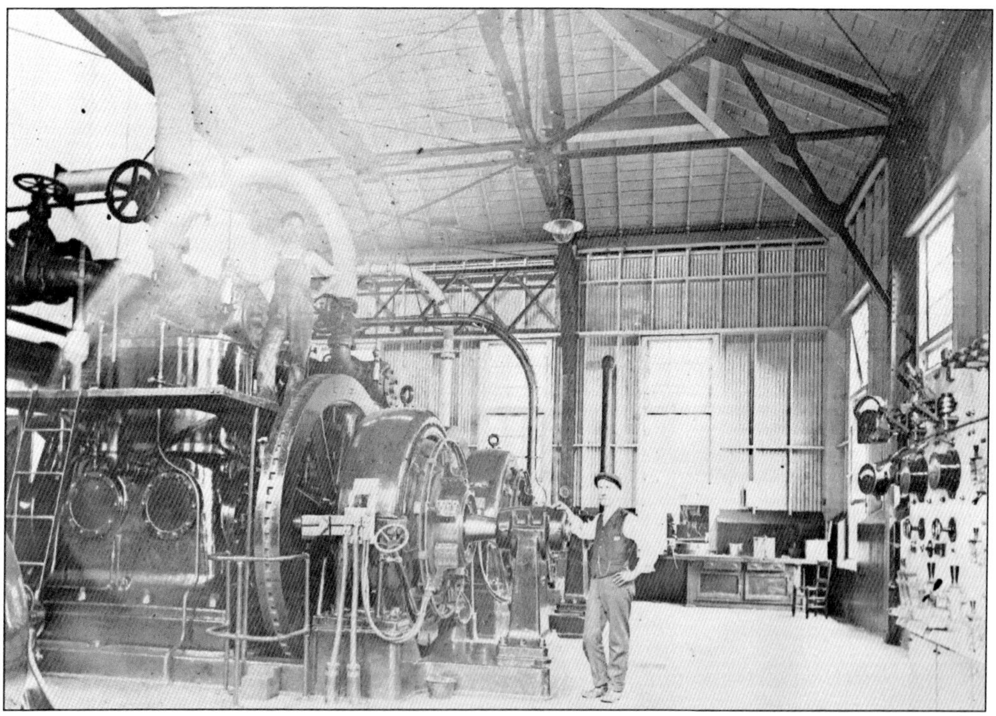

This earlier view shows the original 1896 section of the powerhouse. Note the excess steam escaping from the safety valves. Two 85-foot smokestacks helped draft air for the boilers. The 1926 addition added another four steam-powered boilers, generating a total of 1,100 horsepower for the shops. (North Carolina Division of Archives and History.)

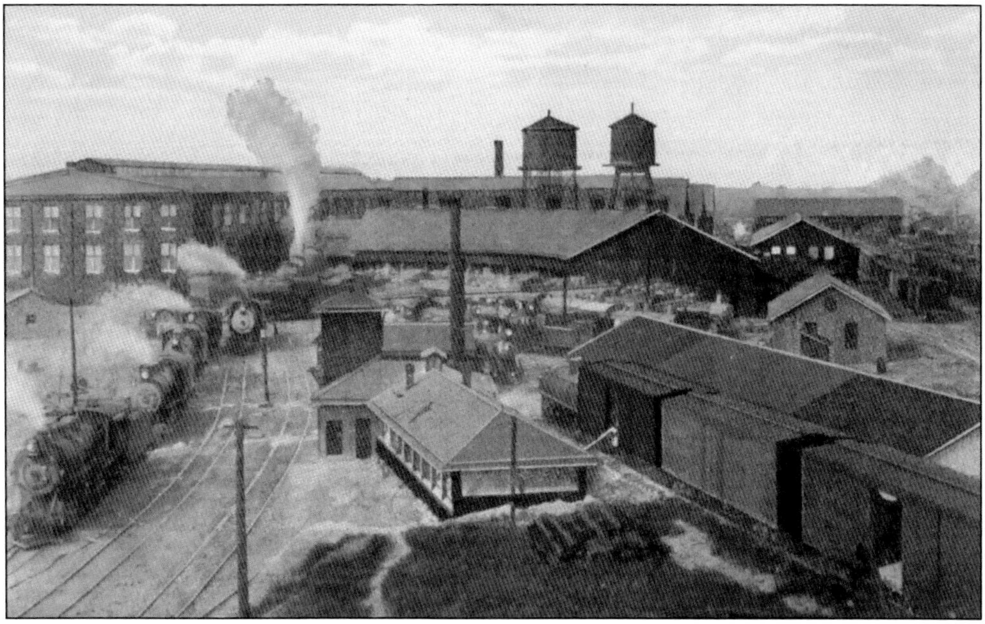

Construction continued in 1896 with the completion of a 15-stall roundhouse, shown some time in the 1910s. John P. Pettyjohn and the W.W. Dorning companies, of Lynchburg, Virginia, handled the construction for most original shop buildings. This roundhouse used a 65-foot turntable, but by 1912, an additional 90-foot turntable was constructed to rotate larger locomotives. (North Carolina State Archives.)

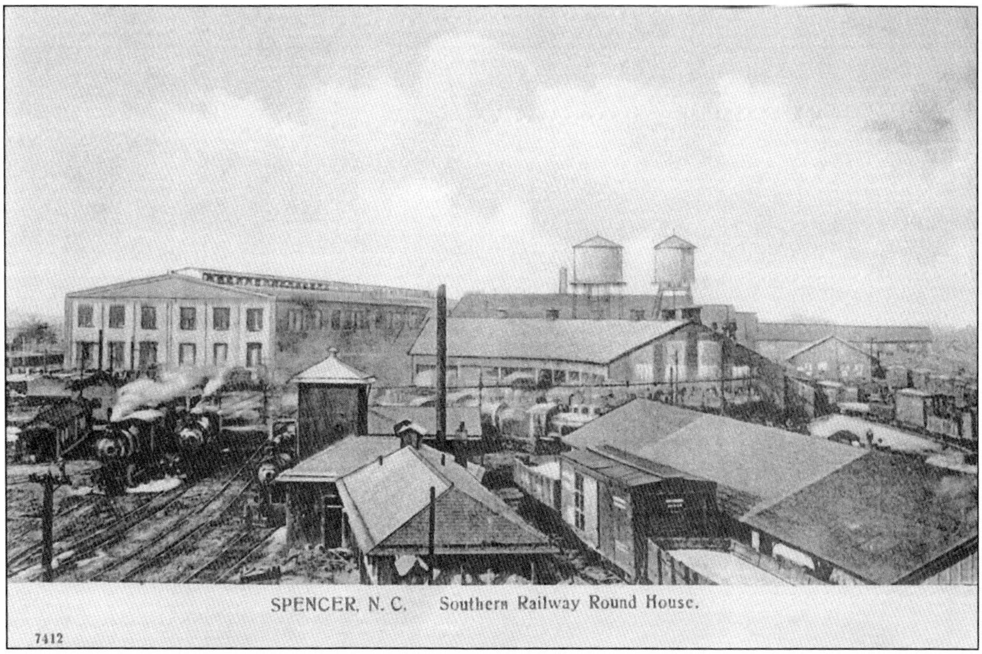

Taken after 1905, here is another view of the 1896 roundhouse. The locomotives on the left could be waiting on service in the roundhouse or awaiting a call for the next train. Note the sand in the cars to the right. Sand was used to help locomotives gain traction when the rails were wet or when pulling a long train. (Rowan Museum Collection.)

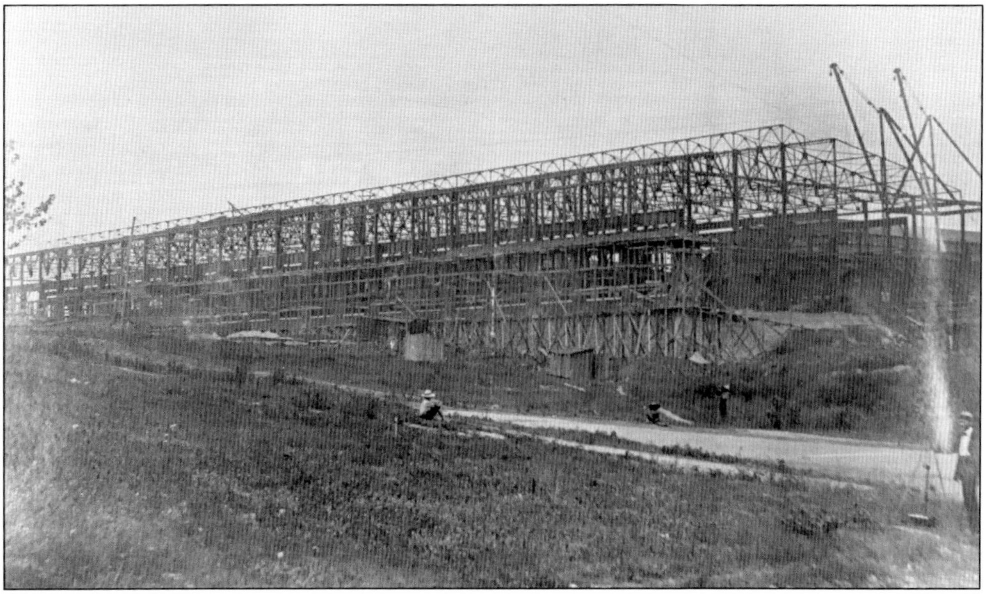

This photograph, taken on June 8, 1904, depicts the construction of the back shop. When completed in 1905, this building was 600 feet long, 150 feet wide, and over two stories high. The building was used for the main overhaul and repair of steam locomotives, each moving the entire length of the structure. Over 15 locomotives were serviced at one time, but at least one had to be returned to service every day. (Rowan Museum Collection.)

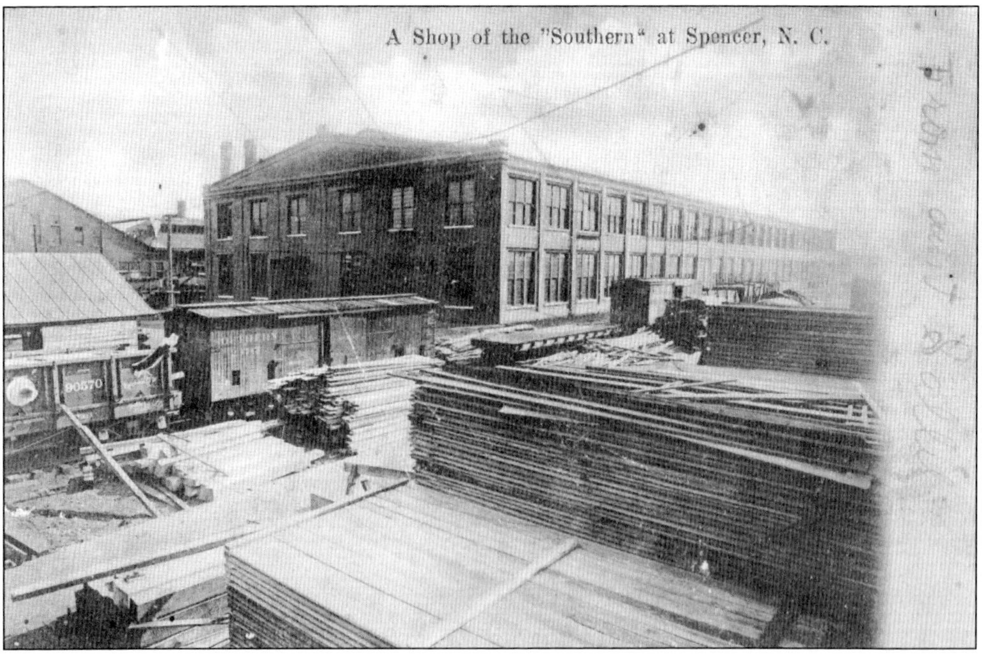

Here is a north-end view of back shop from the early 1900s. Notice all the woodwork on the ground for construction of other buildings. The two buildings in the left background are the woodworking shop and powerhouse with twin stacks. Completed steam locomotives exited the building from this end to be test fired before returning to operation. (North Carolina Division of Archives and History.)

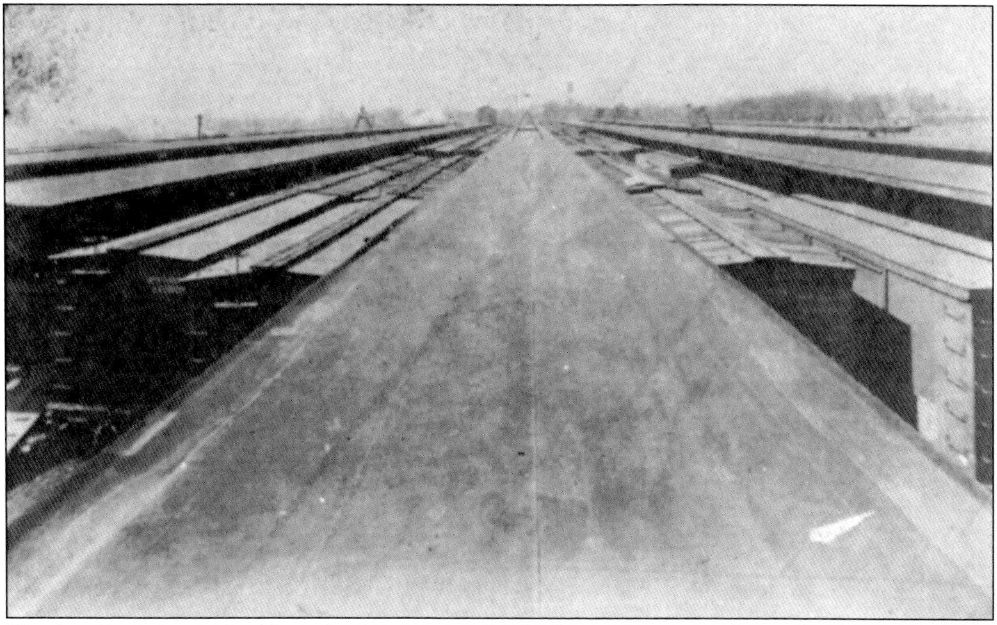

The Southern began building the freight transfer sheds in 1907 one mile south of the shops. The original construction included five sheds that were built at a cost of $29,203. The sheds were designed to accommodate 10 tracks, with a maximum length of 950 feet. The sheds could service between 250 and 350 freight cars a day, which made this one of the largest transfer sheds on the Southern Railway system. Freight could arrive or depart in all directions, north, south, east, or west. (North Carolina State Archives.)

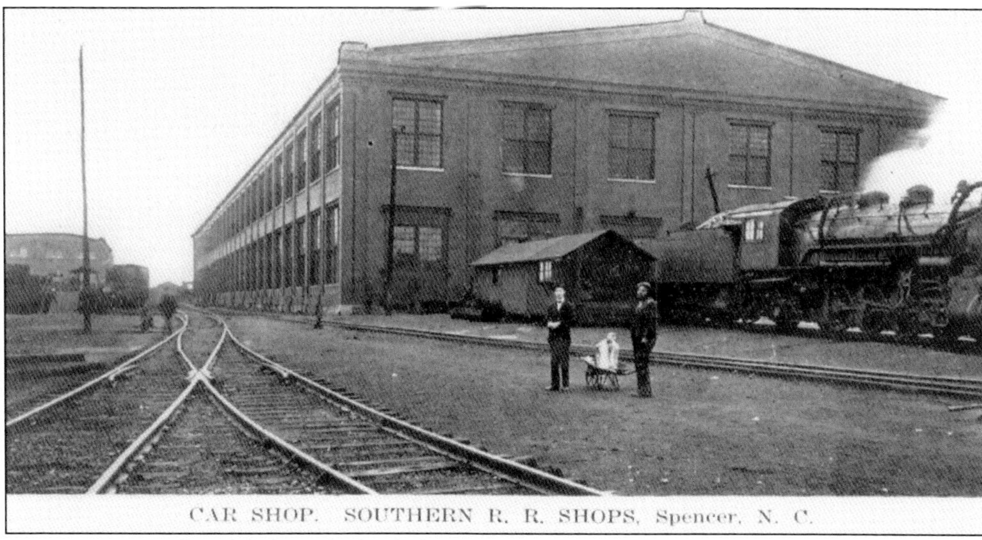

Here is a postcard mislabeling the back shop as a car shop but showing a steam locomotive! This photograph, taken around 1915, shows a Ms-2-class 2-8-2 with an auxiliary tender tractor instead of regular trucks. The extra set of drive wheels gave the locomotives more tractive effort. The powerful locomotives were used between Asheville and Spartanburg over the Saluda grade. Note the large curved pipe to carry steam to the extra cylinders. Only six locomotives, 4535–4539 and 4576, were used for this experiment. The tractor wheels were removed in 1924. (North Carolina Division of Archives and History.)

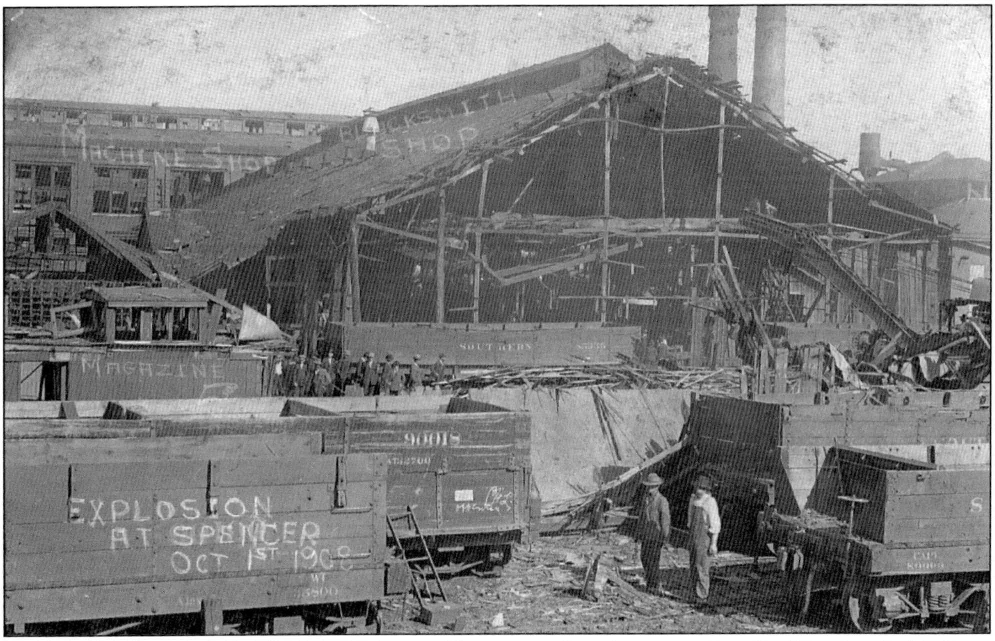

Railroad work was always dangerous, especially in a yard or shop complex. On October 1, 1908, an explosion at the blacksmith shop was strong enough to blow windows out in the back shop, labeled here as the machine shop. There was no record of fatalities. The building, located between the powerhouse and transfer table, was later replaced in 1911 with the boiler shop. (North Carolina Division of Archives and History.)

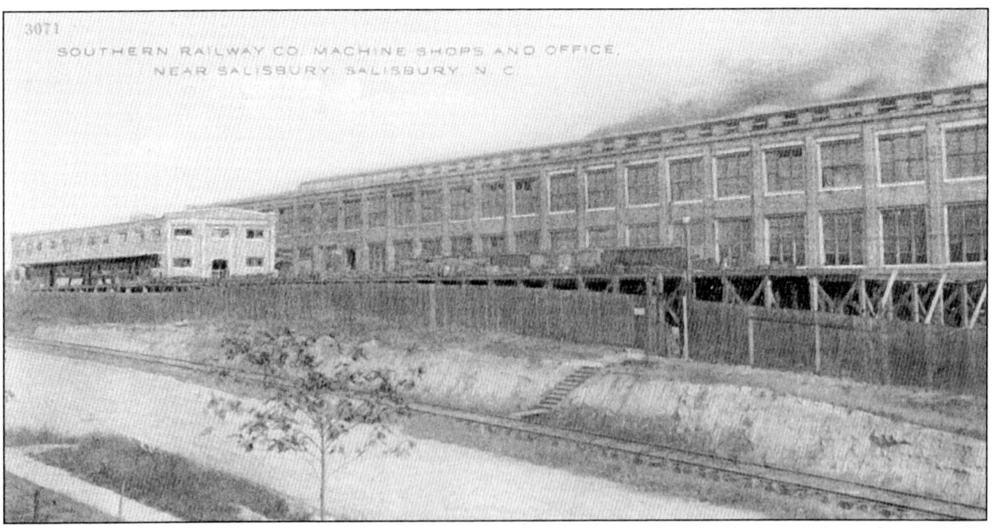

The master mechanic's office, shown at left and completed in 1911, housed the office of the master mechanic, clerks, and a two-story parts storehouse. This view shows how Spencer Shops appeared in the early days with dirt roads, trolley tracks, and impressive shop buildings. (Rowan Museum Collection.)

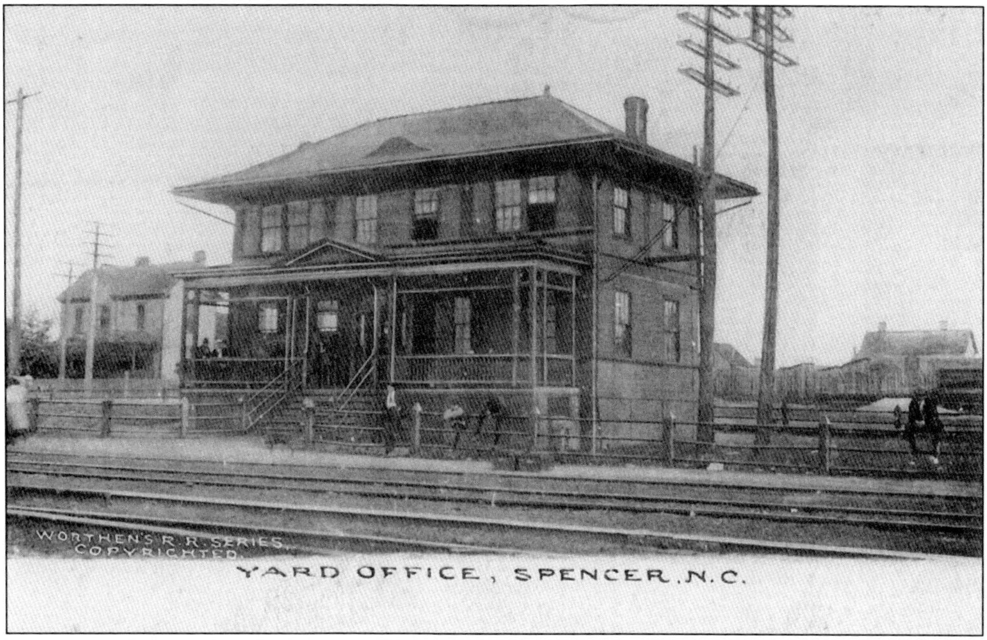

The original yard office for Spencer Shops was located on the East Spencer side of the yard, just south of the ice plant. Clerks in this building kept track of all trains operating in or out of the yard for both locomotives and crews. (Rowan Museum Collection.)

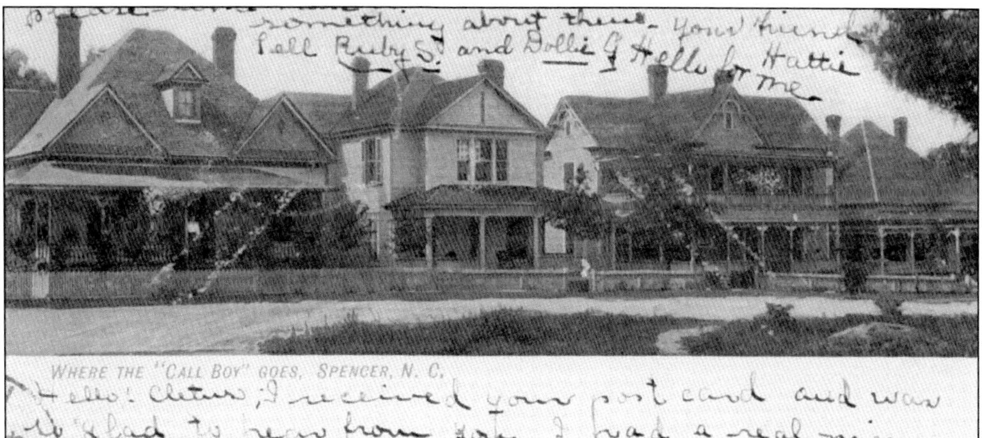

The call boys worked out of the yard office, notifying crews of their assigned trains. They would work their way through Spencer knocking on doors or checking at the YMCA building. This view shows houses located on Yadkin Avenue, behind Spencer Town Park. (Rowan Museum Collection.)

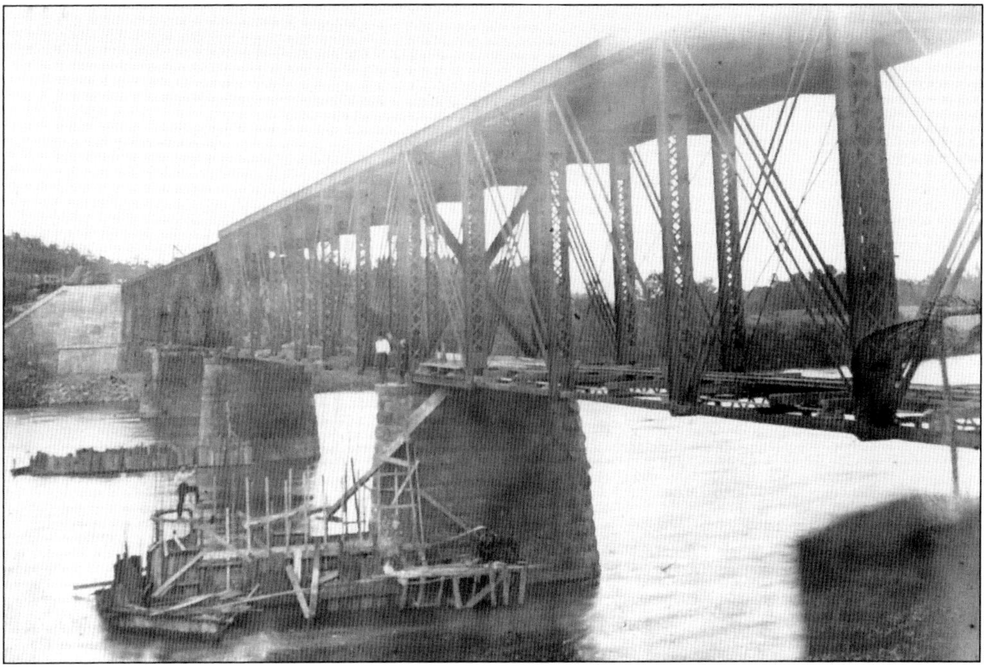

While the Southern Railway was busy constructing the shops, the company was also improving the main line for freight and passenger service. This 1906 photograph shows a second track being added to the Yadkin River Railroad Bridge. By the 1920s, the Southern had double tracked the main line from Washington, DC, to Atlanta, Georgia. (Rowan Museum Collection.)

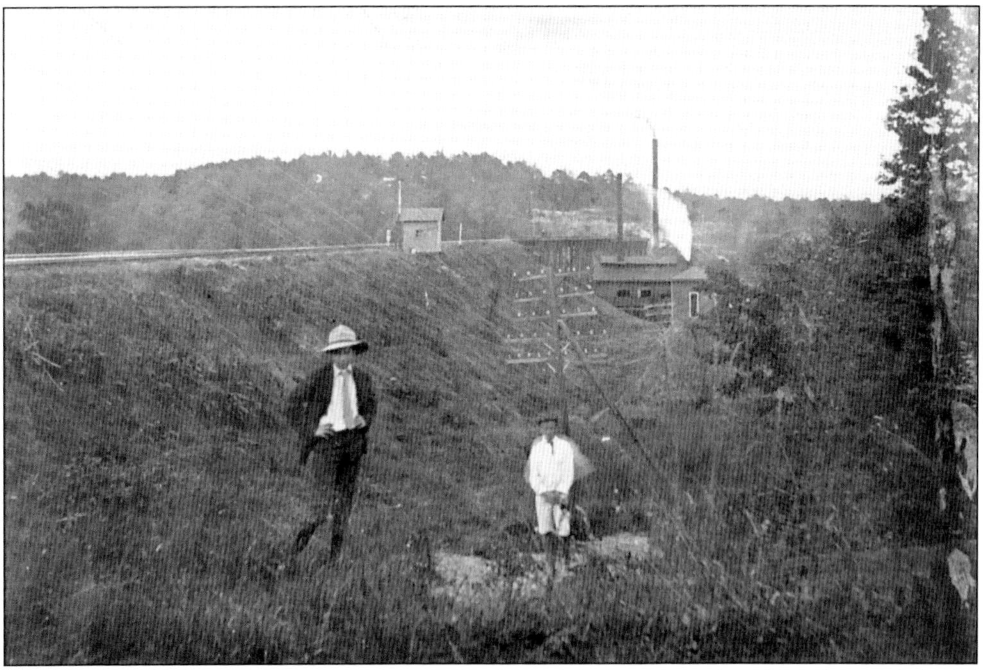

Showing the Southern's pump station in the background, this view, taken from the south bank, is of the Yadkin River Bridge. Francis and Alfred posed for Theodore Buerbaum, who took area photographs for his bookstore. (Rowan Museum Collection.)

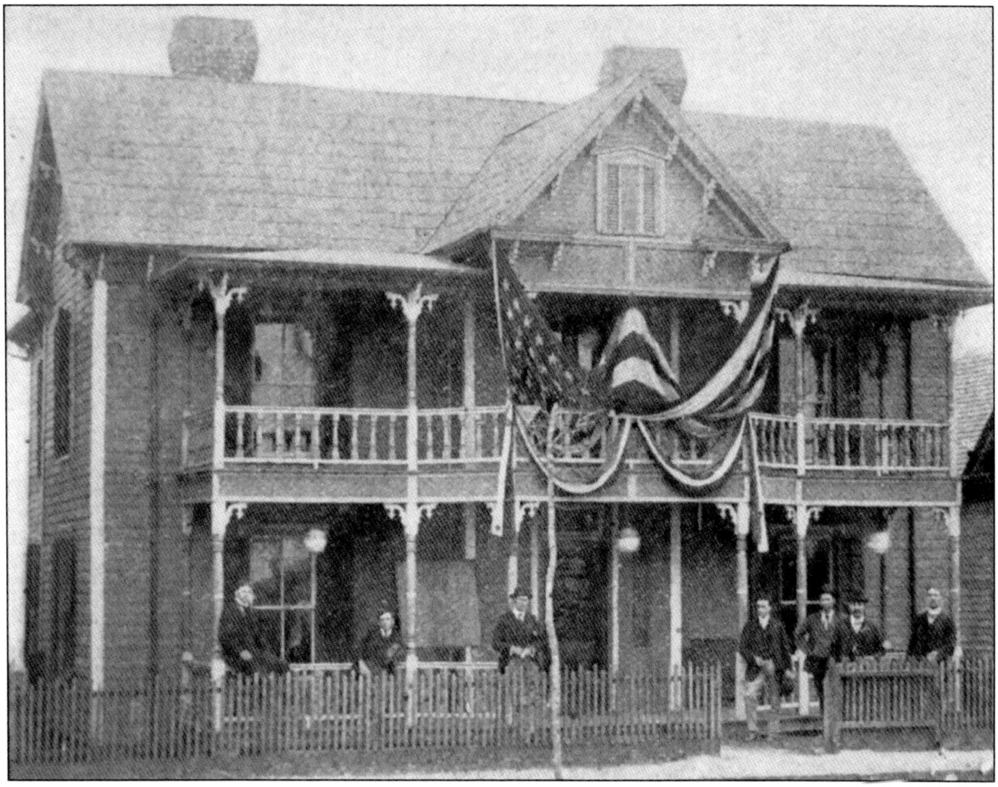

The town of Spencer developed a railroad YMCA for the benefit and recreation of the shop workers. This original building, organized in 1901, was rented from a Spencer resident. It included bedrooms, a game room, a library, and a bathroom with two bathtubs—but no running water. A boiler was used to heat well water, which drained into a nearby ditch. (North Carolina State Archives.)

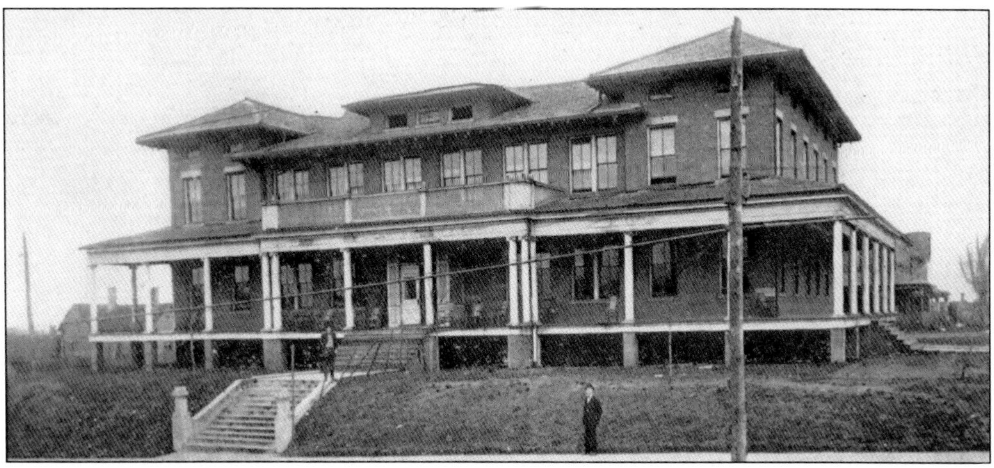

In 1905, noted Southern Railway architect Frank Milburn designed a new building for the YMCA with an estimated construction cost of $20,000. The building opened on March 23, 1907, and included 48 bedrooms, bathrooms with running water, a library, a restaurant, a bowling alley, and a barbershop. Single shop workers, as well as married ones waiting to bring their families to town, lived here. The building was torn down in the late 1960s and replaced by a modern brick structure that serves as city hall today. (North Carolina State Archives.)

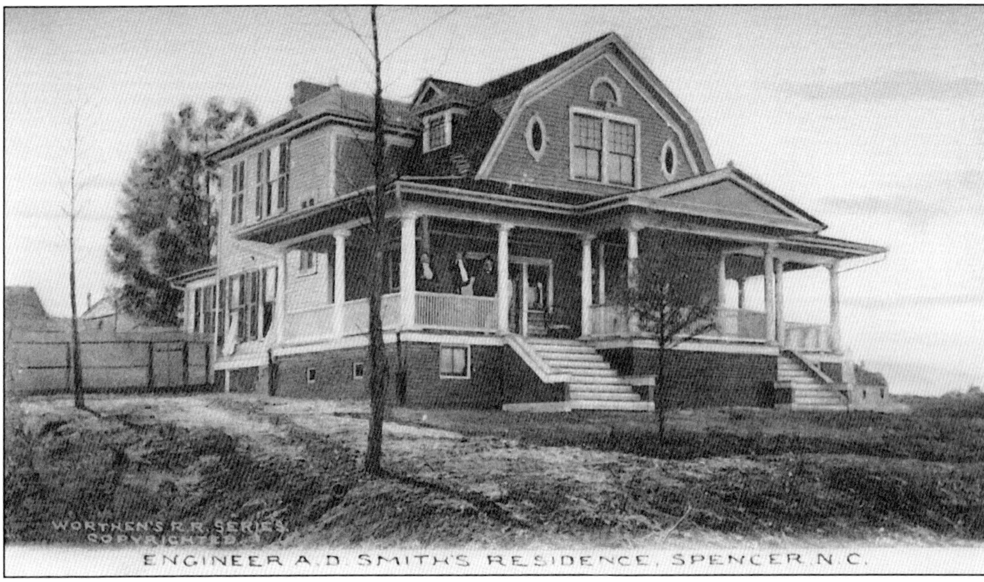

Homes began to appear in Spencer in 1896, as new workers moved into the area. Alexander Boyd Andrews Jr. purchased 85 acres of land from the Southern Railway to develop the town of Spencer. A 50-by-145-foot lot sold for $100 but included some interesting covenants. A house had to be constructed within one year, costing no less than $400, and plans had to be approved by an architect. No alcohol was allowed to be sold in private homes or businesses, and homes could be no closer than 20 feet from the street. (Rowan Museum Collection.)

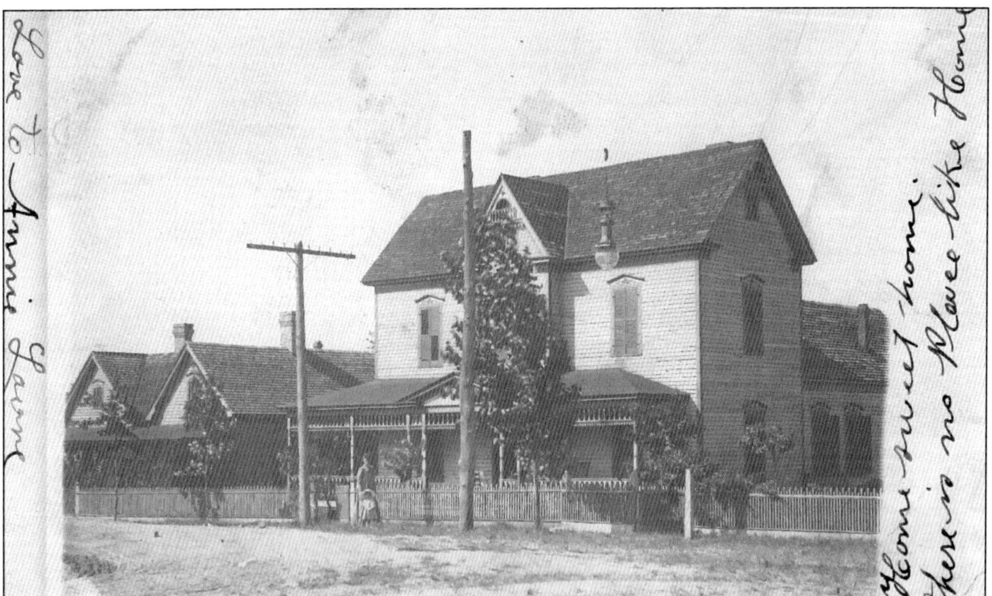

This photograph depicts a typical single-family home in Spencer; W.A. Eagle owned this house. Generally, these larger houses had between 1,800 and 2,300 square feet, two to three bedrooms, one full bath, fireplaces for heat and cooking, and no indoor plumbing. Spencer later developed a community sewer system for the benefit of residents. Homes were constructed with a mix of wood and brick, with most having front and/or wraparound porches, large windows, and electricity. (Rowan Museum Collection.)

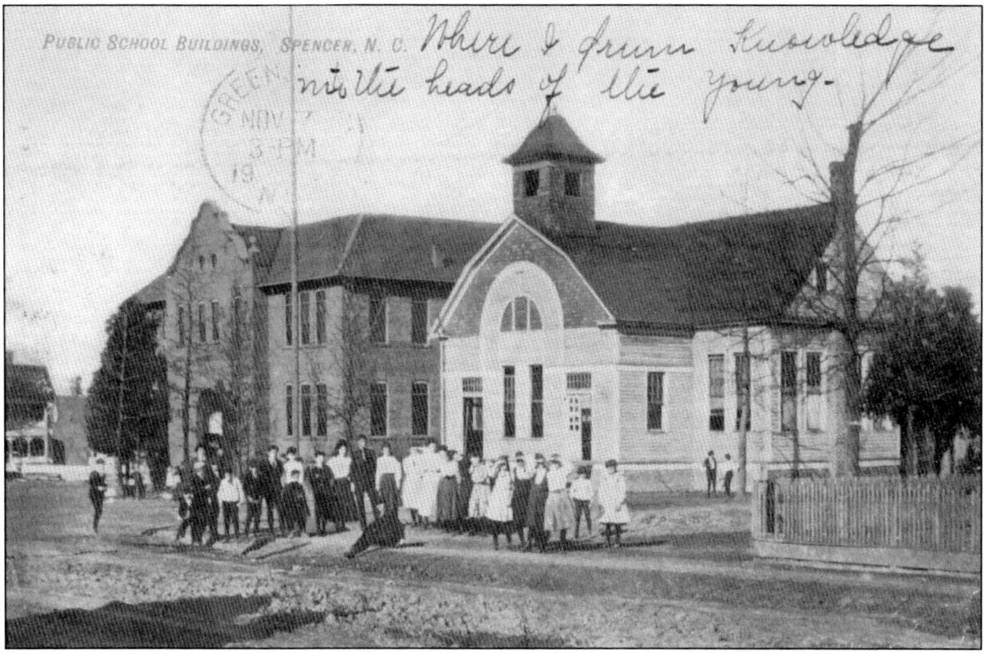

This postcard shows original wooden school building and the brick addition added in 1905. The original building housed grades one through seven, and the new building had grades eight through 11. The school was located between Third and Fourth Streets, bounded by Rowan and Carolina Avenues. The original building was destroyed by fire on March 1, 1925. (Rowan Museum Collection.)

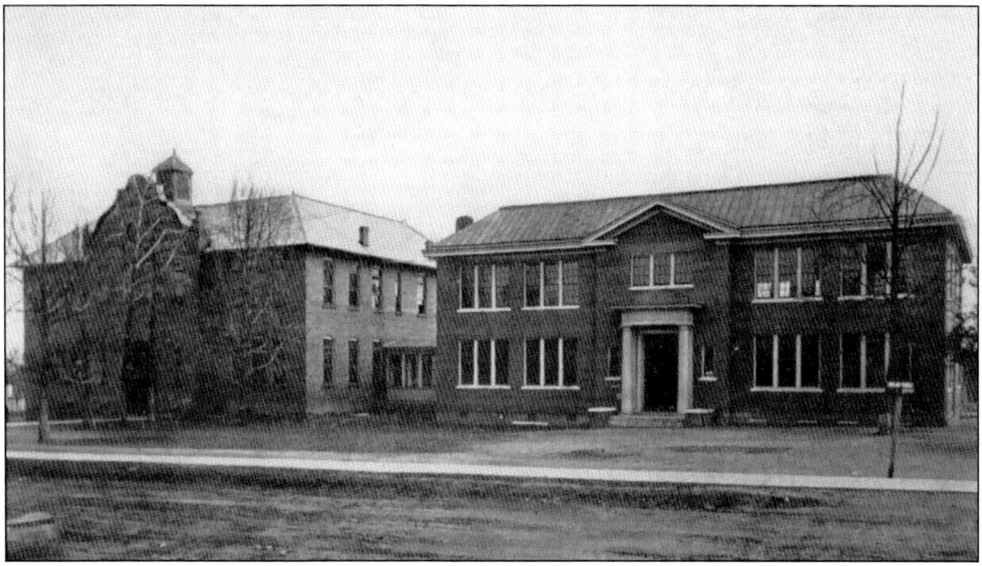

With the completion of a new school building in 1926, Spencer School continued to operate through the 1950s. A walkway connected the two buildings to protect the students and teachers during inclement weather. Baseball games were played at the park across from the shops, while the football field was located off Eighth Street. With new county school construction and reorganization, Spencer High School was replaced by North Rowan High School in 1958. (North Carolina State Archives.)

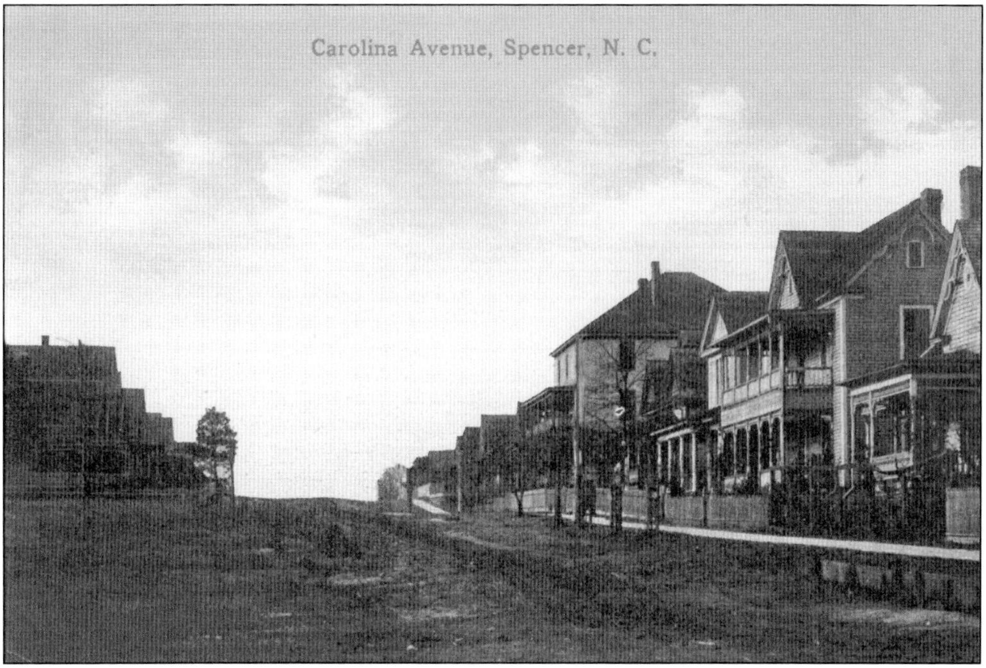

In this early scene of Spencer, one can see the streets are still dirt, but concrete sidewalks and trees line the way. With just enough room for a driveway, though many people parked on the street, these houses were very close to each other. (Rowan Museum Collection.)

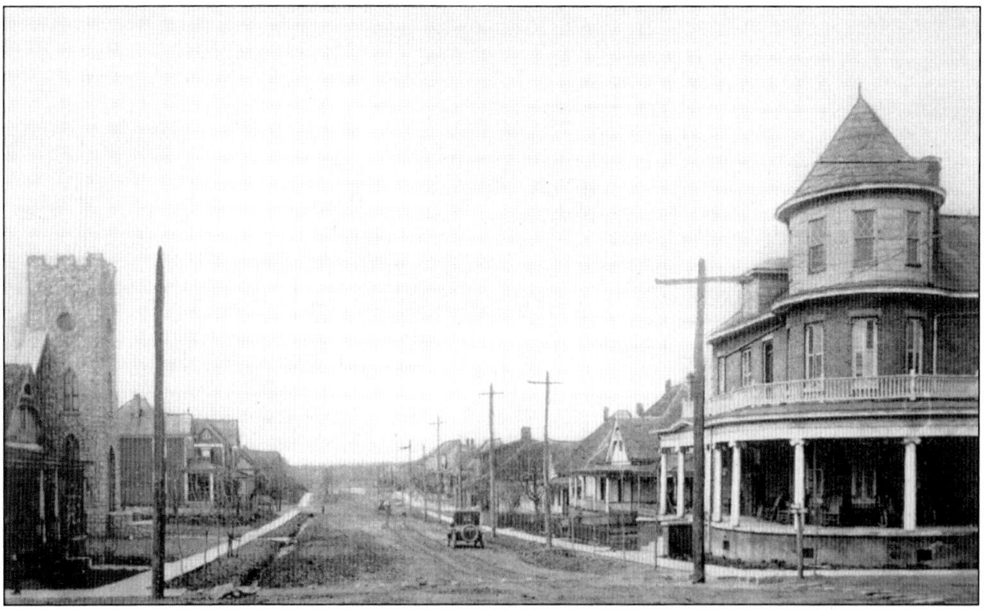

Taken at the intersection with Fifth Street, this view is of Carolina Avenue. The large house on the right was used as a boardinghouse for employees and visitors. Across the street is Spencer Lutheran Church. The church building was replaced in the early 1950s with a circular sanctuary resembling a roundhouse. (North Carolina State Archives.)

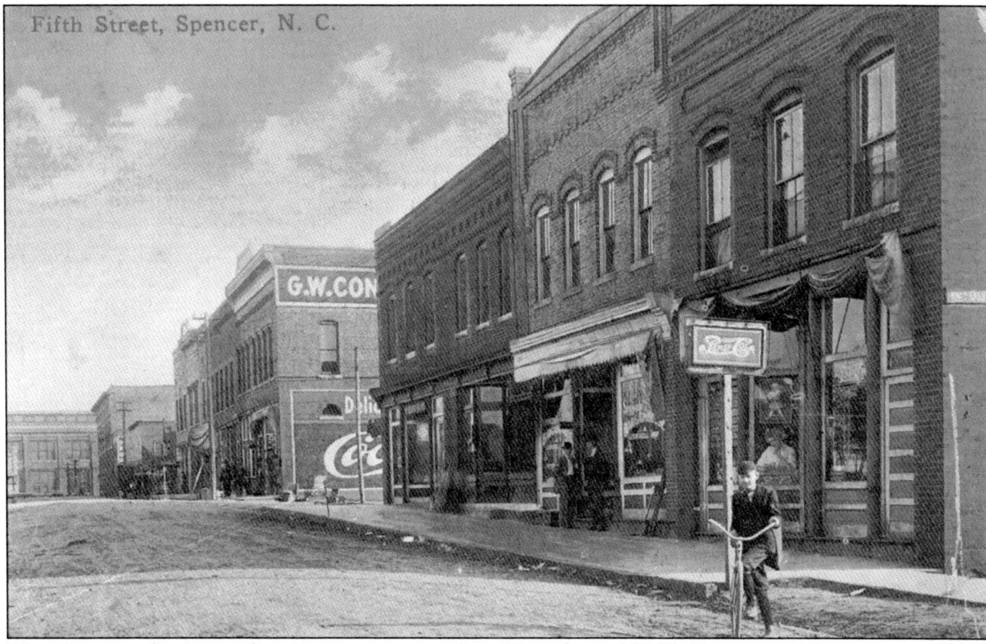

The Spencer business district was centered on Fourth and Fifth Streets, with many buildings constructed before 1910. The Southern Railway did not operate the businesses but did forbid the sale of liquor in town limits through covenants. Pepsi-Cola had a bottling plant in Spencer through the 1920s that was replaced by Boone Rock Bottling Company. (Rowan Museum Collection.)

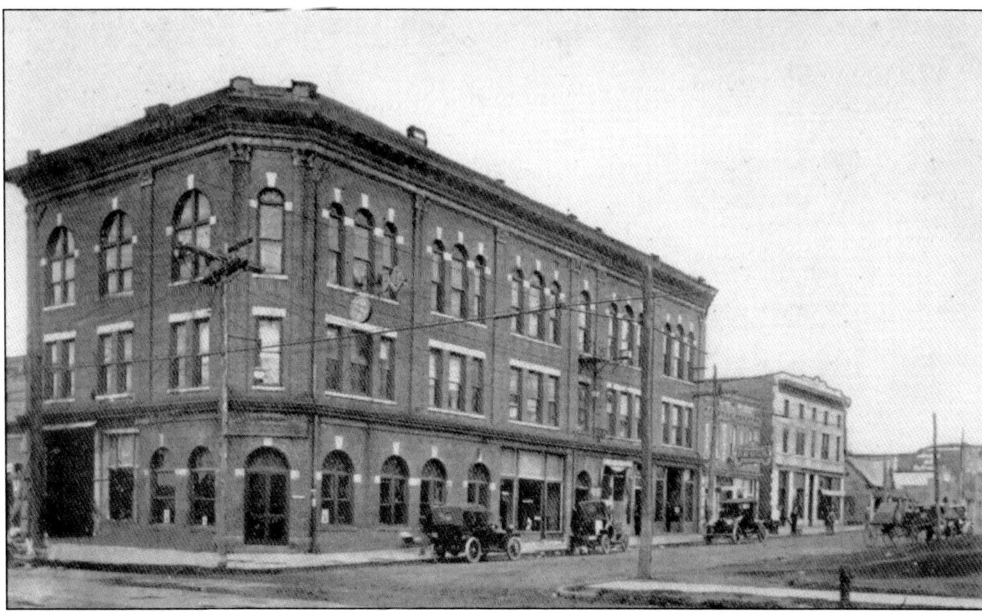
This view of Fifth Street shows the Wachovia Bank Building. Several stores were located on the first floor, and the Masons used the third floor for a temple. Other Spencer businesses included drugstores, livery and feed, furniture, grocery, clothing, and women's hats. (North Carolina State Archives.)

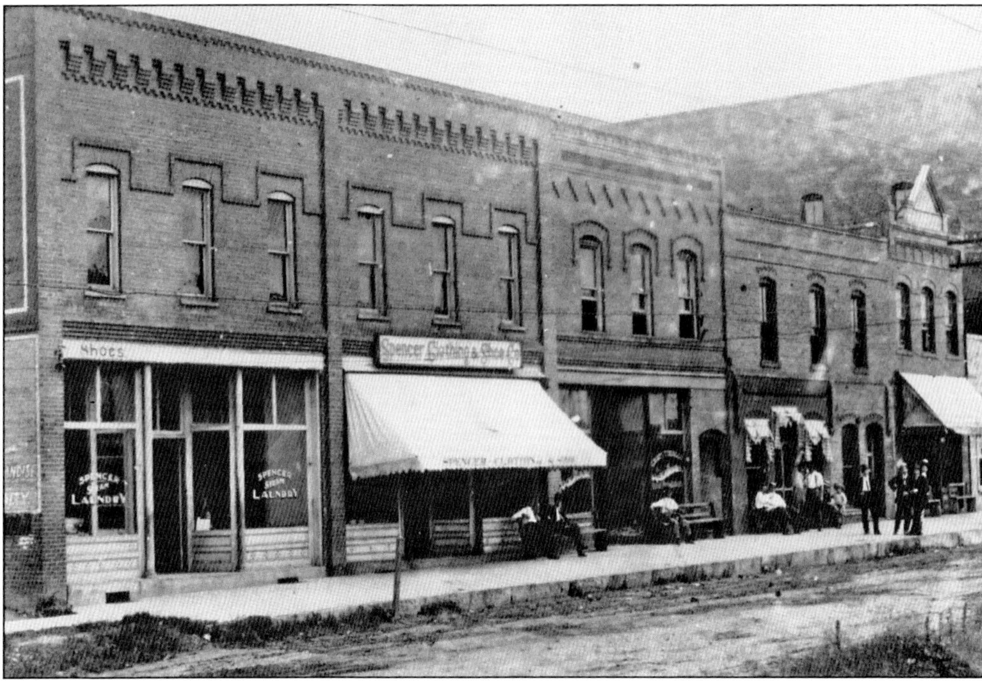

The area between the YMCA and Wachovia Bank contained several interesting stores, all packed closely together. Businesses on Salisbury Avenue stretched between Third and Sixth Streets, roughly the length of Spencer Shops. (North Carolina Division of Archives and History.)

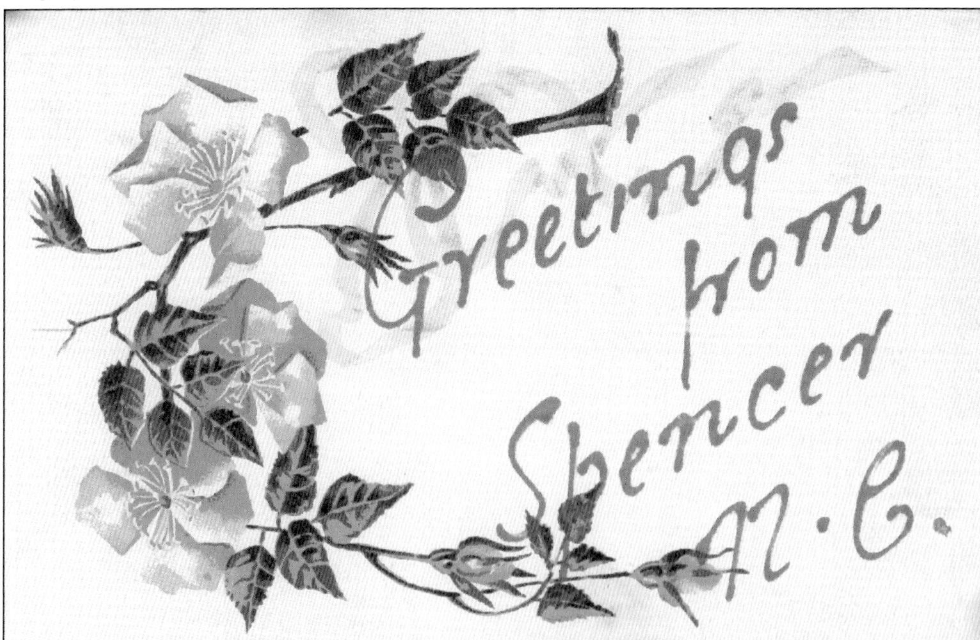

To attract visitors and residents to Spencer, printers designed special postcards during the early 1900s for local businesses to sell. Several showed the buildings and stores of the town, while others offered a slogan. This particular card was mailed from Spencer on April 13, 1909, to Advance, North Carolina. (Rowan Museum Collection.)

The Harry M. Cooke Pharmacy, located on Fifth Street, was one of the oldest original businesses in Spencer. This pharmacy not only offered prescription drugs but also carried household items, cigars, candy, and a soda fountain featuring Coca-Cola. Harry Cooke was also the mayor of Spencer during the 1910s. (North Carolina State Archives.)

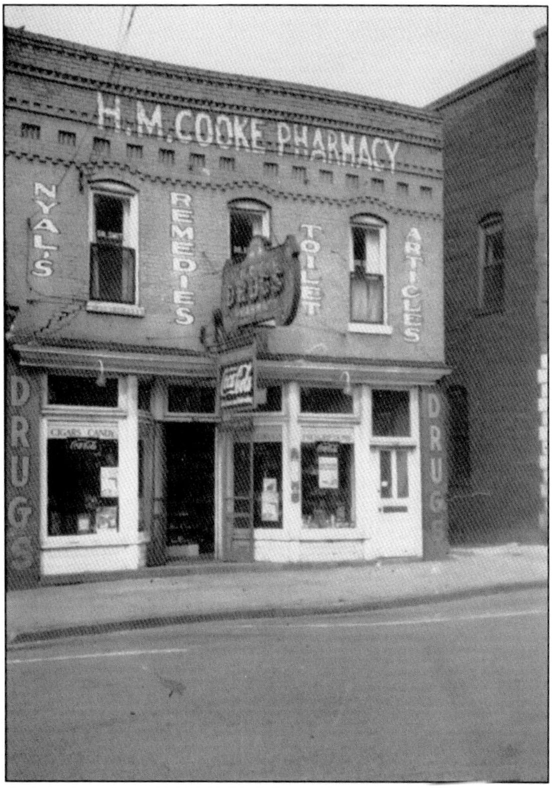

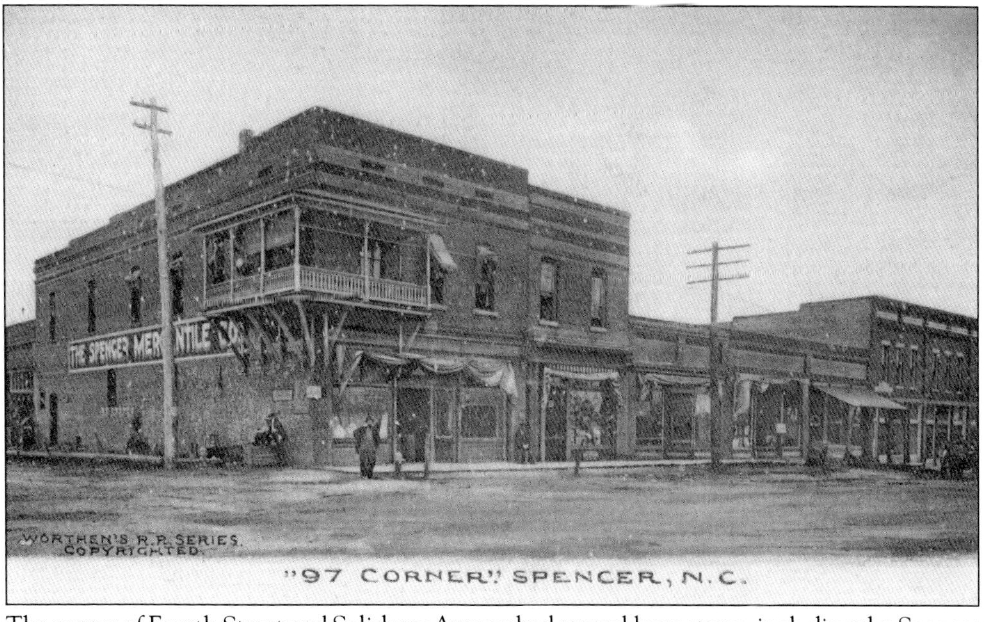

The corner of Fourth Street and Salisbury Avenue had several large stores, including the Spencer Mercantile Company. Opened in 1907, it was a large general store that carried clothes, shoes, groceries, tobacco, and furnishings. The large building to the right was the Harris & Stoudemire furniture store. This business, which also opened in 1907, has been in continuous operation for over 100 years by the Stoudemire family. (Rowan Museum Collection.)

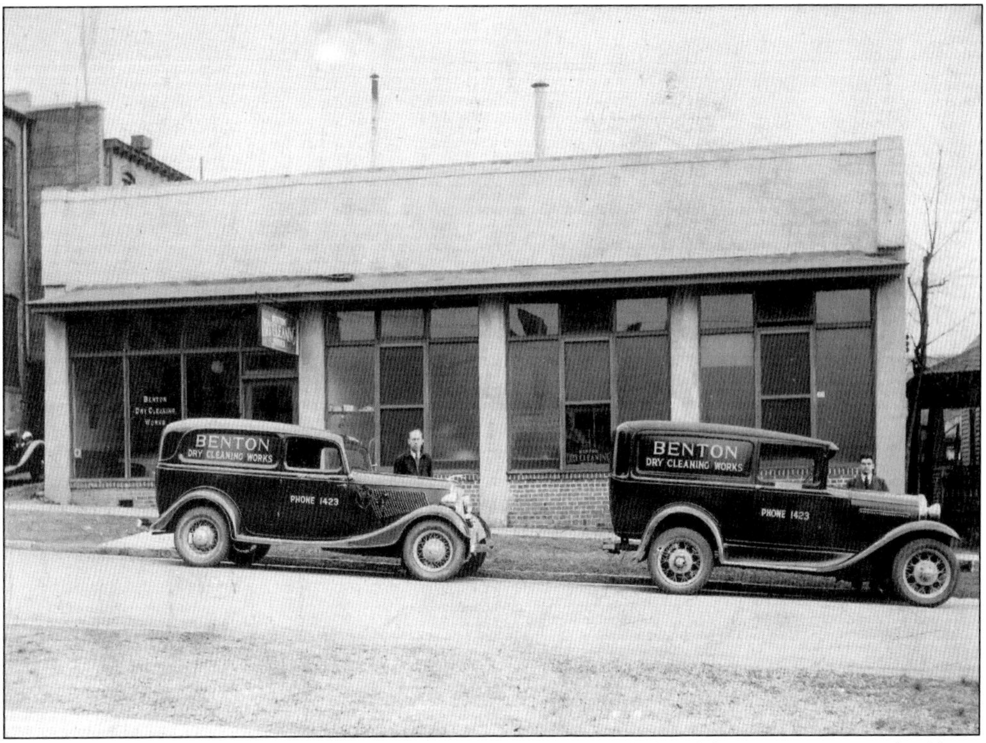

Benton Dry Cleaning was located at 505 South Yadkin Avenue, behind the C.H. Morrison building. Given the dirty nature of railroad work, dry cleaning was very popular in Spencer. During the 1930s, Benton maintained a fleet of Ford panel delivery trucks that were stylishly marked with the company name. By 1961, the phone number had changed to ME 3-2561. The dogs were pets of the owner of the dry cleaning works. (Both, North Carolina State Archives.)

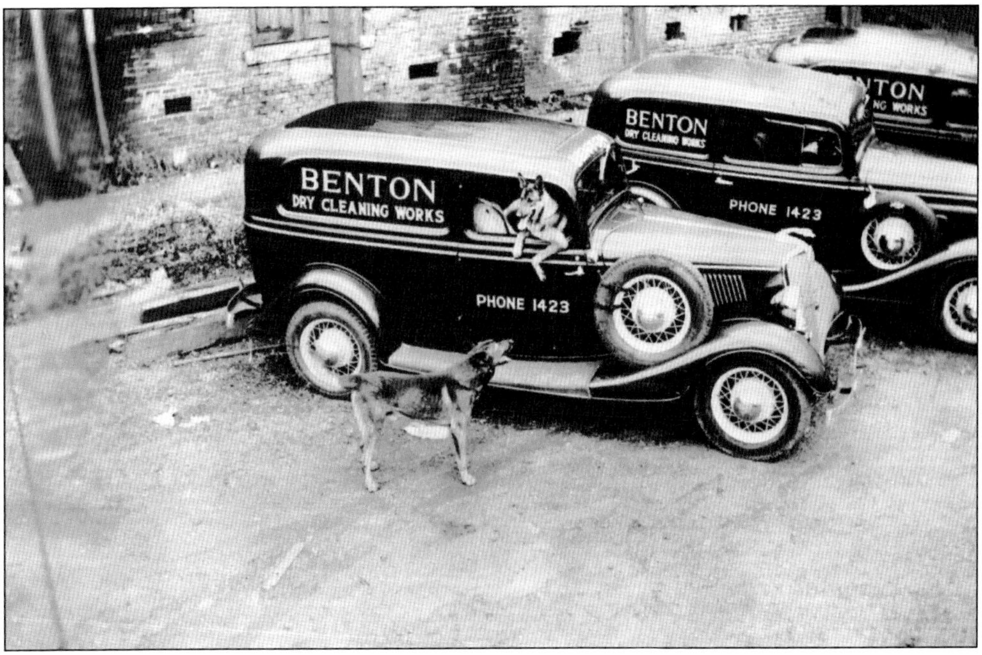

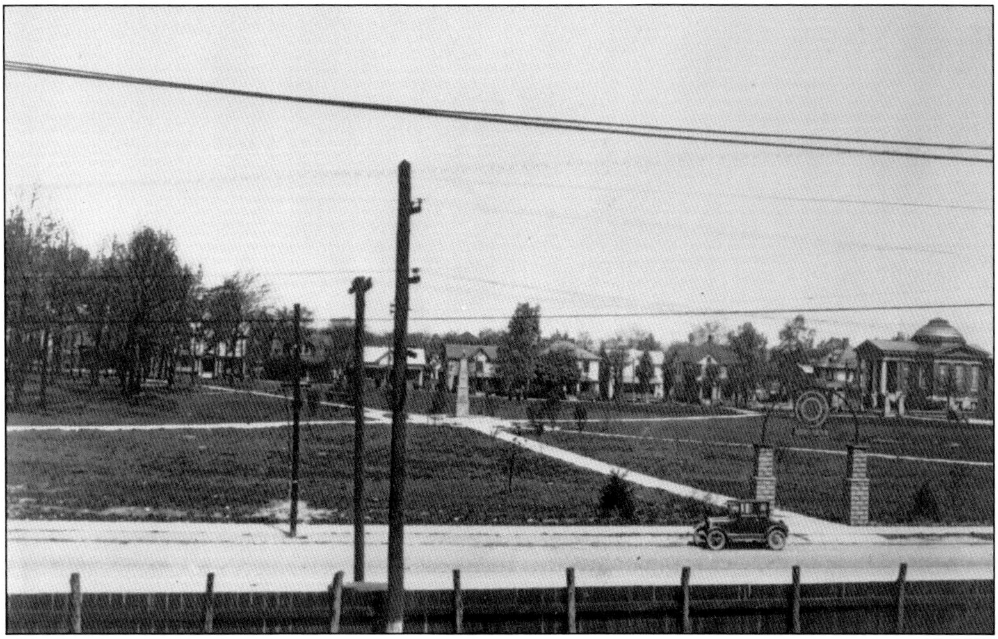

The Southern Railway designed Spencer Town Park to give residents a place for relaxation and community events. Four local churches each adopted a corner to maintain. Trees were planted to line the paths, and a baseball field was constructed by the 1920s. (North Carolina Division of Archives and History.)

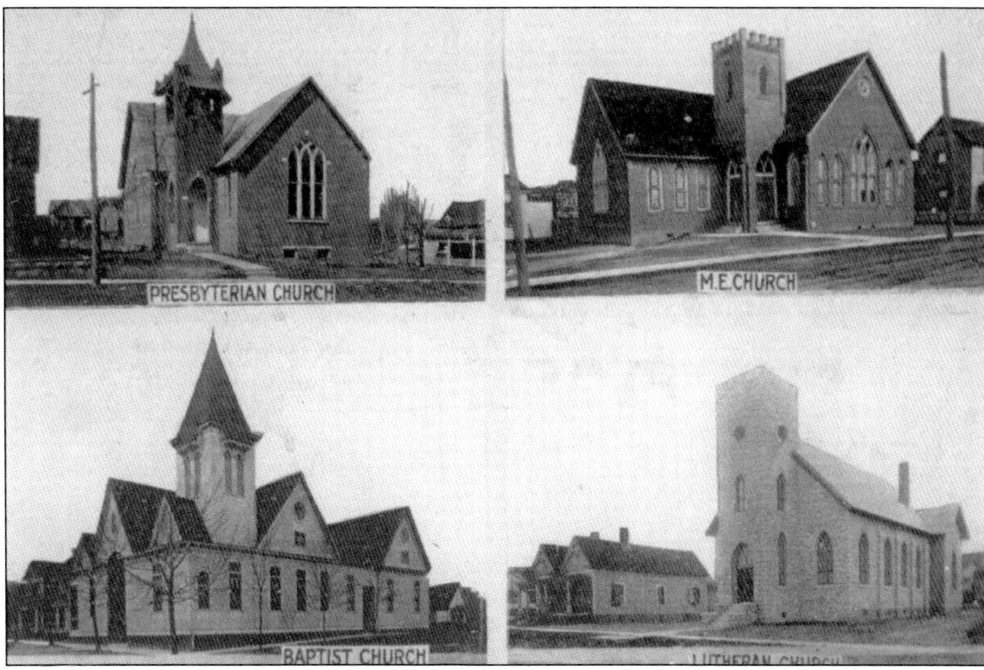

Several different Christian denominations built churches. Christian values were very important to the early leaders of the Southern Railway, as evident by the covenants added to sales of land in Spencer. The Presbyterian church is the only surviving building of this series. The others have been replaced by modern structures. (North Carolina State Archives.)

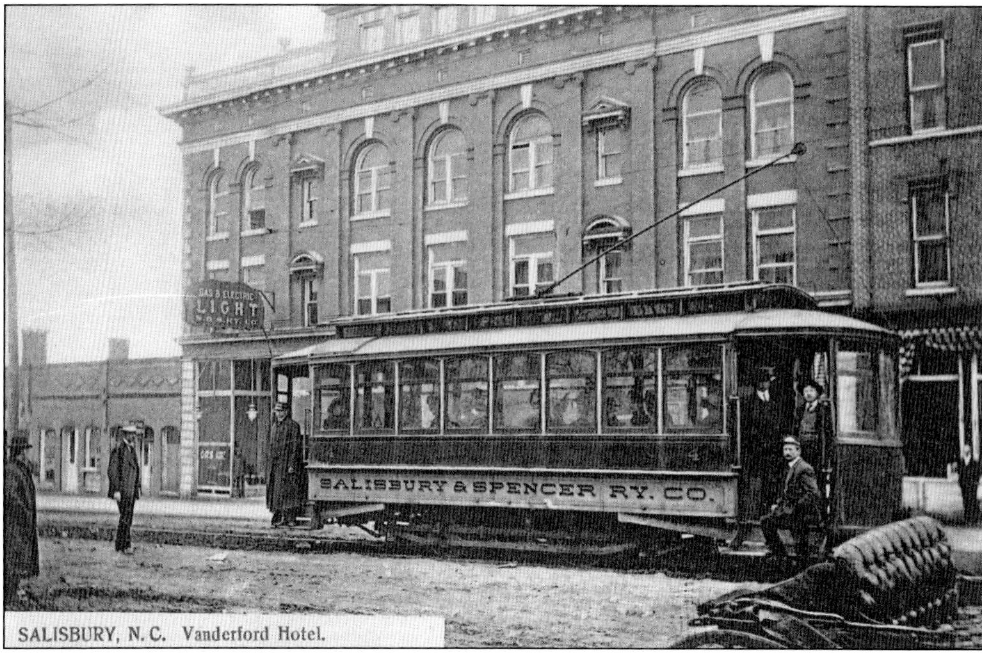

SALISBURY, N. C. Vanderford Hotel.

Some shop workers lived in nearby Salisbury, three miles to the south of Spencer. To aid workers, the Salisbury and Spencer Railway Company built a trolley line between the two communities, terminating in front of the shops. The streetcar system was sold to the North Carolina Public Service Company by 1911 and the Southern Power Company in 1919. The line started in Salisbury at Mitchell Avenue and then extended onto the town's Main Street to Salisbury Avenue in Spencer. (North Carolina Division of Archives and History.)

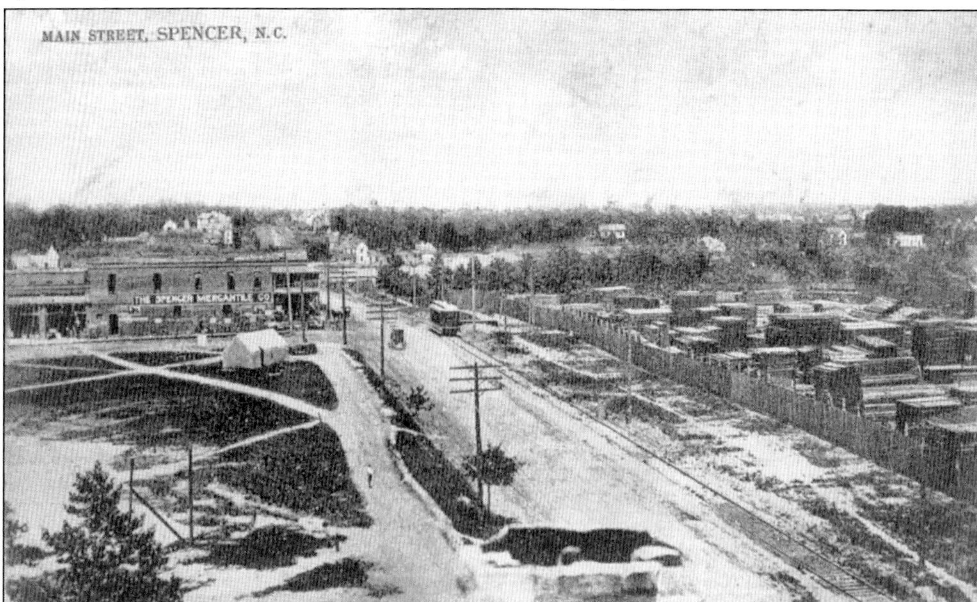

MAIN STREET, SPENCER, N. C.

In this view of Spencer from around 1910, one can see the trolley and track alongside the road and shops. The track was laid with the ties almost on top of the road surface, giving it an uneven look and fairly bumpy ride. (North Carolina Division of Archives and History.)

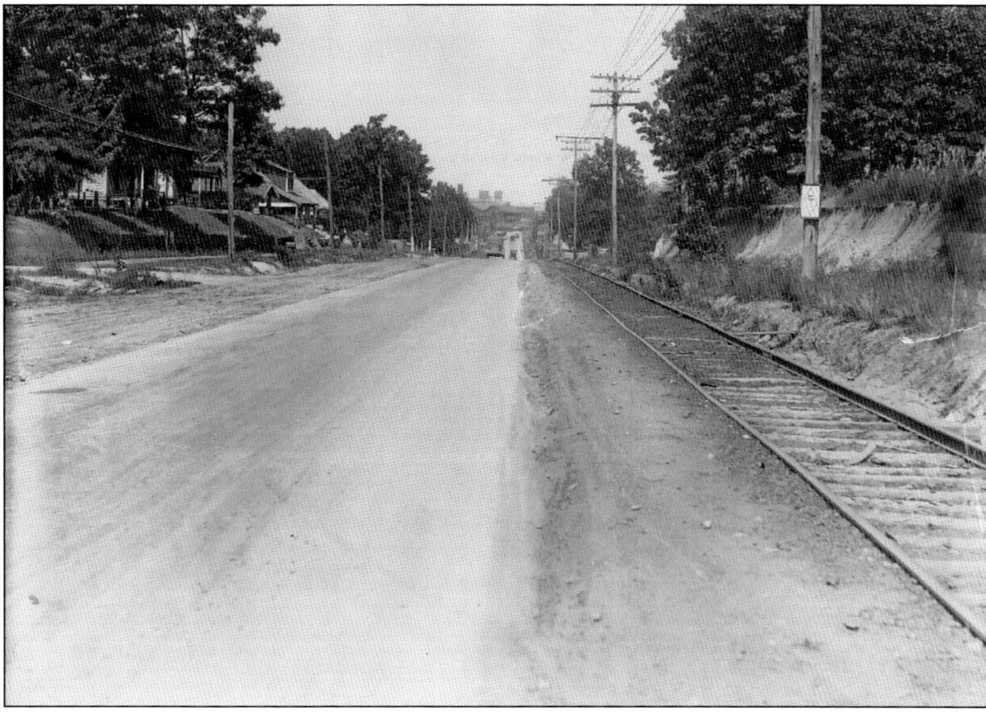

Here is a June 28, 1925, view of Salisbury Avenue and the trolley line. The highway marker on the right marks this road as North Carolina Highway 10, which was changed to Highway 29 through Rowan County. The trolley tracks were not removed after paving in some sections, including Salisbury Avenue in downtown Spencer. (North Carolina Division of Archives and History.)

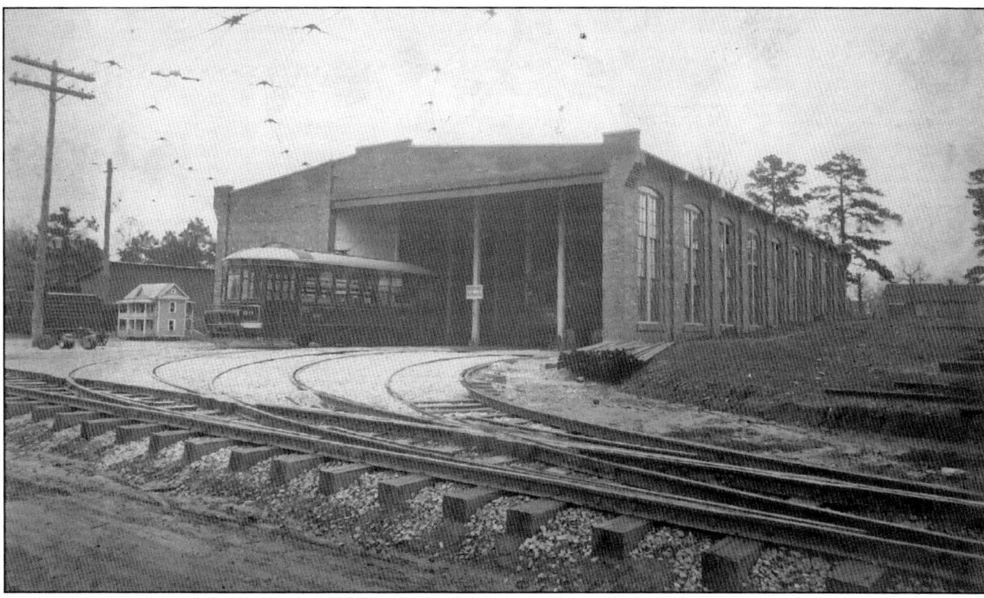

The trolley barn was located between Salisbury and Spencer, with three service tracks entering the building. Southern Power Company, which was renamed Duke Power Company in 1924, continued to use the building for other purposes after trolley service was discontinued in 1938. (North Carolina Division of Archives and History.)

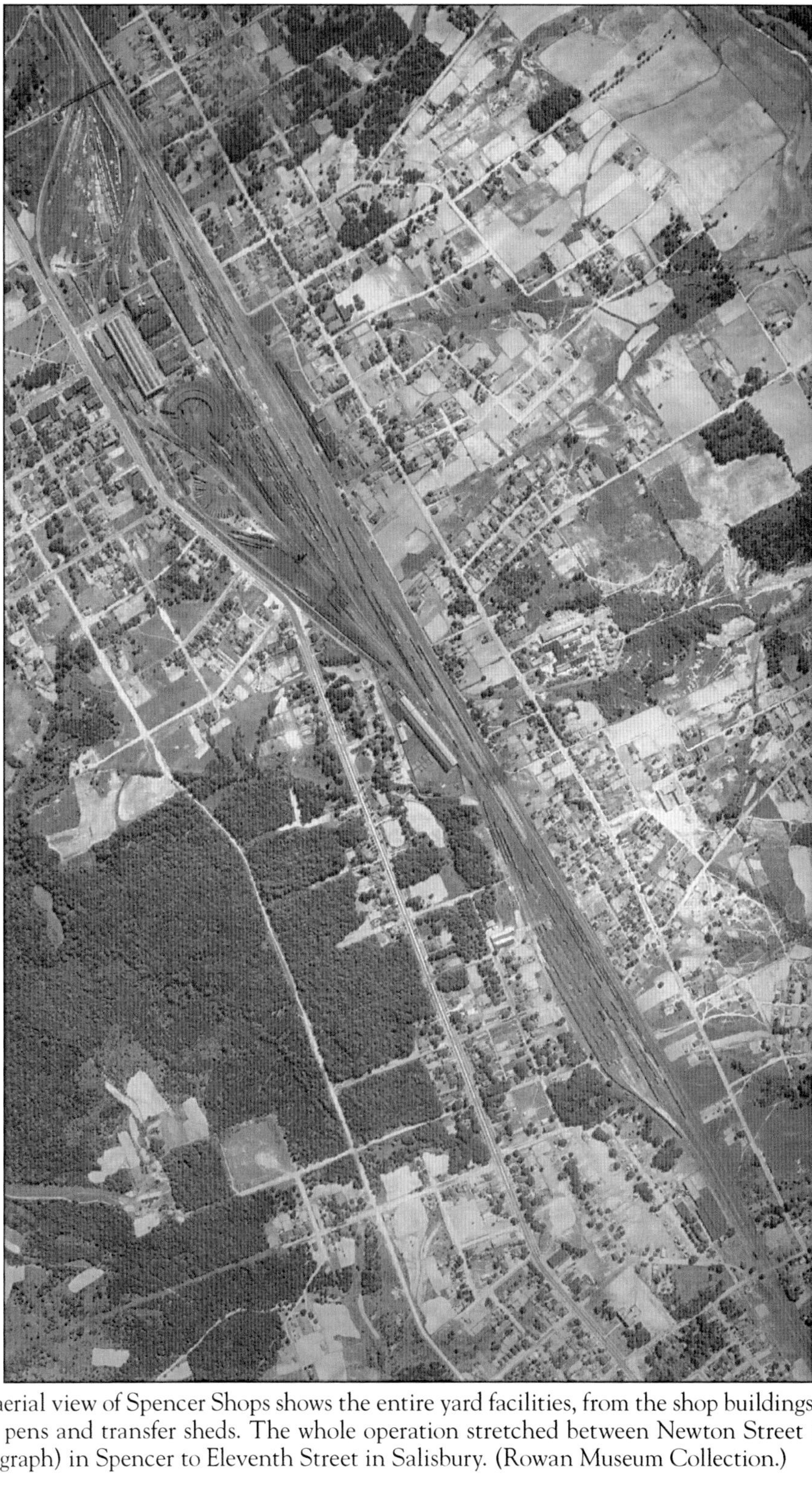

This aerial view of Spencer Shops shows the entire yard facilities, from the shop buildings to the cattle pens and transfer sheds. The whole operation stretched between Newton Street (top of photograph) in Spencer to Eleventh Street in Salisbury. (Rowan Museum Collection.)

Two

Steam Locomotive Repair and Operation

The Southern Railway maintained steam locomotives at Spencer Shops from 1896 until converting to diesels by 1953. These state-of-the-art shops utilized the latest knowledge and technology to maintain locomotives operating between Washington, DC, and Atlanta, Georgia.

The back shop, completed in 1905, was one of the newest and most advanced buildings in the United States for locomotive maintenance. New technology included electric motors to operate machinery, longitudinal design for maintenance similar to an assembly line, and compartmental work areas. At 600 feet in length, the building could easily accommodate 10 to 15 locomotives across four tracks, two through tracks and two stub work tracks. When the building opened, it took two to four weeks to overhaul a steam locomotive.

The new 37-stall roundhouse, with its 100-foot electric turntable, opened in 1924. It could easily hold the largest locomotives through Spencer, which were 2-10-2 Santa Fe types numbered in the 5000 series. To insure the roundhouse was used to full capacity, locomotive work was divided by type of locomotive, work required, and time needed for repairs. Locomotives could not remain in the roundhouse for more than three days, regardless of the work being done.

Spencer Shops eventually became one of the largest and most respected locomotive maintenance facilities on the entire Southern Railway system.

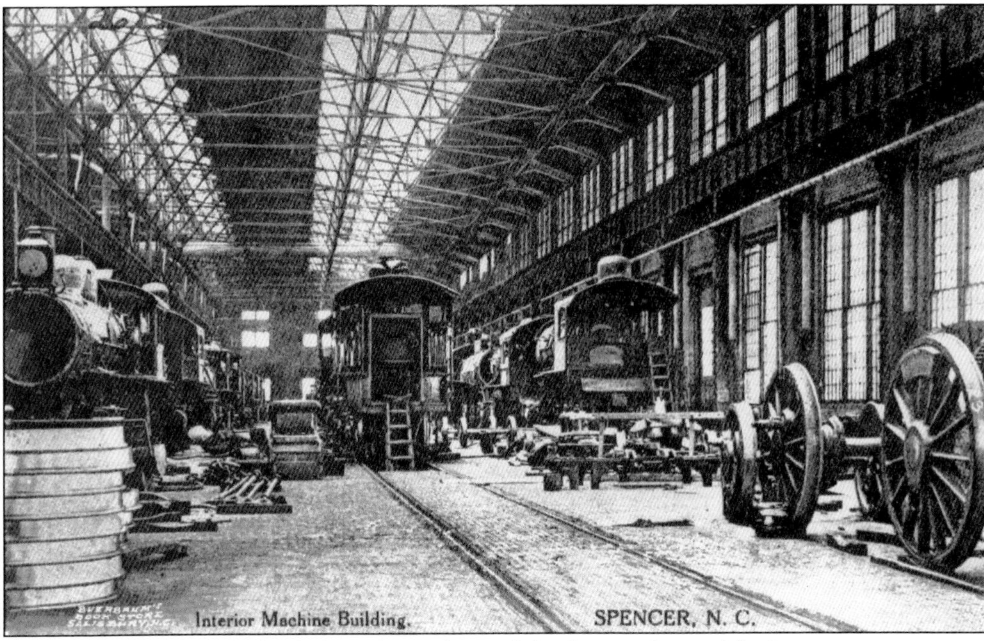

This interior view of the back shop shows three of the four tracks used for locomotive servicing. Locomotives entered the south end of the building and worked their way through repair stations. The skylights and large side windows let in natural light, allowing electricity to be used for machinery rather than lighting. (North Carolina Division of Archives and History.)

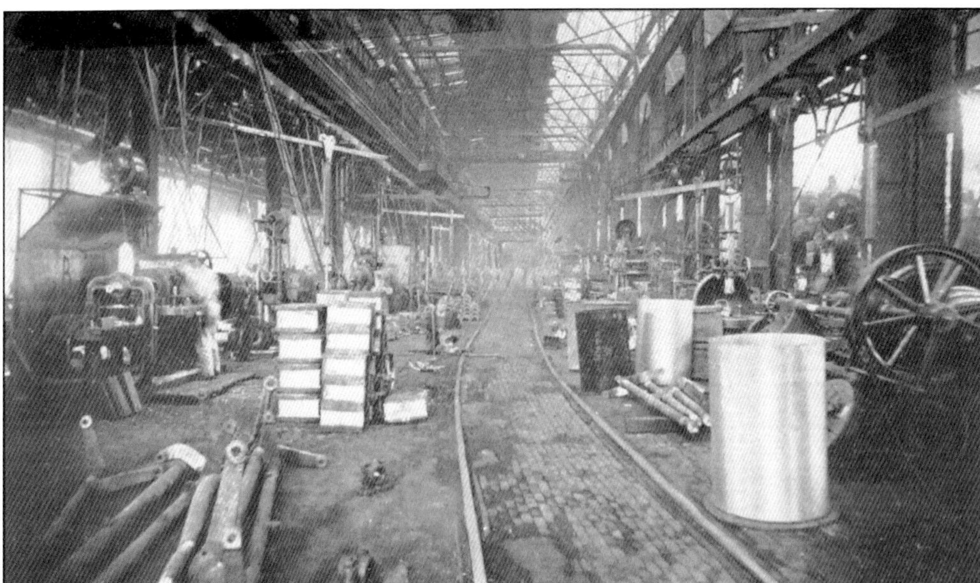

The back shop was divided, with one side for locomotives and the other for machinery. This view shows the line shafts and belts used to operate many of the machines. Small electric motors mounted on the steel columns were used to power the line shafts. (North Carolina Division of Archives and History.)

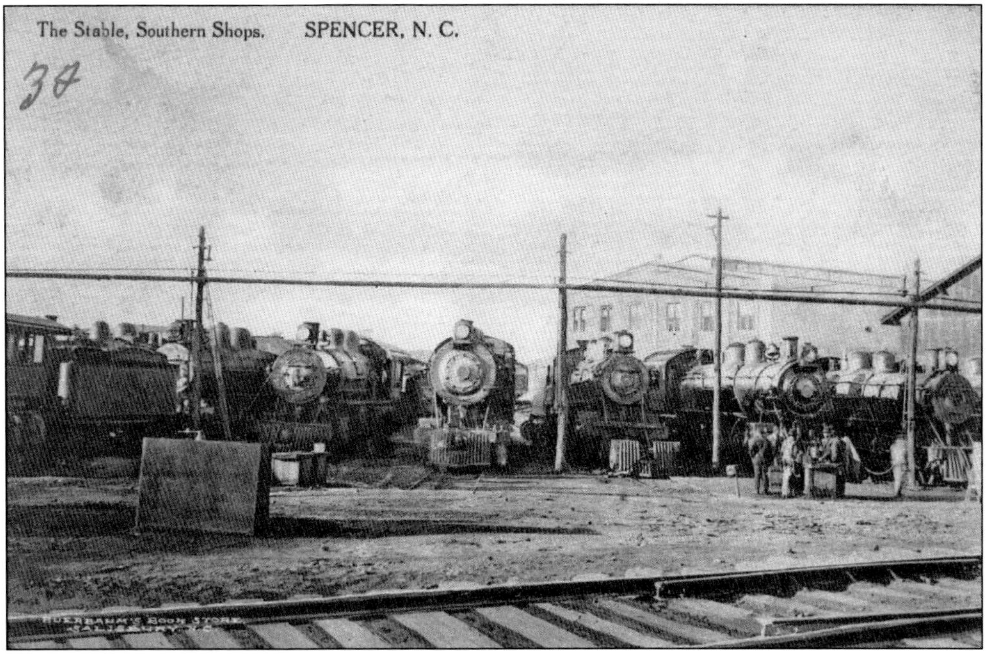

Locomotives are seen arranged on the garden tracks surrounding the turntable. A second turntable was constructed nearby and could accommodate locomotives up to 90 feet in length. A second roundhouse was planned for this turntable but was never built. (North Carolina Division of Archives and History.)

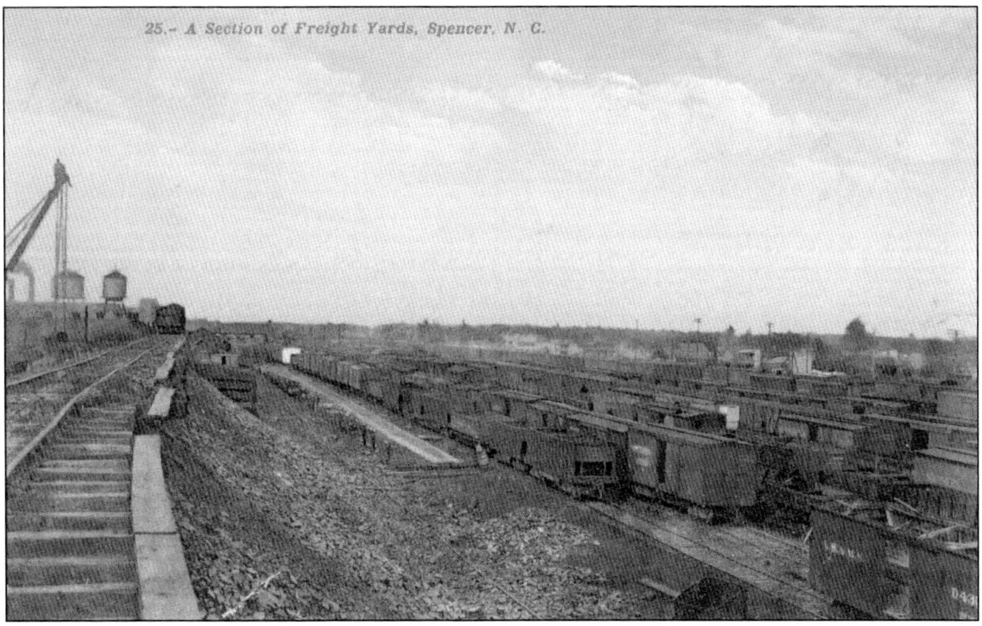

The original coaling dock was located adjacent to the freight classification yard. A crane, visible on the extreme left, shoveled coal from the pile into a tender. Though efficient, this became outdated and was subsequently replaced by a large coaling tower by the 1920s. The tower could load four locomotives with coal at once. (Rowan Museum Collection.)

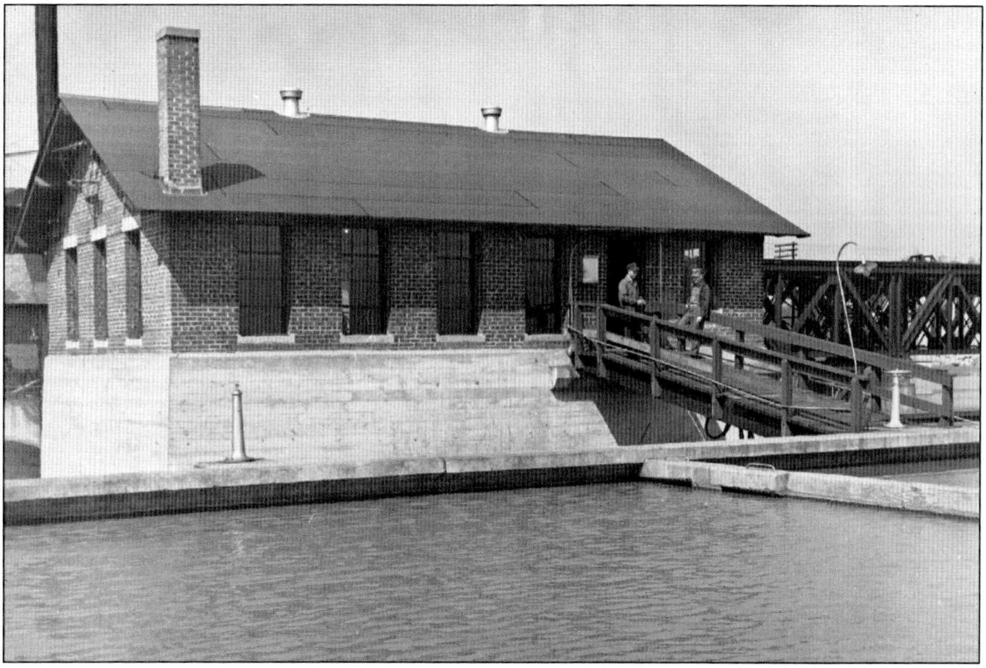

Steam locomotives not only needed coal to operate but also plenty of water. The Southern Railway built a water treatment plant alongside its bridge on the Yadkin River. Water that was collected from the river was treated to prevent boiler corrosion and piped to the shops and stored in tanks. (North Carolina Division of Archives and History.)

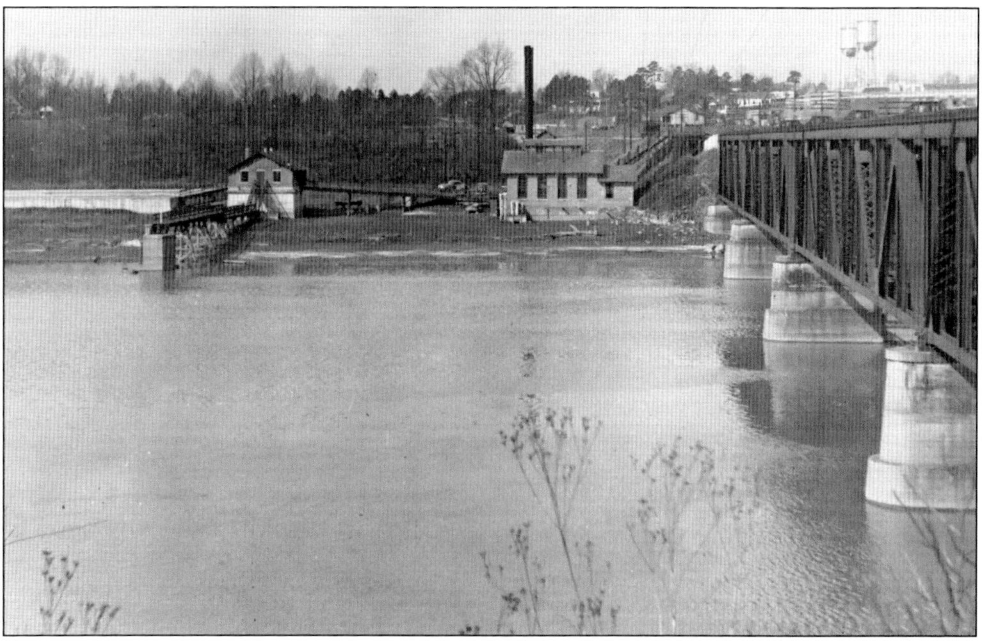

Here is a view taken beside the Southern Railway bridge over the Yadkin River of the pump station. Concrete pools held water awaiting treatment. Water from the river was also pumped to Spencer Shops for use in fire prevention and stored in tanks near the master mechanic's office. (North Carolina State Archives.)

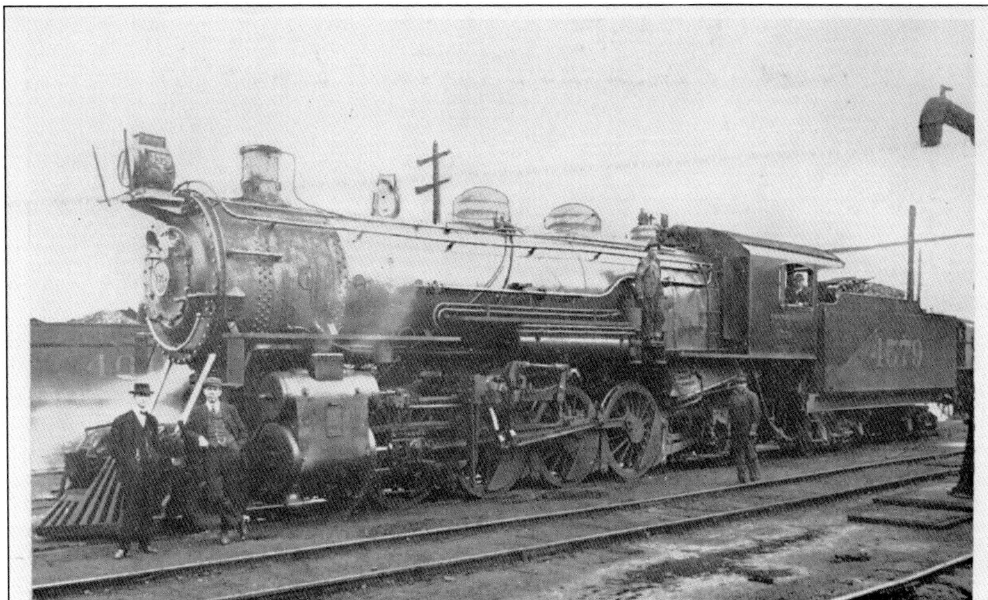

NO. 4579—ONE OF THE GIANTS. D. V. BARGUS, ENGINEER, Spencer, N. C.

Baldwin Locomotive Works constructed Southern Ms-class 2-8-2 Mikado No. 4579 in 1914. The locomotives were used for freight service on both the main and branch lines of the Southern Railway. When engineers were assigned to engines, they added ornamentation, such as the two "candlesticks" bracketing the headlight. (North Carolina Division of Archives and History.)

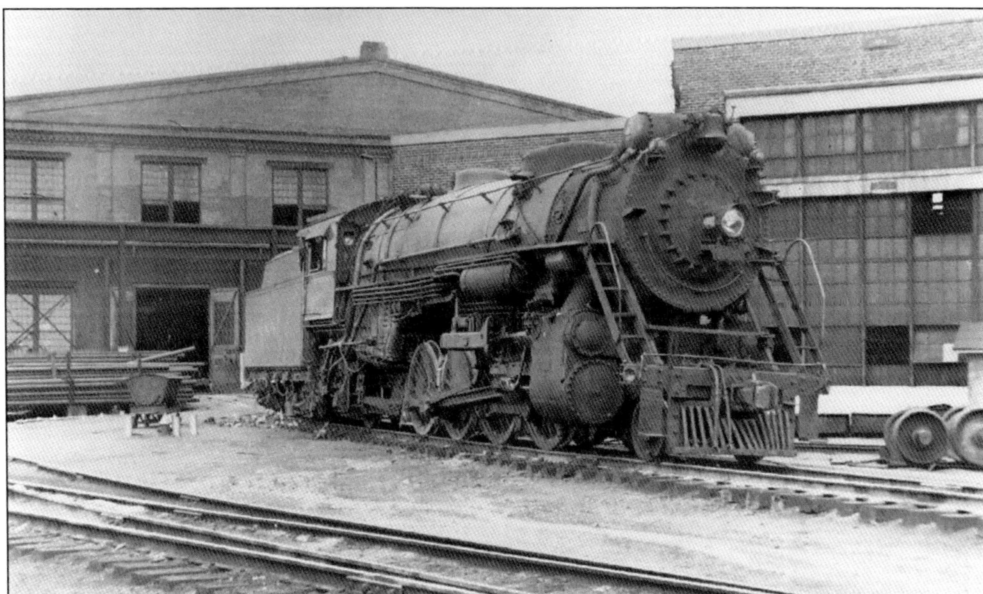

Southern 4881, a Ms-4-class 2-8-2, is awaiting work in the back shop during the 1940s. From this point, the locomotive would be separated from the tender and enter the building facing south. The tracks beside the roundhouse were also used for temporary storage and work on locomotives by roundhouse crews. On average, a locomotive entering the back shop would require two to four weeks for overhaul. The back shop accommodated up to 15 locomotives at one time. (North Carolina Division of Archives and History.)

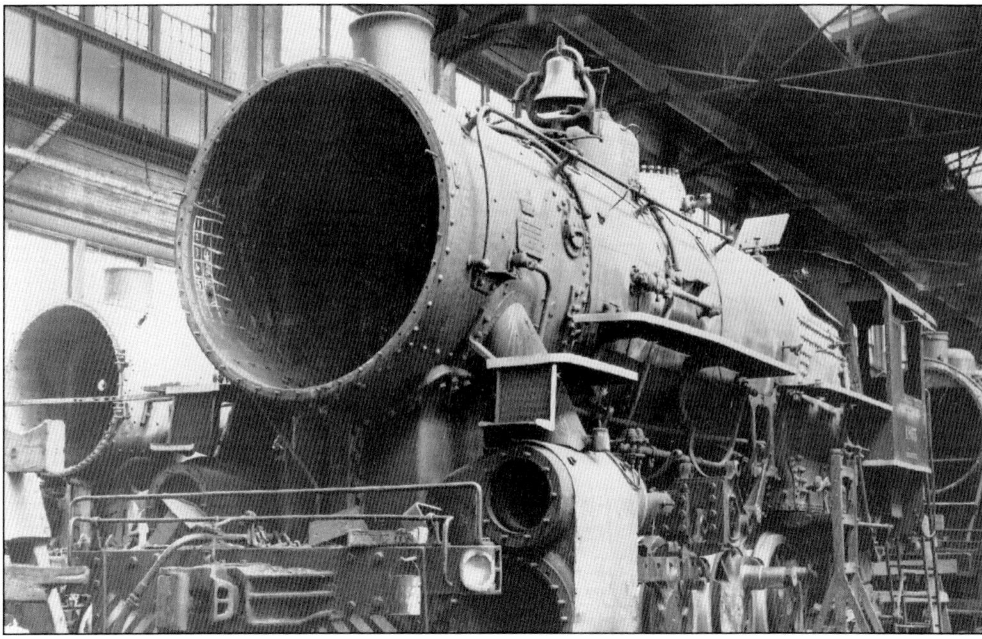

This is a typical view of a steam locomotive inside the back shop. Parts that needed repair were removed and sent to other buildings near the back shop. Wheelsets could also be removed and serviced in this building or sent to the machine shop. Heavy cranes moved locomotives from the communication track (main track through the building) to erecting tracks (side tracks used to store locomotives under repair) to allow more locomotives to be serviced. (North Carolina State Archives.)

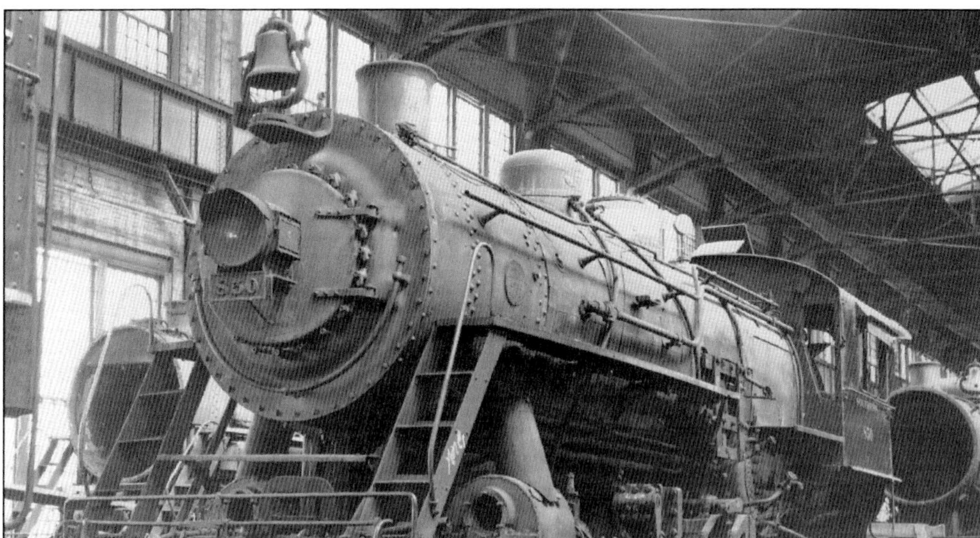

This locomotive, bracketed by two other locomotives, has not experienced total disassembly, since it still has the boiler front and headlight in place. Note that cylinder covers and drive rods have been removed. One easy way to spot a Spencer locomotive was the walkway step handrails and the triangular bell bracket—all of which were made to the same design. Each railroad shop on the Southern personalized certain parts that gave the locomotives a local identity. (North Carolina State Archives.)

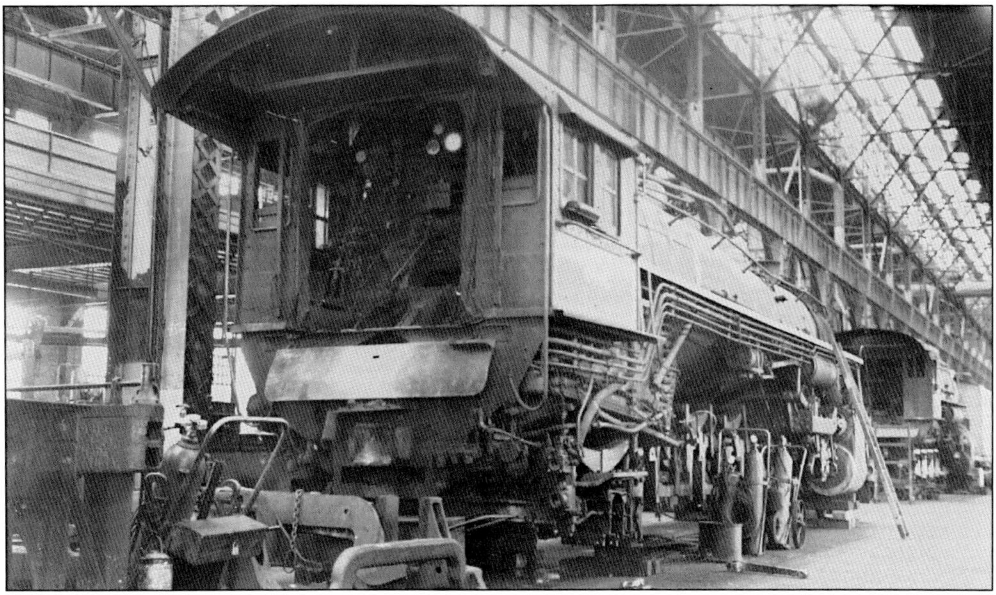

A locomotive in the back shop could be stripped down to the boiler and frame if necessary to complete the overhaul. In this particular case, an unknown locomotive has had all the wheelsets removed and wooden blocks added to support the weight. In some cases, workers removed the cab if the interior woodwork needed to be replaced. (North Carolina Division of Archives and History.)

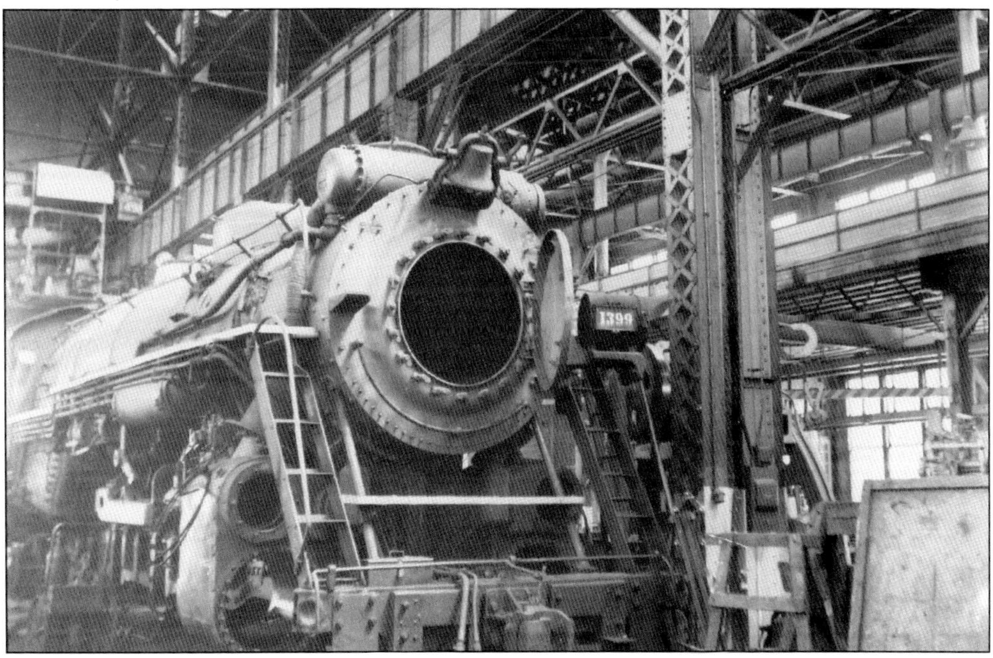

Here is another locomotive receiving a complete overhaul. The wheelsets have been removed, as well as the cylinder covers. This was passenger locomotive 1399, a Ps-4 4-6-2 Pacific built in 1926. It had 73-inch drivers and an Elesco Feedwater Heater (used to preheat water before adding it to the boiler) mounted across the smokebox. The Ps-4 locomotives were used to pull the *Crescent* between Washington, DC, and Atlanta. (North Carolina Division of Archives and History.)

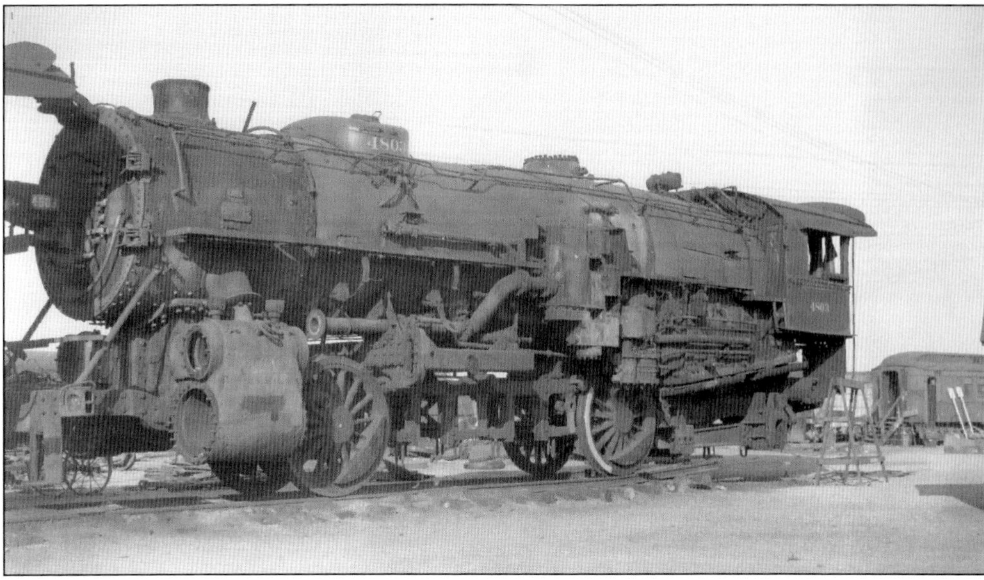

Due to limited space, some locomotives undergoing overhaul in the back shop were removed and stored around the property. Locomotive 4803, above, was stripped of several parts, including most wheelsets, driving rods, and valve gear. Locomotive 5072, below, sits on a roundhouse garden track awaiting work on the cab and flues, as evidenced by open access to the smokebox. (Photographs by C.K. Marsh; both, Marvin Rogers's collection.)

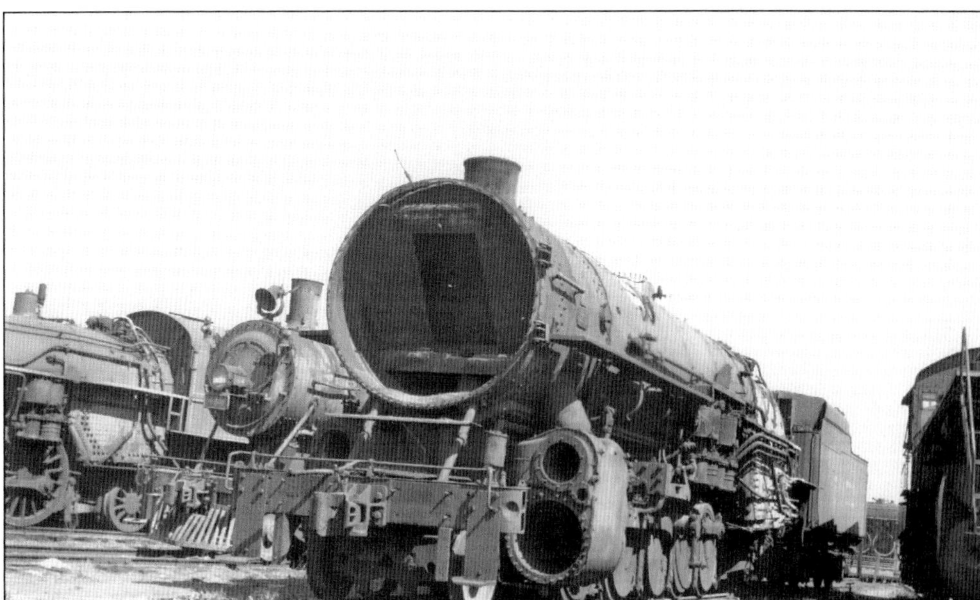

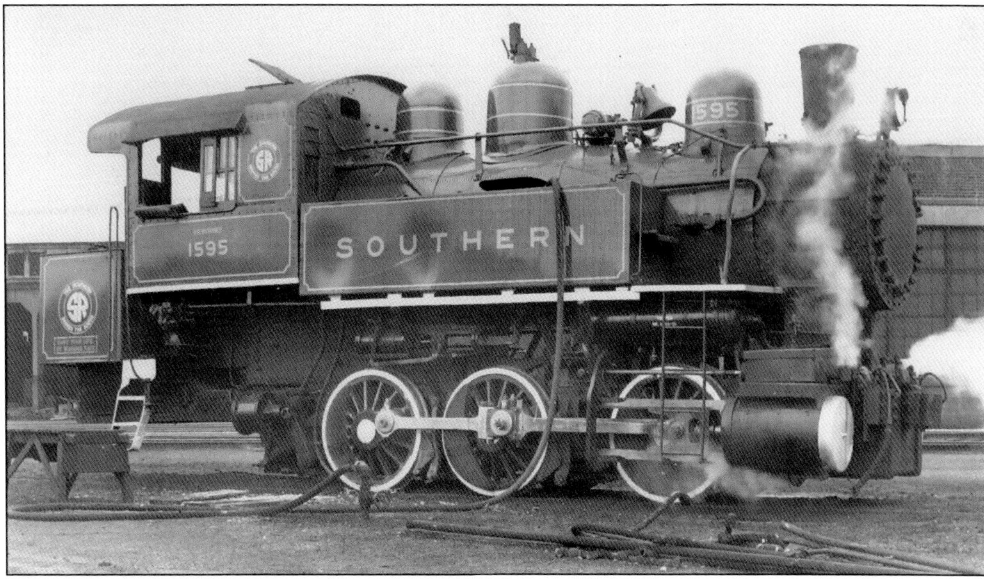

The Southern converted three 0-6-0 steam switch locomotives into yard goats to move locomotives around the property. The locomotives were numbered 1573, 1575, and 1595. The original tender was replaced with a small coal bunker behind the cab, and water tanks were added to the sides of the boiler. When this photograph of 1595 was made at the roundhouse, the cab had been lettered for engineer O.R. Wagoner. (Marvin Rogers's collection.)

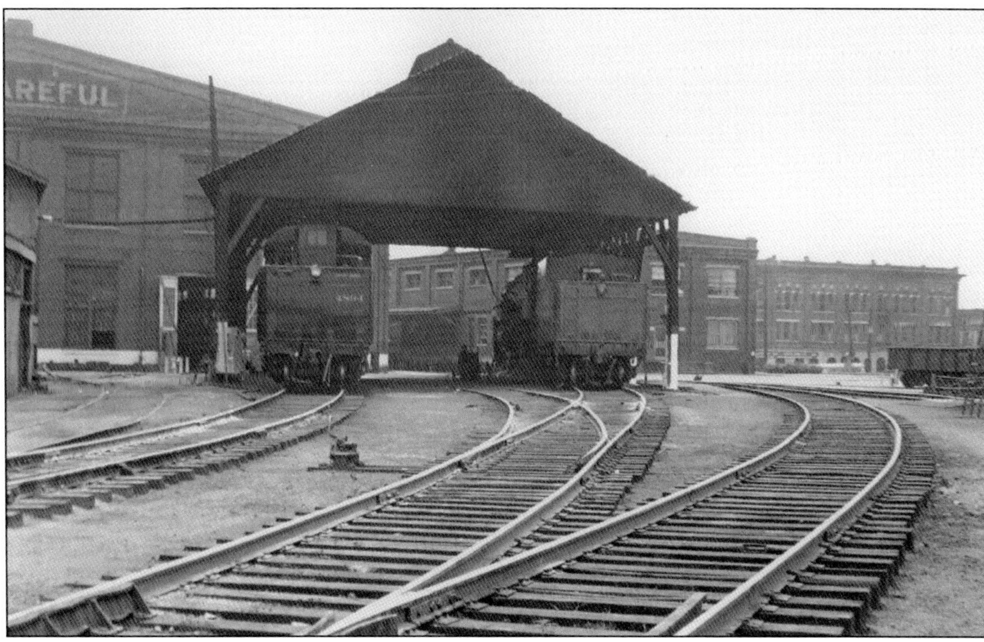

Once a steam locomotive was finished in the back shop, it was moved to the firing-up shed, the small building at the bottom of the photograph. Once it was mated back with its tender, the locomotive would be test fired under the shed. From there, the locomotive was operated around the shops and then moved to the main line. If everything passed, it was taken to the service area south of the roundhouse for coal and water and placed on the ready tracks. (Photograph by David Driscoll; J. Marvin Black's collection.)

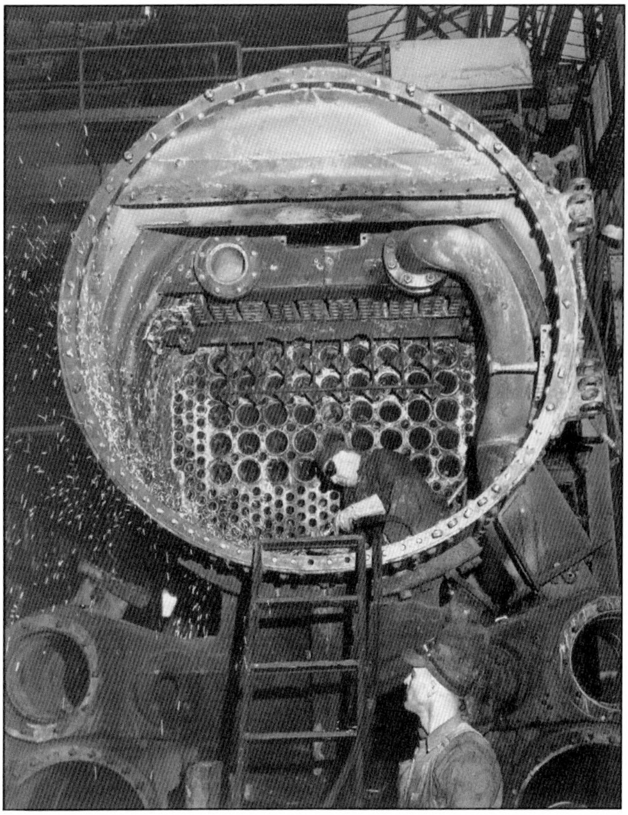

Two areas that needed special attention were the smokebox and front flue sheet. The smokebox was checked for corrosion, and the flues were inspected for cracks or broken welds. All work was performed according to Federal Railroad Administration guidelines. H.W. Guffey is seen using a cutting torch while J.W. Hedge watches. (Photograph by the Southern Railway; collection of North Carolina State Archives.)

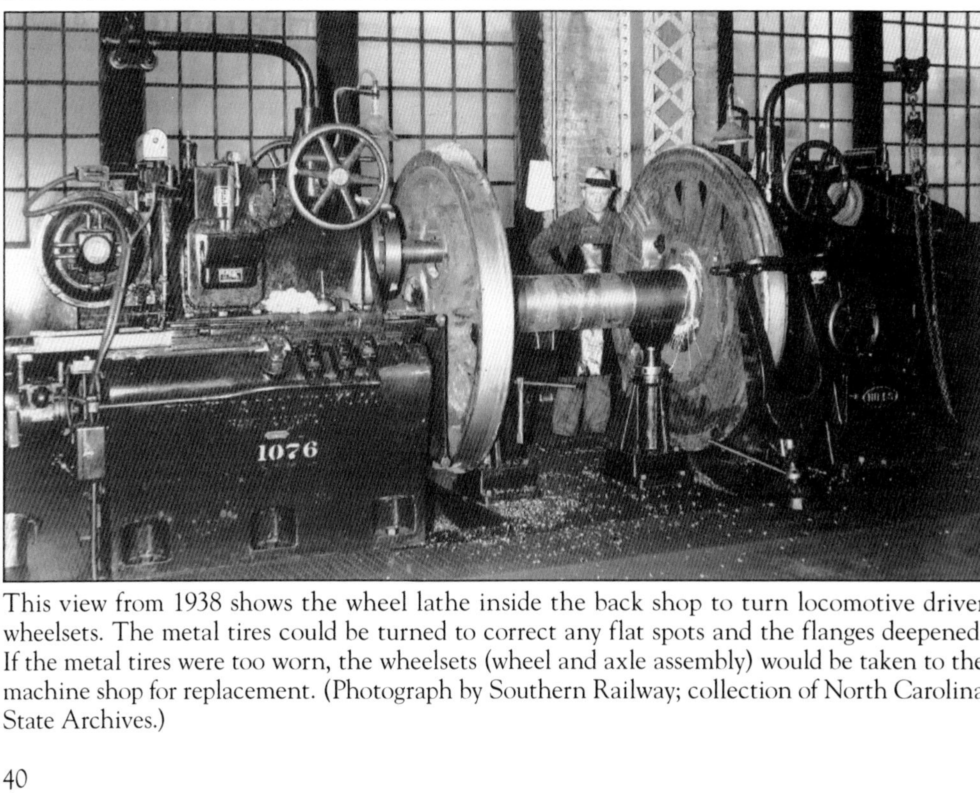

This view from 1938 shows the wheel lathe inside the back shop to turn locomotive driver wheelsets. The metal tires could be turned to correct any flat spots and the flanges deepened. If the metal tires were too worn, the wheelsets (wheel and axle assembly) would be taken to the machine shop for replacement. (Photograph by Southern Railway; collection of North Carolina State Archives.)

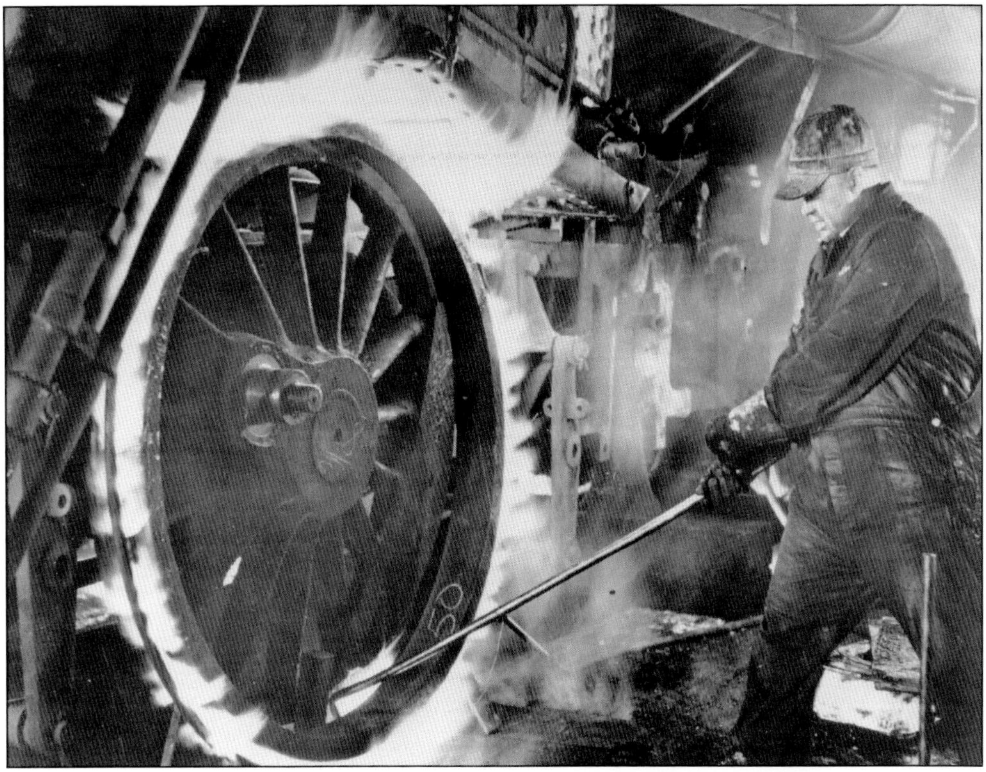

Replacing a locomotive drive tire was a very hot process! First, the old tire was heated using a fire ring until it was red hot. The old tire was removed, and the new tire, also preheated, was pressed into place. Once cooled, the new tire would be locked in place due to the metal tightening around the rim. This process could be performed while the wheelset was still on the locomotive, as illustrated by this photograph. (North Carolina Division of Archives and History.)

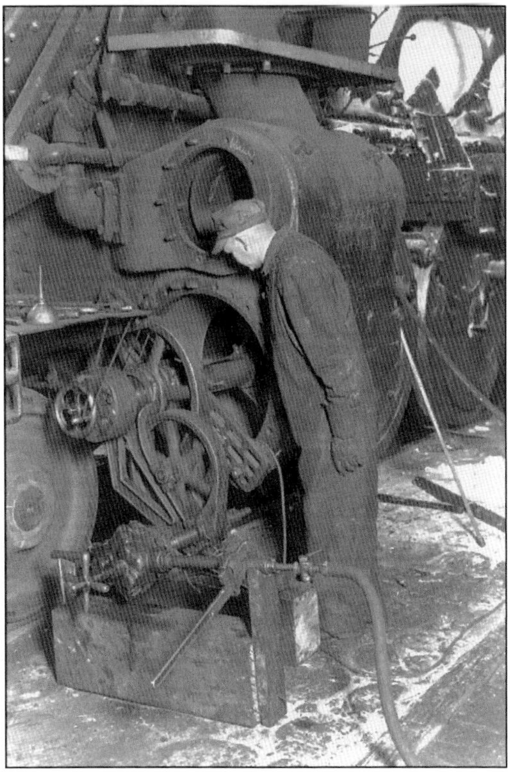

Other machine work performed in the back shop included cylinder cleaning and boring. This boring machine would clean the cylinder walls to insure a smooth surface during overhaul. The workers assigned to this task would work their way down the line of locomotives with a portable lathe. (North Carolina Division of Archives and History.)

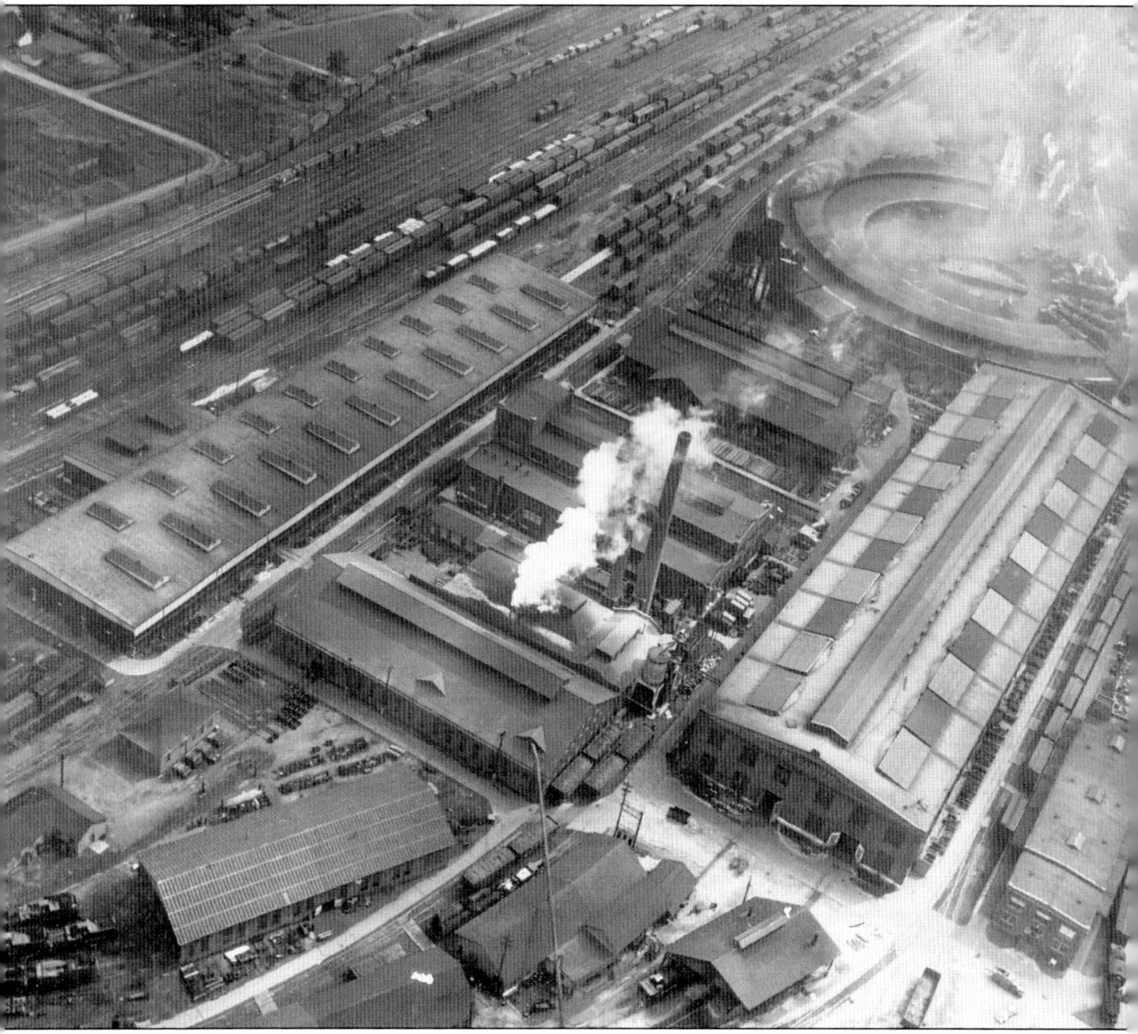

This overhead view shows the primary shop buildings during the late 1940s. From left to right are the car repair shed, woodworking shop, powerhouse, boiler shop, machine shop, back shop, and master mechanic's office. The buildings in the lower left corner include the tender repair building (later converted to a paint shop) and the firing-up shed, located just below the back shop. The roundhouse is visible in the upper right corner. This photograph was made during the steam-to-diesel transition and shows a diesel switcher working in the yard. (North Carolina State Archives.)

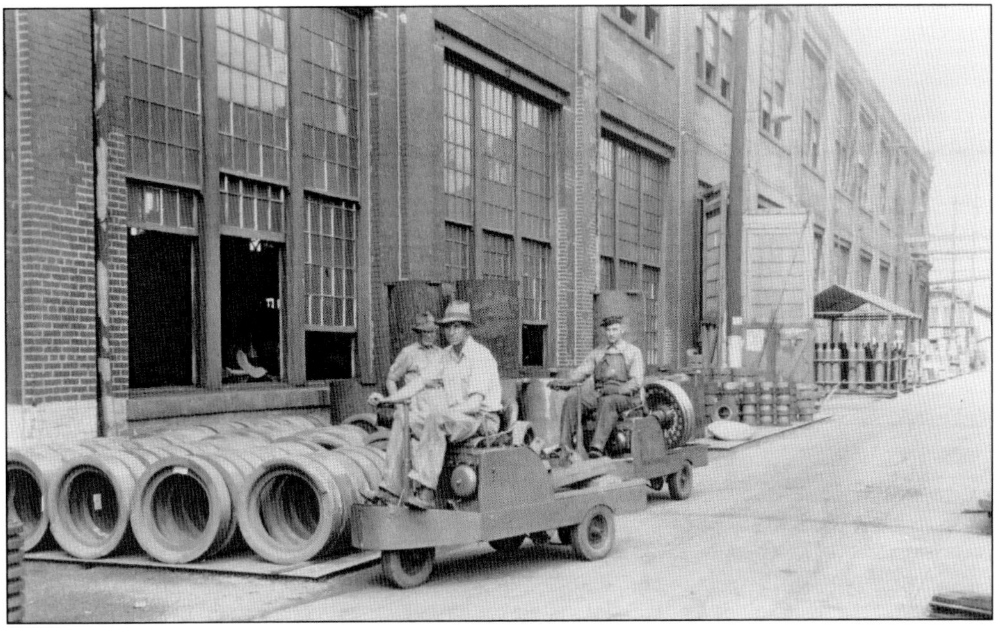

When the back shop was opened in 1905, special tracked carts were used to ferry parts and tools between the buildings. These were later replaced by motorized rubber-tired vehicles, which are shown beside the east end of the building. With these carts, parts could easily be taken to the boiler shop, machine shop, or other building as needed. Note the bell to warn people when entering buildings. (North Carolina Division of Archives and History.)

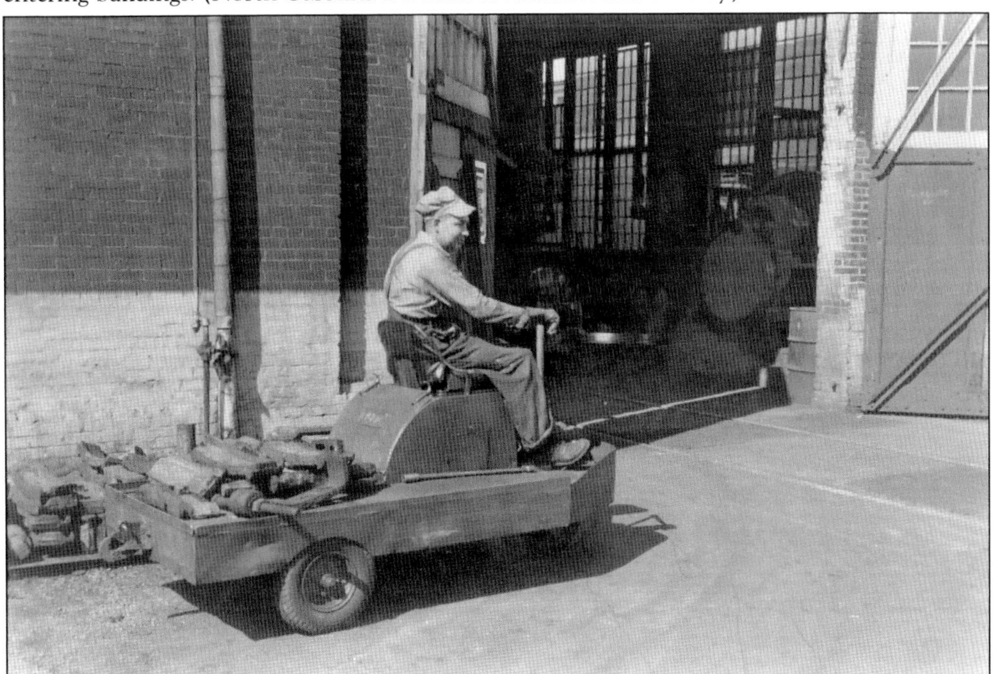

Here is a close up view of one of these motorized carts. The original track through the machine side of the back shop was still used until the building closed in 1960. (North Carolina Division of Archives and History.)

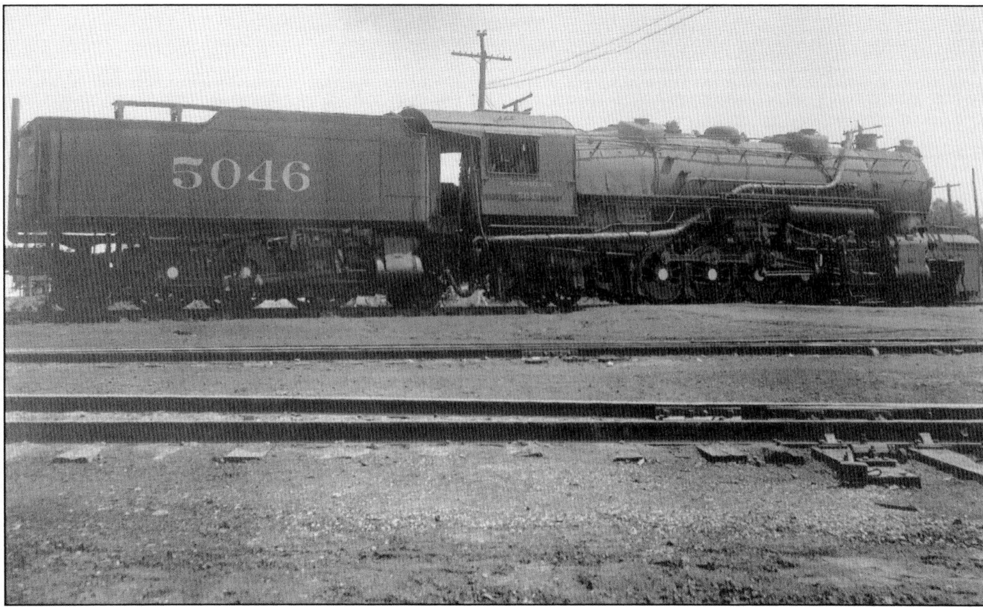

The workers at Spencer Shops not only performed routine overhauls of steam locomotives but could also totally rebuild them. Southern Ss-class 2-10-2 5046 was the only locomotive of this type to receive a tractor motor under the tender. Note the large pipe from the boiler to power the extra cylinders. This experiment lasted until 1926, when the tractor motor was removed. The Asheville Division used these special locomotives between Asheville and Salisbury and over the Saluda grade, which was between Asheville and Spartanburg, South Carolina. (North Carolina Division of Archives and History.)

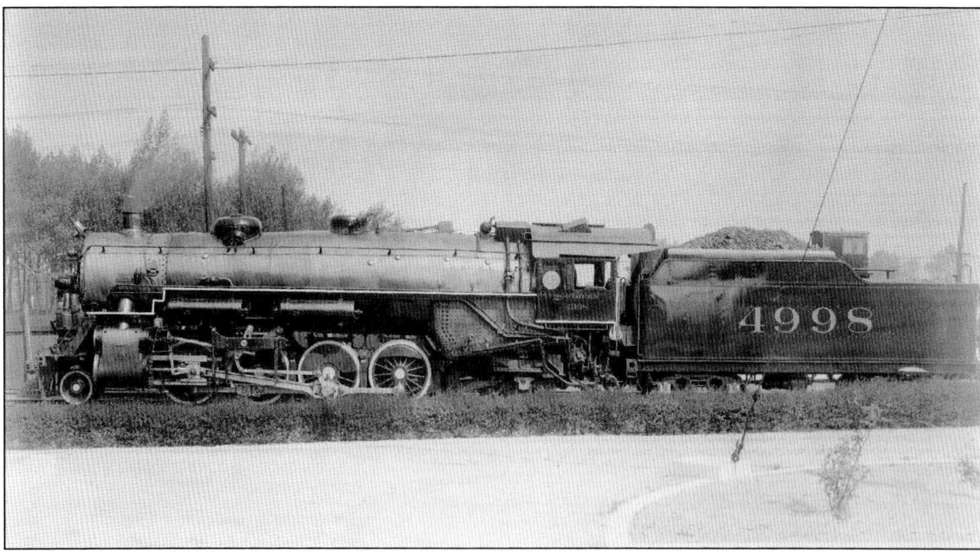

Southern 4998 started out as Ss-1-class 2-10-2 No. 5234, built in 1918. Starting in 1929, the Southern began a program to rebuild surplus 2-10-2 locomotives into 2-8-2 Mikados. No. 4998 was the first such locomotive completed at Spencer Shops, redesignated the Ms-5 class. This locomotive was given 63-inch drivers to operate fast freight service and passenger trains between Washington, DC, and Atlanta. Only four other locomotives were rebuilt between 1929 and 1931 due to conditions of the Great Depression. (Rowan Public Library Collection.)

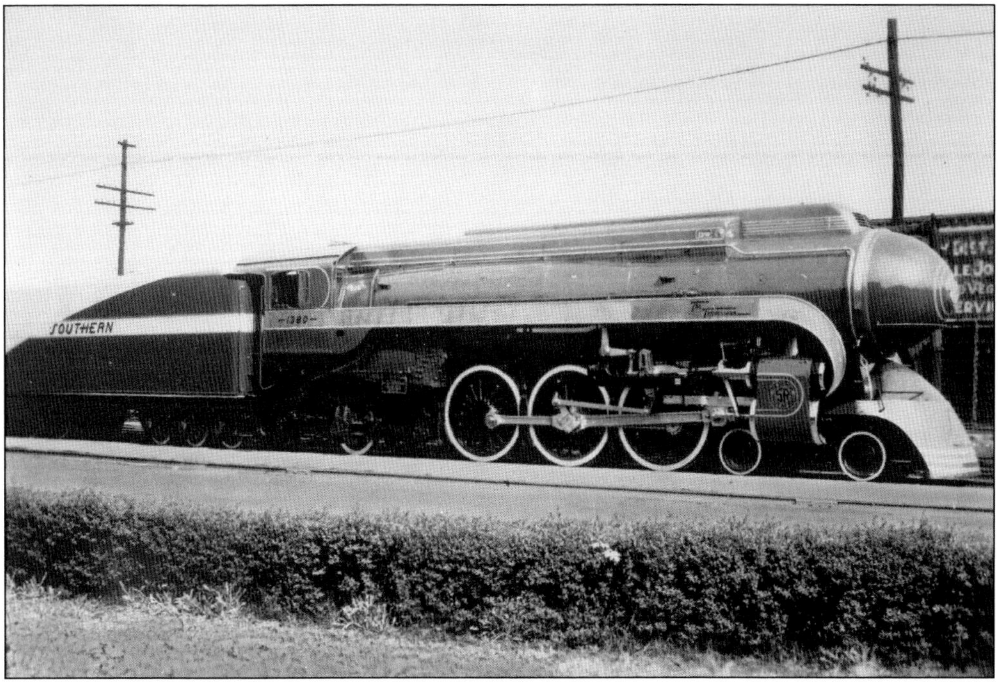

One of the most famous locomotives to come from Spencer Shops was the streamlined Ps-4-class No. 1380. This Pacific-type locomotive was designed to operate on the *Tennessean* passenger train between Washington, DC, and Monroe, Virginia. The famed Art Deco stylist Otto Kuhler designed the metal shroud (shown on upper half of the locomotive), which made the 4-6-2 locomotive look similar to the Norfolk & Western 4-8-4 J class that pulled the train between Bristol, Tennessee, and Lynchburg, Virginia. (North Carolina State Archives.)

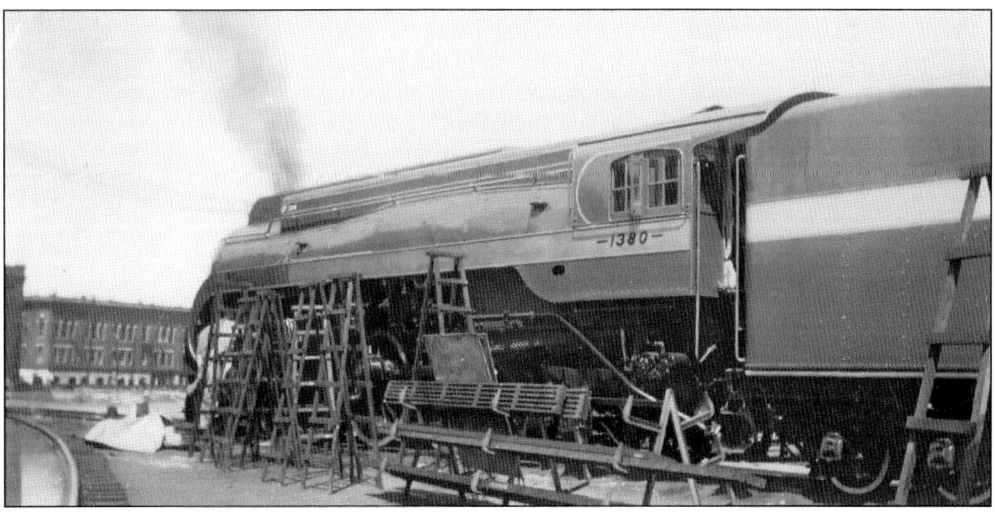

Spencer Shops continued to service the 1380 through its working life. With the metal shroud in place, it was difficult for workers to access the side and top of the boiler. Notice the large number of ladders and platforms needed for the repair. After the 1380 was replaced by diesels on the *Tennessean*, it continued to pull passenger and freight trains between Washington, DC, and Salisbury, North Carolina. (North Carolina Division of Archives and History.)

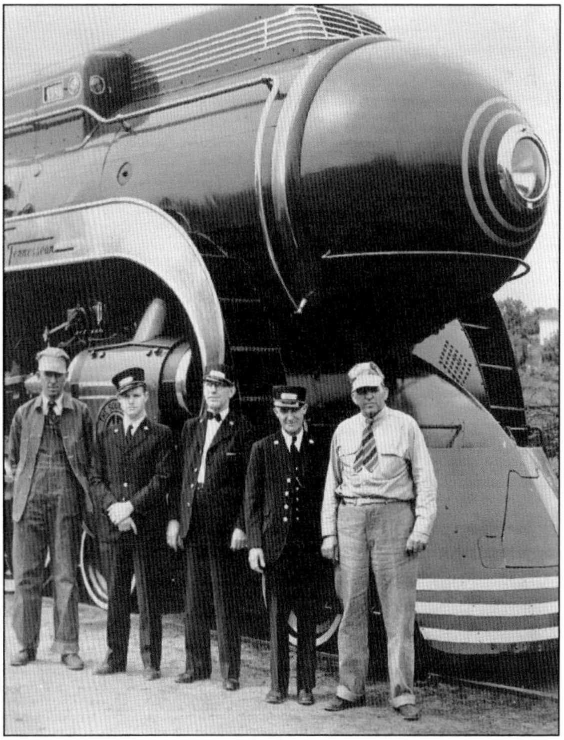

The crews who worked on the 1380 and the *Tennessean* train took great pride in its operation. The entire crew, including the fireman, brakeman, flagman, conductor, and engineer, posed for this photograph. The 1380 pulled the train for about a decade before diesels overtook main line passenger service. (North Carolina State Archives.)

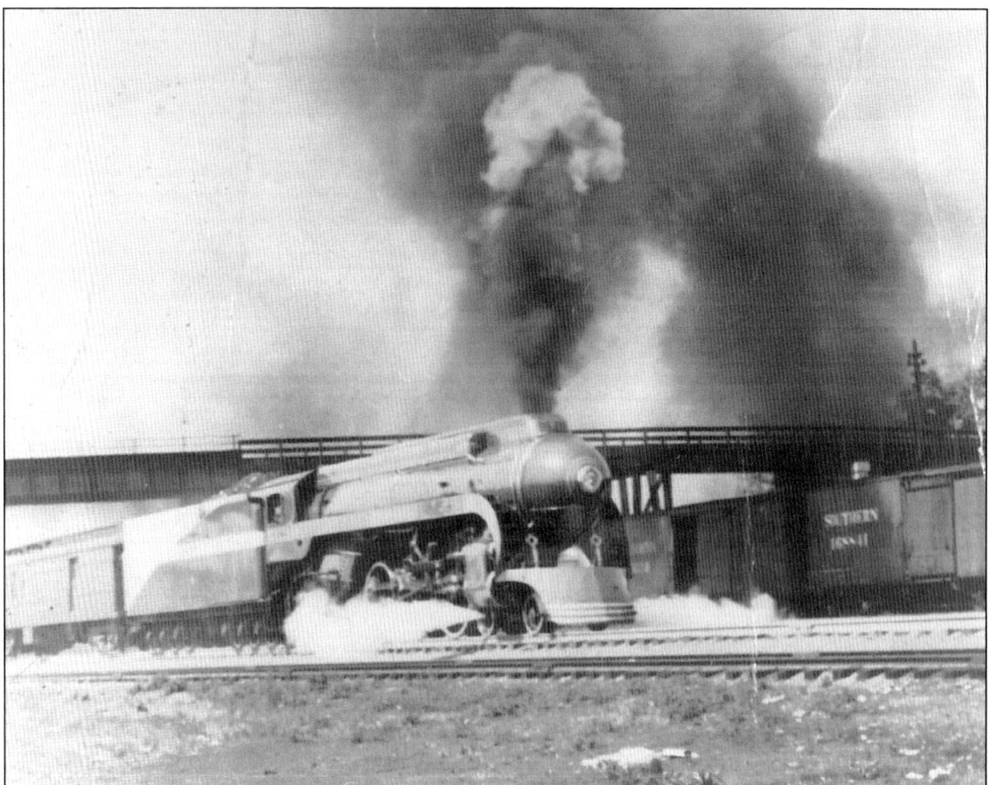

The 1380 is seen just north of Spencer Shops, near the Spencer depot. By this time, the locomotive had been relegated to pulling local passenger and freight trains between Washington, DC, and Salisbury. Despite the new assignment, the 1380 still maintained its streamline appearance and striking paint scheme. (North Carolina Division of Archives and History.)

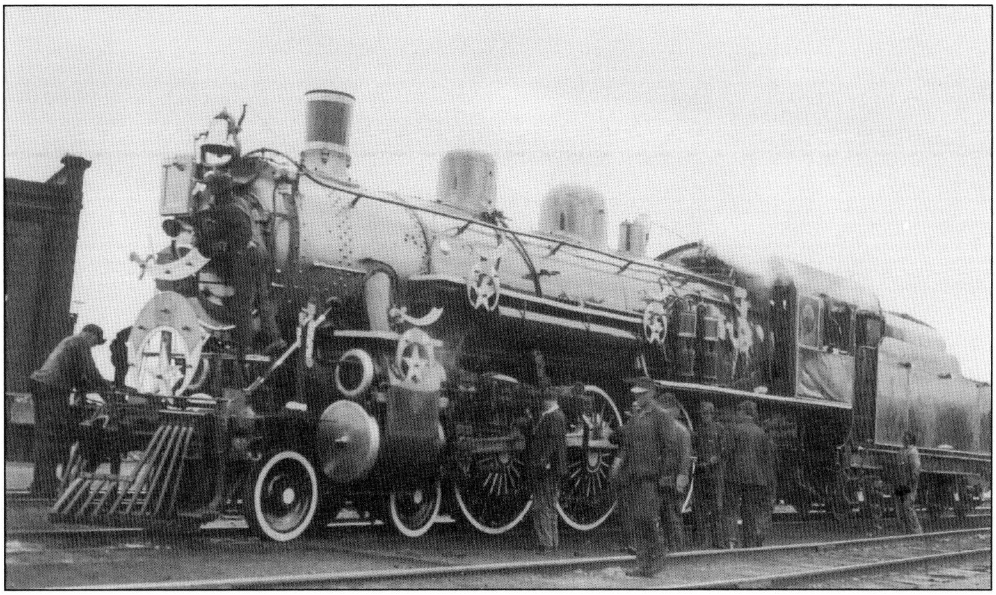

Some locomotives were decorated more for fun than practicality. Here is Ps-class 4-6-2 Pacific No. 1361 decorated for a special Shrine Club train in 1928. As one can see, the decoration covers most of the locomotive. It appears the Shriner emblems on the front could be lit as well as the headlight. What a sight this would make on the main line! (North Carolina Division of Archives and History.)

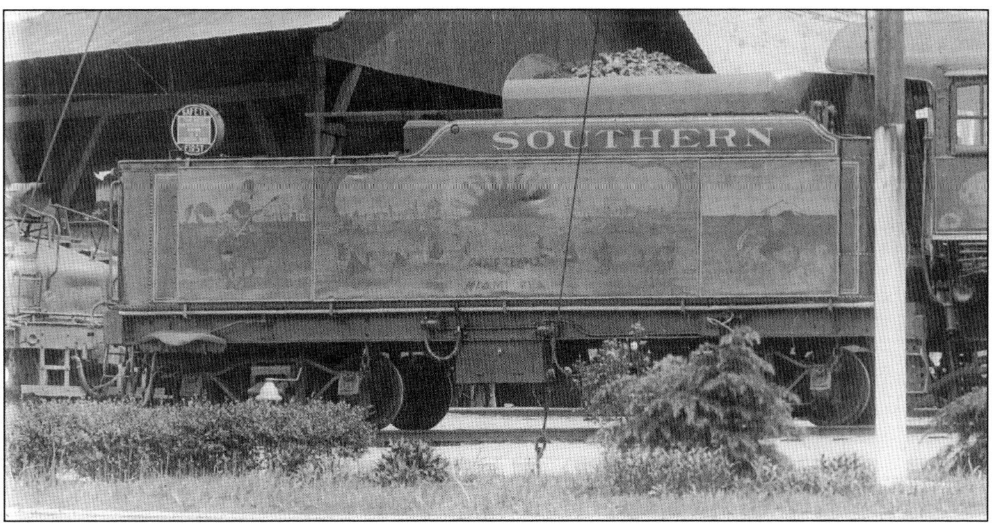

This tender received exquisitely painted murals on both sides. The scenes illustrate some of the Shriner values and the meeting's destination, Miami, Florida. Between 1910 and 1935, it was common to see some type of decoration applied to steam locomotives by engineers, but it was not common for the artwork to be this elaborate. (Photograph by Shelby Lowe; Vernon Lane's collection.)

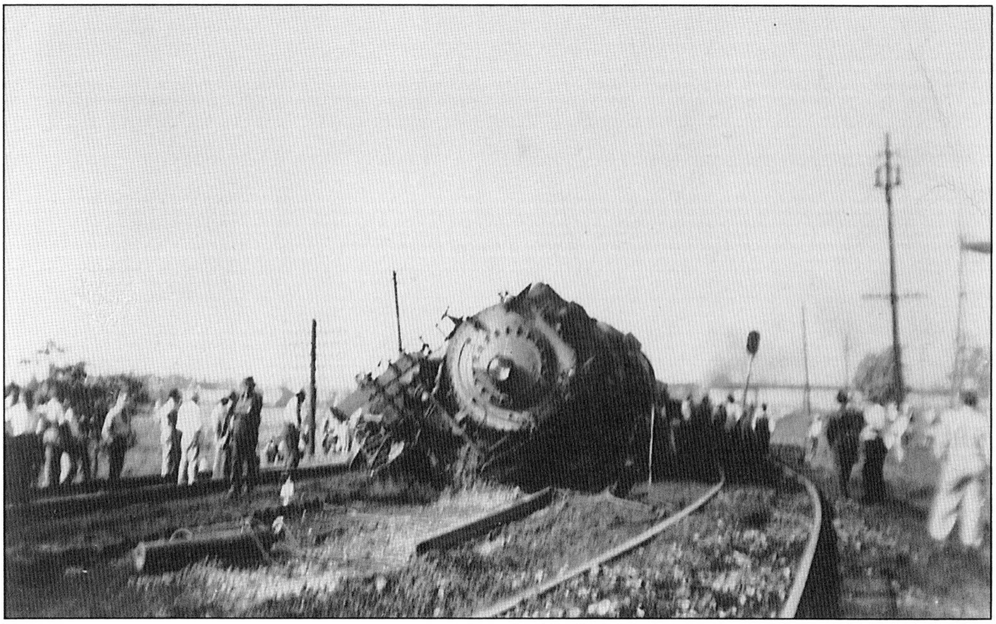

Locomotives damaged as a result of derailments or accidents were sent to Spencer Shops for repairs. Here, a locomotive must have found a bad rail and started to roll. Once returned to the tracks by a wreck crane, it was towed to Spencer and overhauled in the back shop. (North Carolina Division of Archives and History.)

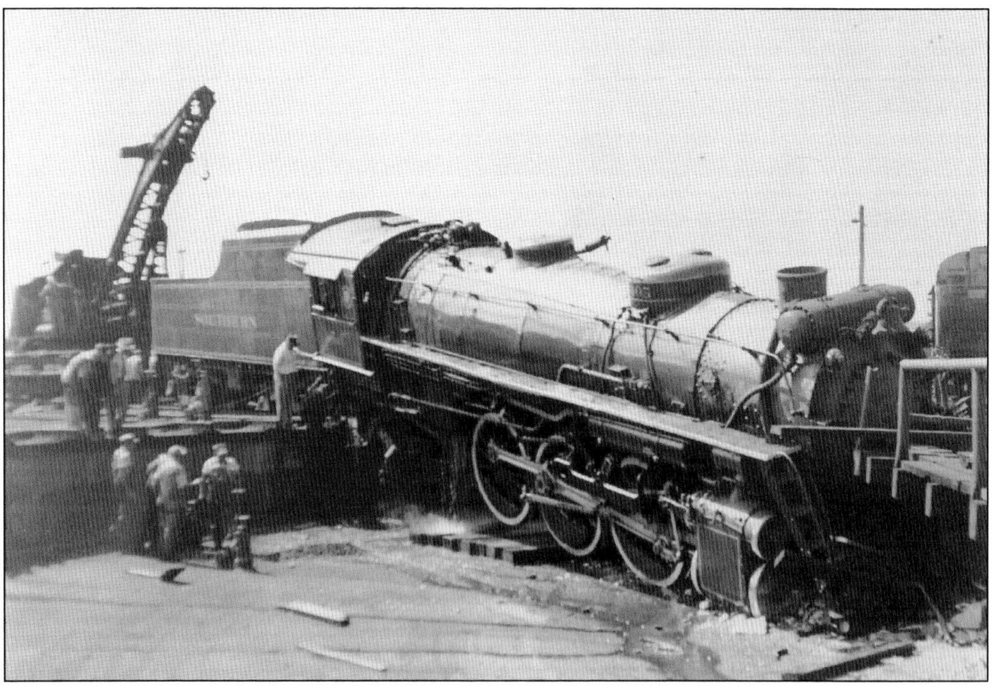

Spencer was not immune to accidents around the shops. An engineer possibly left the throttle cracked open enough for this locomotive to roll into the turntable pit. If the throttle was not entirely closed, a locomotive could "walk" as the steam entered the piston chamber. The turntable pit still has the marks from this derailment. (North Carolina Division of Archives and History.)

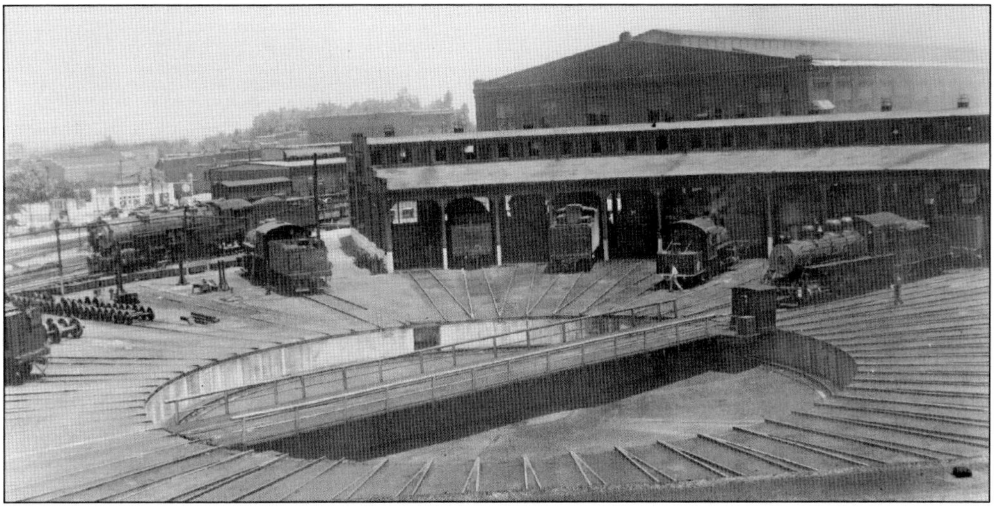

The 1924 roundhouse dramatically changed the way locomotives were serviced for daily operation. The building had 37 stalls and a 100-foot electric turntable, easily able to accommodate the largest locomotives operating in the area. The final cost of the building was $500,000, which included potbellied stoves between the stalls, smokejack openings in the ceiling, and new electric motors in the attached machine shop. Special terra-cotta tiles were added in the roof for decoration. Wood-block floors were installed to contain liquid spills and provide comfort for worker's feet. Water removed from boilers was recycled and used for steam locomotives around the property. (North Carolina Division of Archives and History.)

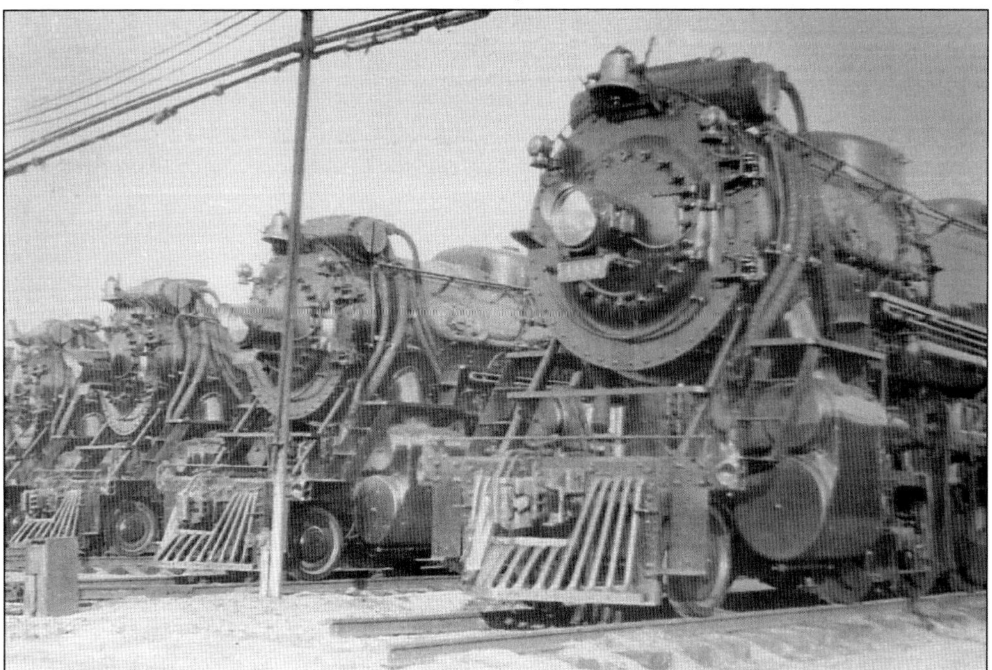

The Southern Ms-4-class 2-8-2 Mikado became one of the main locomotives used for freight service between Washington, DC, and Atlanta. Here are 4889 and her sisters on display at Spencer Shops. Baldwin Locomotive Works built the locomotives in 1928, equipped with Elesco feedwater heaters. (Photograph by *Salisbury Post*; collection of North Carolina Division of Archives and History.)

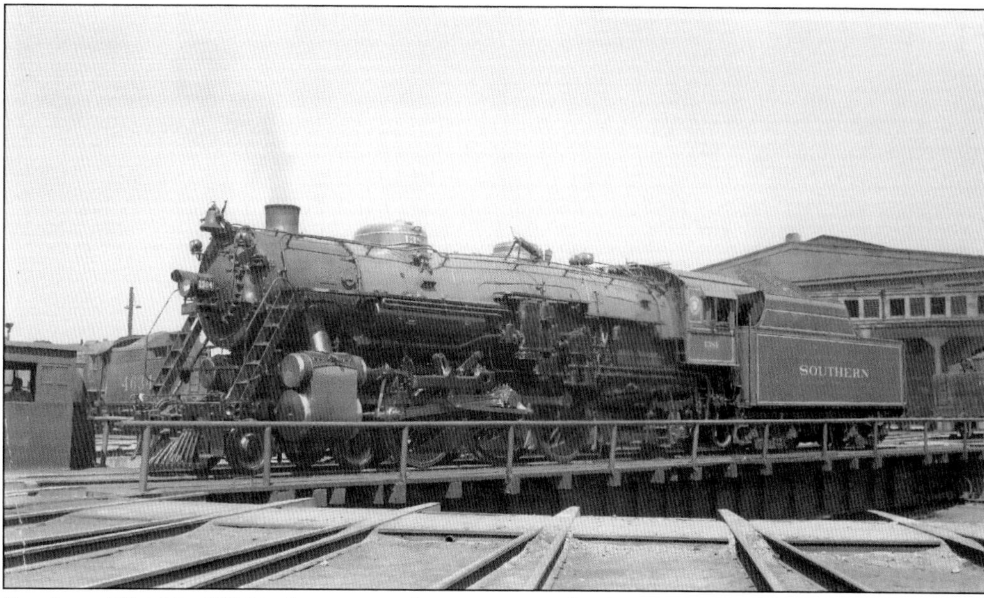

Southern PS-4 No. 1384 is shown in a classic pose on the Spencer turntable. It is moving under its own power to the ready tracks behind the yard office to await another run. (Photograph by C.K. Marsh; Marvin Rogers's collection.)

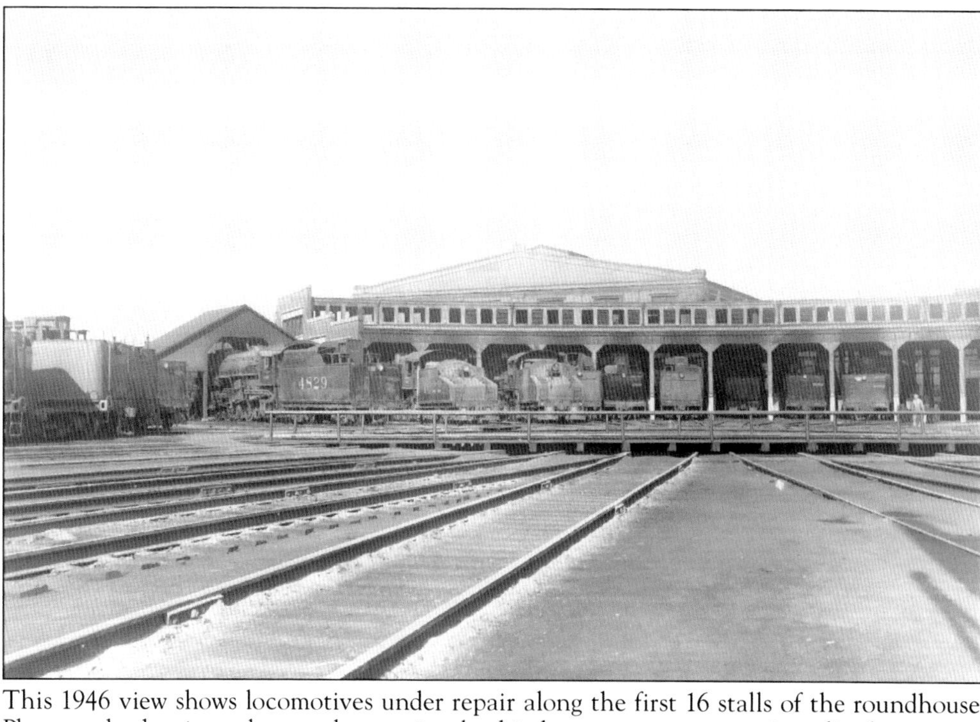

This 1946 view shows locomotives under repair along the first 16 stalls of the roundhouse. Photographs showing only steam locomotives by this date were uncommon, since dieselization was well underway on the Southern. (Photograph by David Driscoll; J. Marvin Black's collection.)

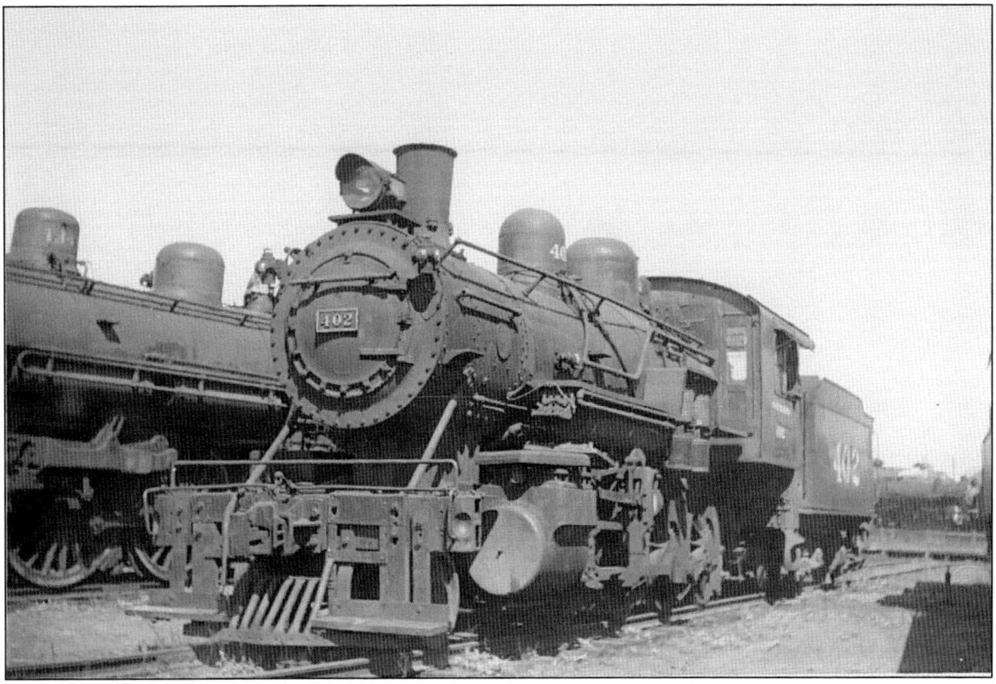

Spencer Shops serviced a variety of steam locomotives over the years, from small 2-8-0 consolidations to the 2-10-2 Santa Fe style. As follows, the roundhouse stalls were divided based on the locomotive type for servicing: 3–11 had wheel drop pits, 12–15 for yard locomotives, 16–24 for passenger, and 25–37 for freight locomotives. This division changed through the years, and locomotives could be serviced in any open stall if needed. The photograph above shows 2-8-0 No. 402 on one of the roundhouse garden tracks, while the photograph below shows 2-8-2 No. 4762 preparing to pull a freight train. (Above, photograph by Richard D. Patton; below, photograph by August A. Thieme; both, Marvin Rogers's collection.)

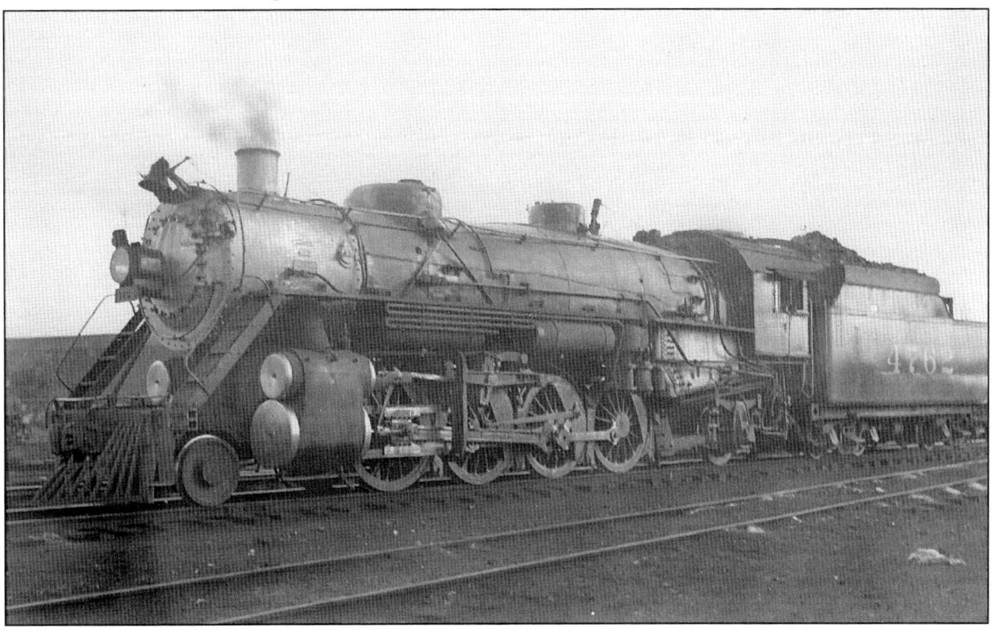

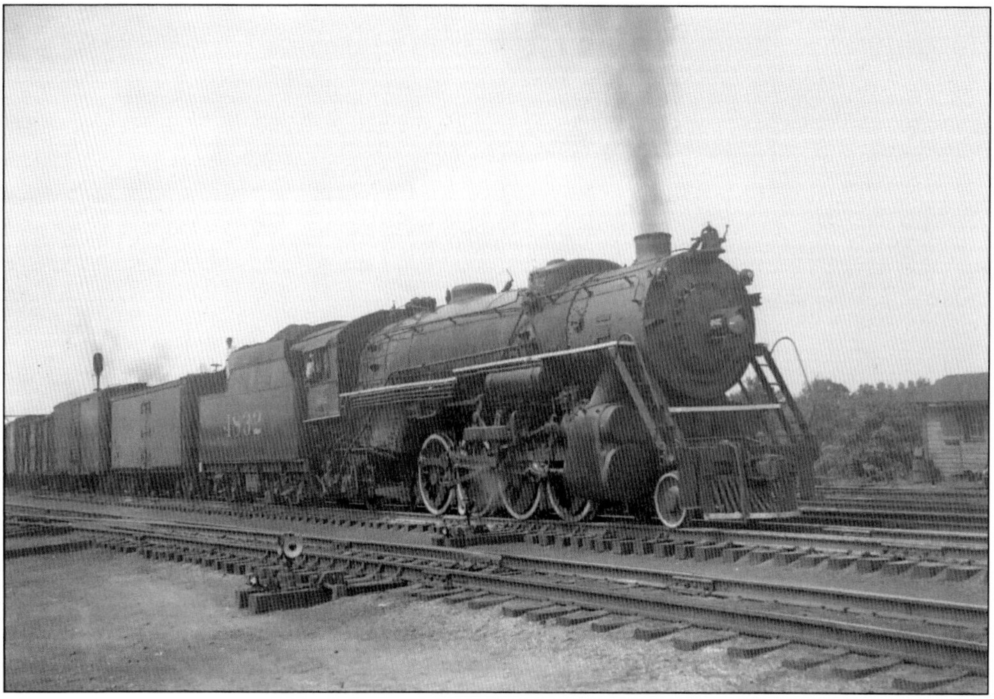

The Ms-4 2-8-2 Mikado steam locomotive, based on plans developed during World War I, became the main freight power across the Southern Railway system. The locomotives were numbered 4800–4914 and constructed between 1924 and 1926. Spencer Shops maintained these locomotives assigned to the Danville and Charlotte Divisions through the early 1950s. No. 4832 (above) was built in 1923, and No. 4856 (below) was built in 1924. Both are shown at Spencer during the 1940s. (Photographs by Richard D. Patton; both, Marvin Rogers's collection.)

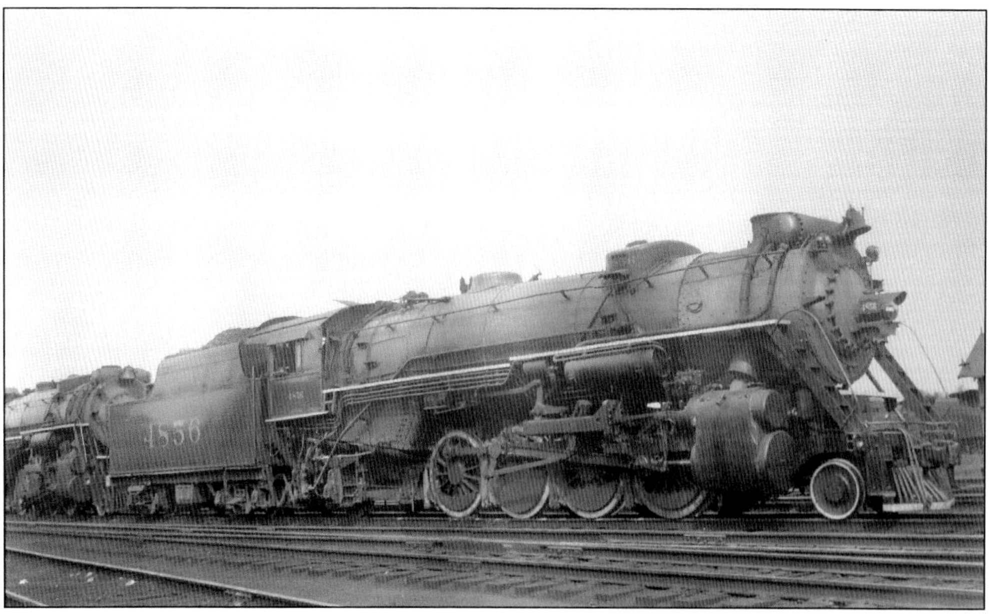

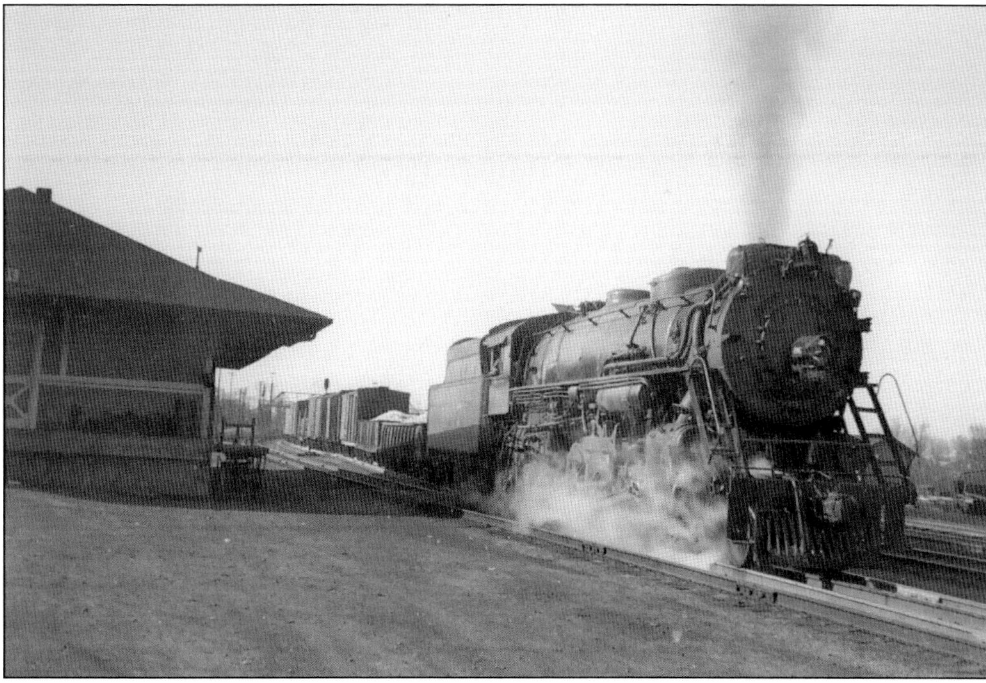

Ms-4 No. 4907 heads north out of Spencer by the depot. Unlike most railroad stations that are located in the center of town, this building was just north of town on the opposite side of the tracks. This allowed the station to serve both Spencer and East Spencer. (Photograph by Richard D. Patton; Marvin Rogers's collection.)

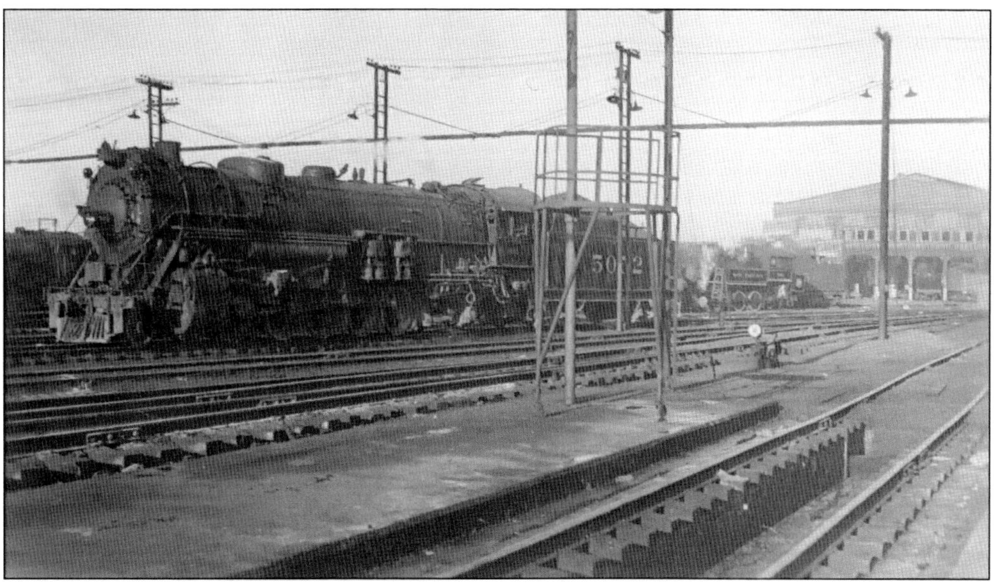

Southern Ss-class 2-10-2 No. 5072 awaits the next assignment in the ready tracks at Spencer. The Southern used these locomotives between Salisbury and Asheville due to the heavy grade west of Old Fort. These were the heaviest locomotives maintained by Spencer. The use of these locomotives was one of the reasons why the larger roundhouse and turntable were built in 1924. (Photograph by C.K. Marsh; Marvin Rogers's collection.)

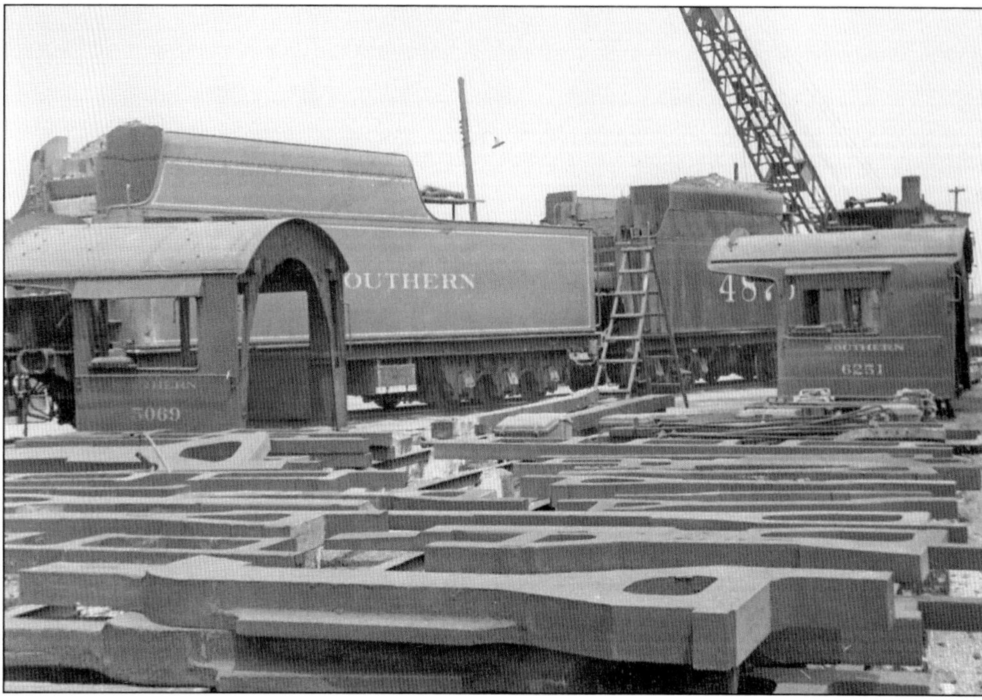

Spencer Shops began a shift in the late 1940s from repairing and maintaining steam locomotives to scrapping them. These photographs show a little bit of the process, which included the removal of cabs, drive rods (above), and cylinder castings (below). The locomotives would be stripped to the boiler and frame, which could be transported to other facilities and melted down to recycle the metal. (Above, photograph by David Driscoll; below, photograph by R.B. Carneal; both, J. Marvin Black's collection.)

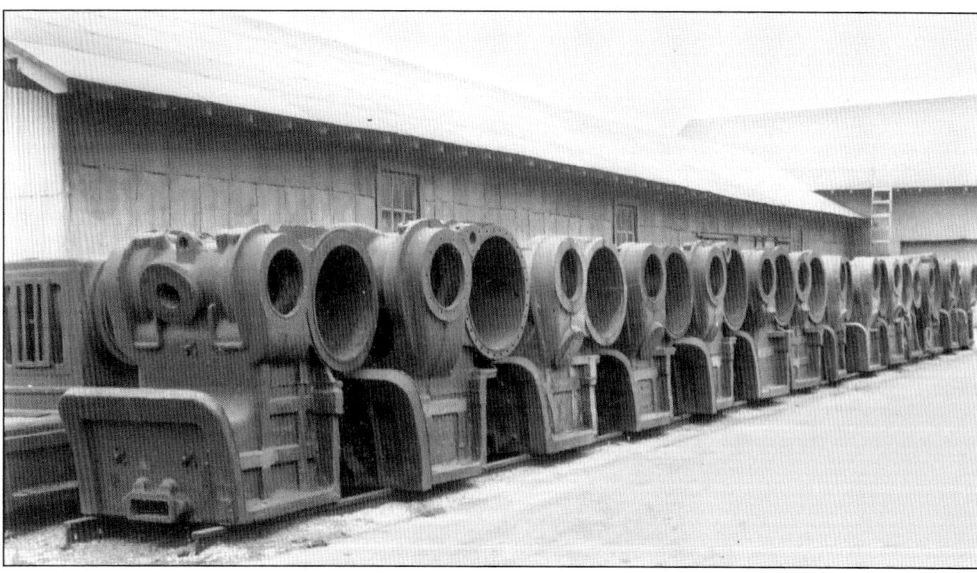

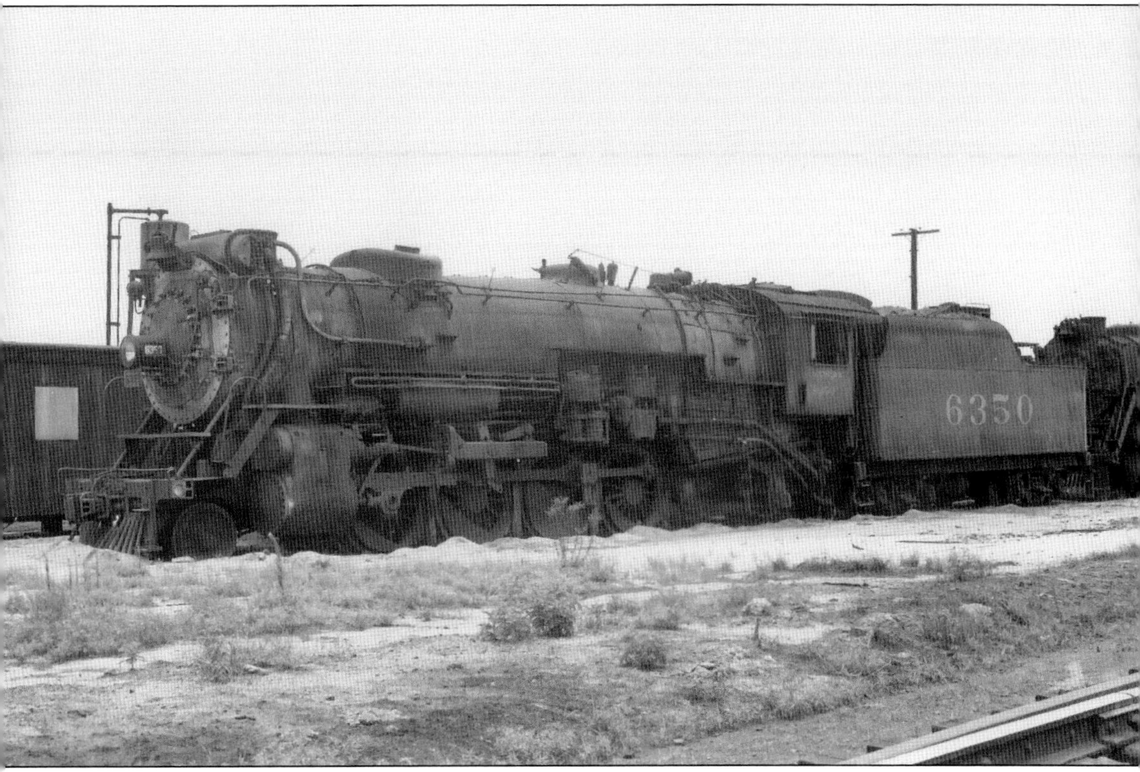

Locomotive 6350, an Ms-4 Mikado, sits at Spencer on July 9, 1950, waiting to be scrapped. Some of the drive rods have been removed to allow this locomotive to be pulled from Spencer in a dedicated train of retired steam locomotives. These long "funeral trains" of steam locomotives were a common sight at Spencer during the early 1950s. (Photograph by C.K. Marsh; Marvin Rogers's collection.)

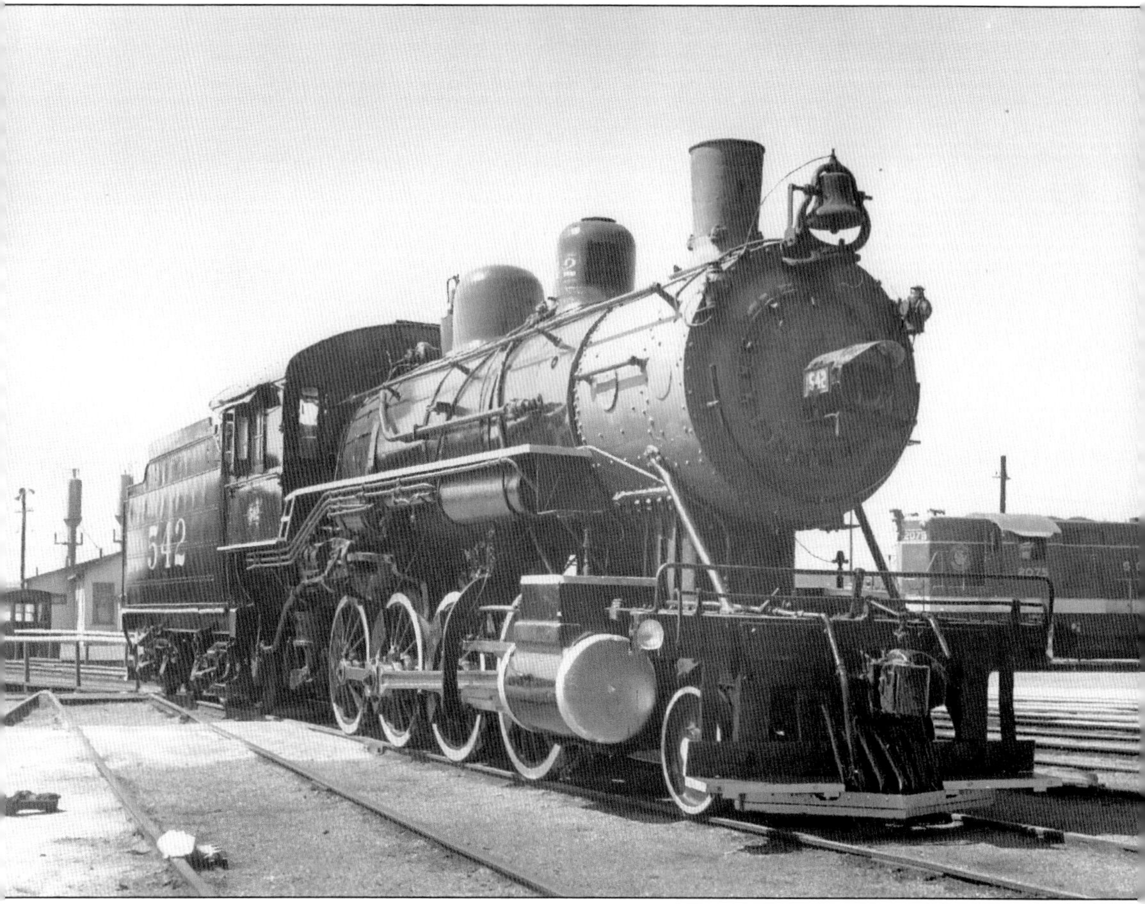

The Southern Railway understood the importance of the steam locomotive to Spencer and the surrounding areas and promoted some preservation during the early 1950s. Locomotive 542, a 2-8-0 consolidation, was placed on display at Tanglewood Park in Clemmons, west of Winston-Salem, in 1954. Spencer also worked on locomotive 544 for display at the North Carolina State Fair in 1953 as part of Rowan County's 200th anniversary. No. 542 had worked for many years in the Spencer area, switching local freight trains between Statesville and Winston-Salem. The locomotive was later returned to Spencer in 1991 with a grant form the Winston-Salem Chapter of the National Railway Historical Society for display at the North Carolina Transportation Museum. The locomotive was cosmetically restored in 2011 with a grant from the Greensboro Chapter of the National Railway Historical Society. (J. Marvin Black's collection.)

Three

Diesel Locomotive Repair and Operation

When the diesel locomotive first arrived at Spencer Shops, the new motive power signaled both an ending and beginning for railroad operation on the Southern Railway. In order for the shops to remain open, the workers adapted the existing facilities to prove Spencer would still be viable. This process began in the mid-1940s and culminated with the last steam locomotive operation in 1953.

The Southern Railway began purchasing diesel locomotives in 1939, with further purchases through the early 1940s. At first, these were a novelty to the workers at Spencer Shops, who continued to repair and maintain the large fleet of steam locomotives. As more and more diesels took over train assignments, it became apparent the new locomotives were here to stay.

A brand new locomotive servicing building was planned for Spencer in 1947, but instead, the railroad extensively modified the roundhouse and back shop. Of the two, the roundhouse received the most modifications, primarily to the last half of the building.

The first 16 stalls were used only for large parts storage. Stalls 17–20 had concrete floors installed and cinder-block walls built to convert the area for locomotive battery storage. Stalls 21–26 had some tracks removed to convert them into a light repair work area and machine shop. The final stalls, 27–37, had the largest number of modifications done, with the floors lowered and platforms installed. Metal roll-up doors were installed during the 1960s covering stalls 29–32, while 33–37 kept the steam-era wooden swinging doors.

The back shop retained the communication and erecting tracks in place but created an assembly line area for diesel prime movers to replace the machine shop area below the mezzanine. In the new design, workers moved a diesel in the south end of the building and removed the prime mover (diesel engine) by crane and other large parts for overhaul. The diesel body was placed on an erecting track, which was where the rest of the work was performed. Once the work was completed, the diesel locomotive was reassembled, cranked, and moved from the building under its own power.

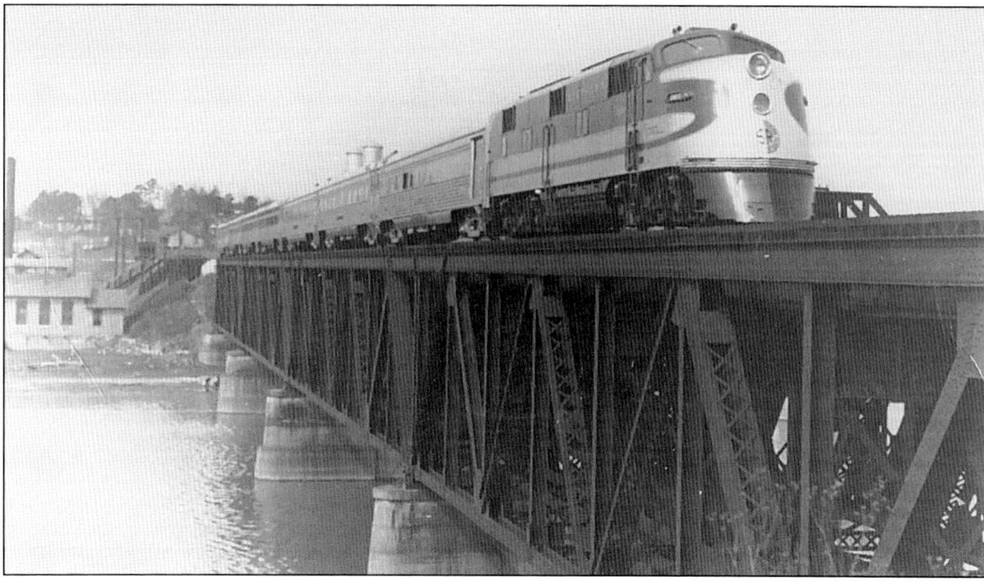

One of the earliest diesel locomotives to visit Spencer Shops was E-6 No. 2801 pulling the new passenger streamliner *Southerner* in 1941. The Southern Railway purchased three E-6 locomotives, numbered 2800–2802, and two seven-car train sets to operate this train between Washington, DC, and New Orleans, Louisiana. The train is shown northbound at the Yadkin River. Note the railroad pump station in the background. (North Carolina Division of Archives and History.)

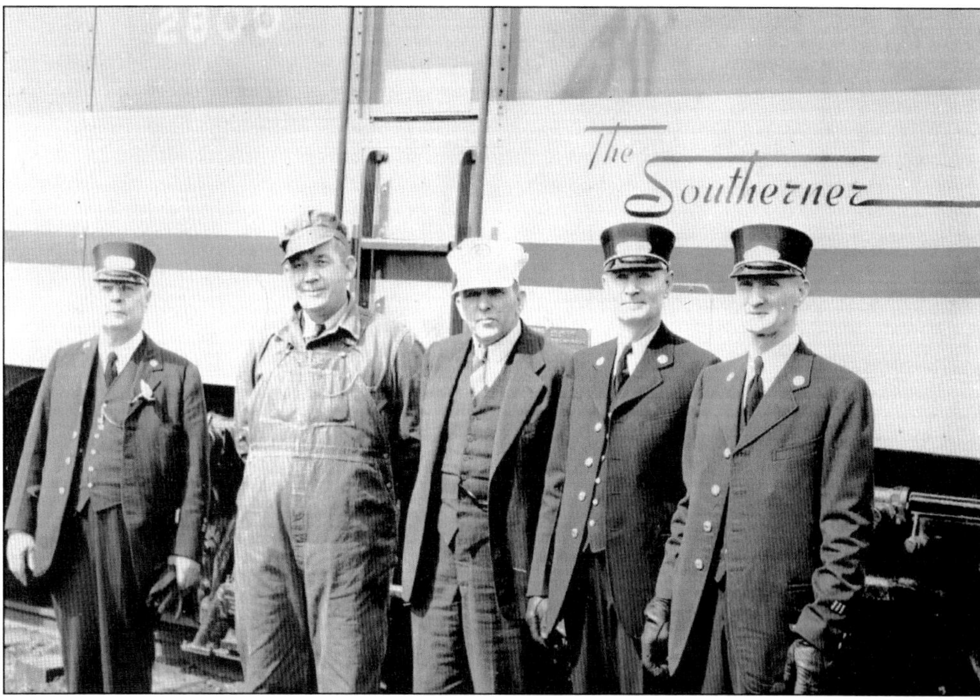

The *Southerner* train held a publicity stop at the Salisbury station in 1941. Salisbury was a crew change point, and here, the new crew is ready for a run. Those pictured are, from left to right, J.B. Jordon, conductor; Tom Albricht, fireman; W.D. Stallings, engineer; and L.C. Cook and C.W. Jones, trainmen. (North Carolina State Archives.)

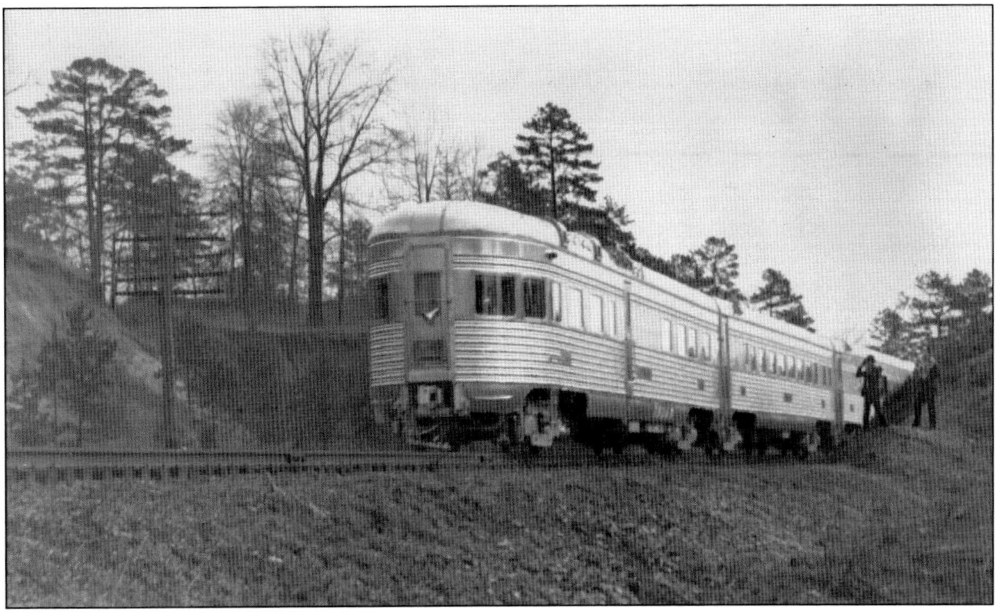

This view shows the *Southerner* heading out of Spencer. The new lightweight bodies were made of stainless steel, and the fluting paid tribute to the Art Deco period of the 1930s. Salisbury would remain a stop even after the train was combined with the *Crescent* in 1970. (North Carolina State Archives.)

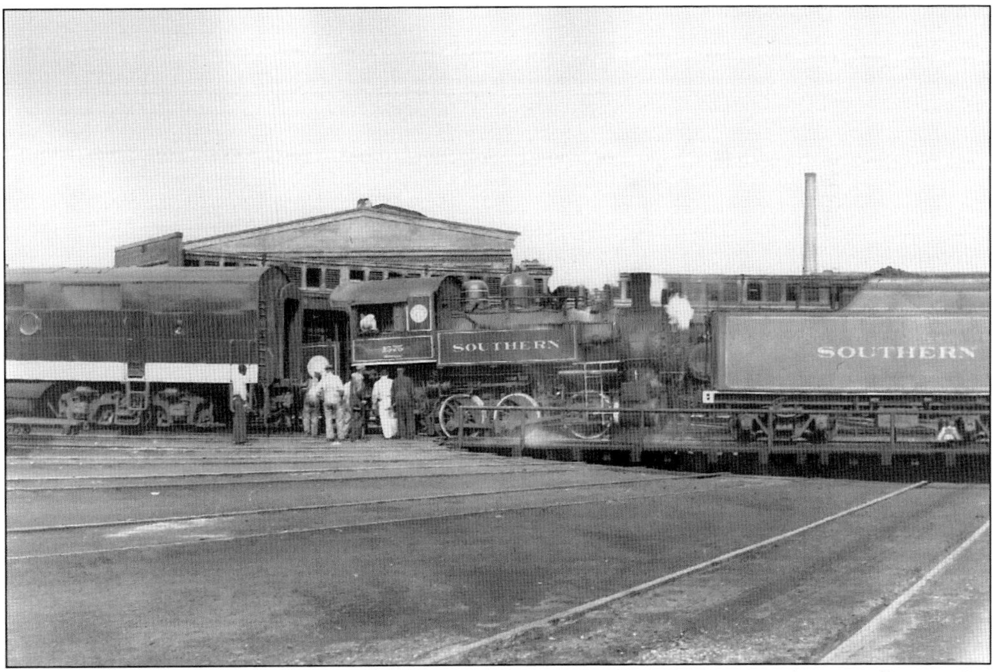

The length of locomotives sometimes caused problems for the operators at the roundhouse. On October 14, 1945, the shop goat 1575 had moved steam locomotive No. 1479 onto the turntable and was in the process of moving it to another track when the end of the goat, while spinning around, struck FT B unit No. 4307. The collision caused four drive wheels of 1575 to derail. (Photograph by David Driscoll; J. Marvin Black's collection.)

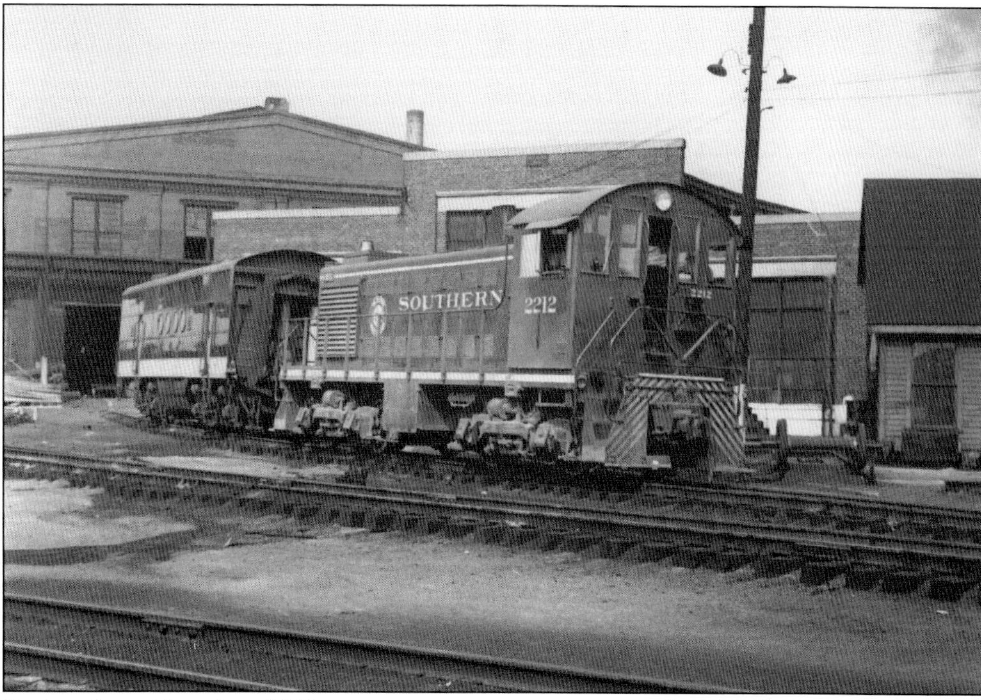

During the mid- to late 1940s, it was not uncommon to see diesel and stream locomotives alongside each other in the back shop. This image from 1946 shows an FT B being shoved into the back shop by 2212, an S-2 switch locomotive. Both of these locomotives were delivered to the Southern Railway during World War II and are still wearing the delivered black freight scheme. (Photograph by David Driscoll; J. Marvin Black's collection.)

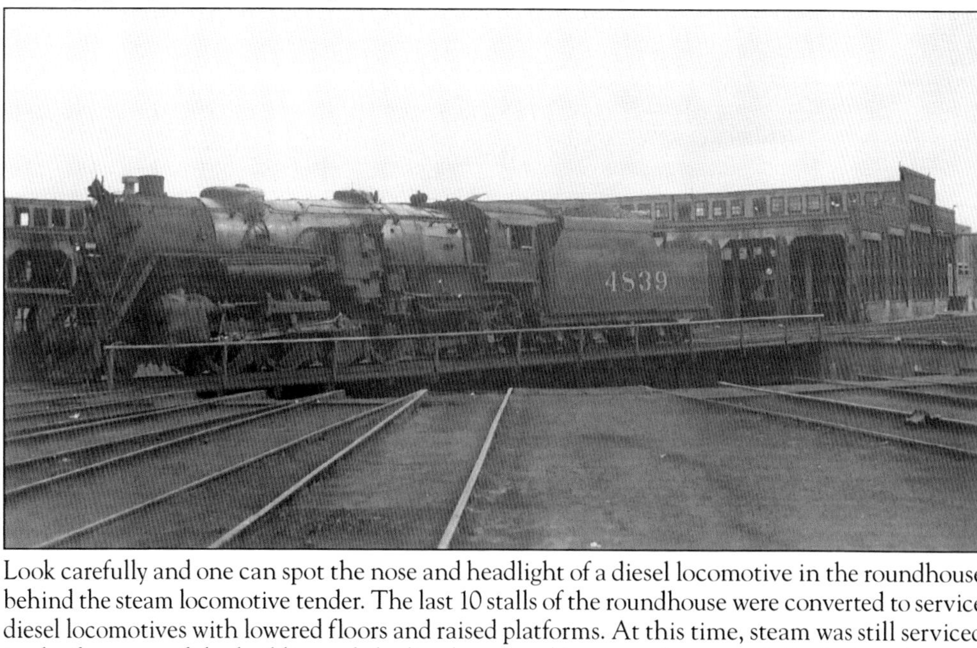

Look carefully and one can spot the nose and headlight of a diesel locomotive in the roundhouse behind the steam locomotive tender. The last 10 stalls of the roundhouse were converted to service diesel locomotives with lowered floors and raised platforms. At this time, steam was still serviced in the first part of the building, while diesels were taking over the second. Such views became more common into the early 1950s. (North Carolina Division of Archives and History.)

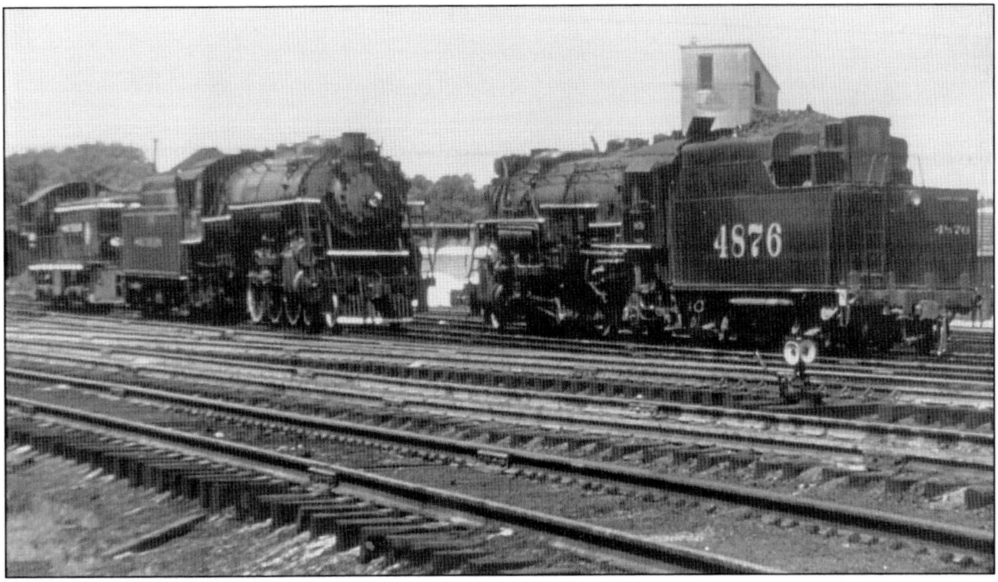

Steam was still prominent in this 1940s view, though the diesel in the background was an omen of the future. The switch locomotive, an early Alco switcher, moves these locomotives between the sand house and coal tower, which is out of view to the left. Once serviced, they would be moved to the ready tracks to await their next train. (Photograph by Shelby Lowe; Marvin Rogers's collection.)

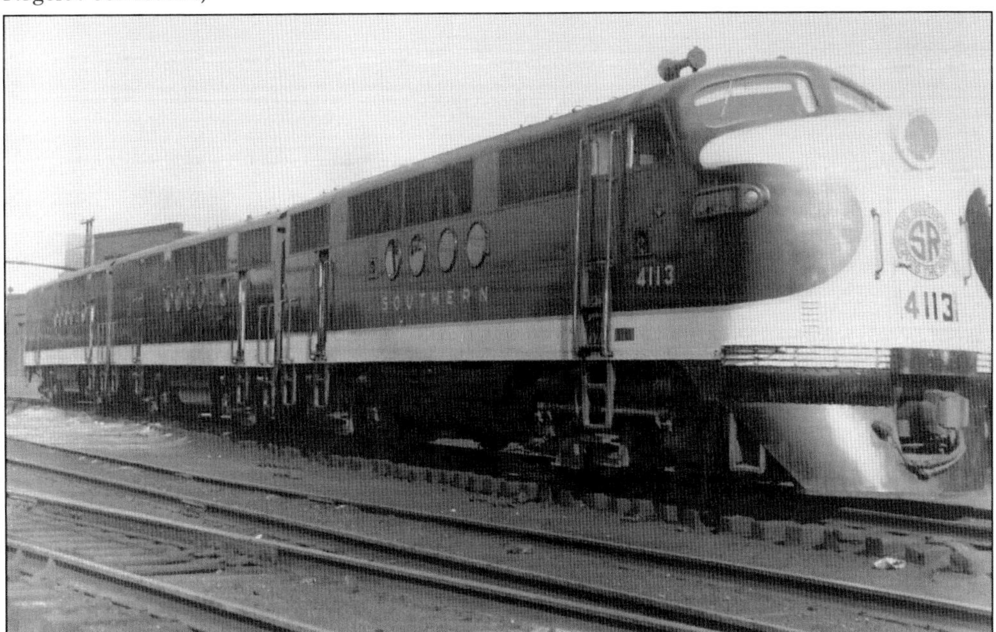

The Southern Railway was impressed with the FT locomotive produced by the Electro-Motive Corporation, a division of General Motors. Thanks to help from the War Production Board, the Southern began receiving A-B-B-A locomotive sets in 1943. The A units had a complete cab, while the B units were controlled from the A units. FT 4113 and the two B units are painted in the delivered black-and-imitation-aluminum scheme, which was replaced with green by 1949. (North Carolina State Archives.)

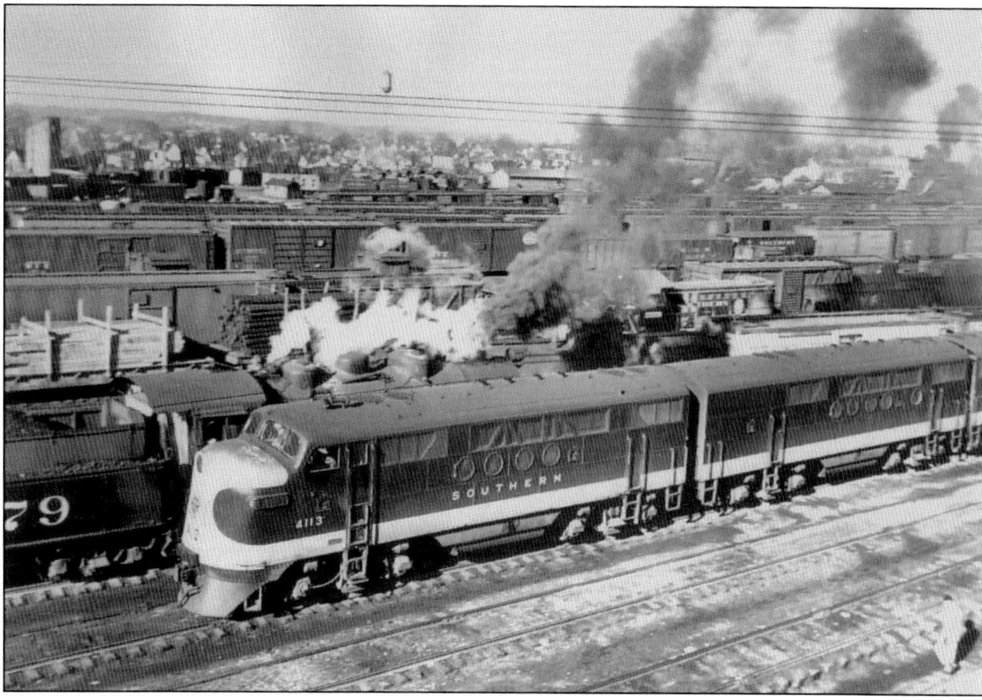

The Southern Railway received permission from the War Production Board during World War II to receive Electro-Motive Corporation FT diesel locomotives due to the high freight traffic between Washington, DC, and Atlanta. FT 4113 is shown leading other FT locomotives into Spencer Yard alongside a steam switch locomotive during the late 1940s. The sand tower is visible in the background. (Photograph by the Southern Railway; J. Marvin Black's collection.)

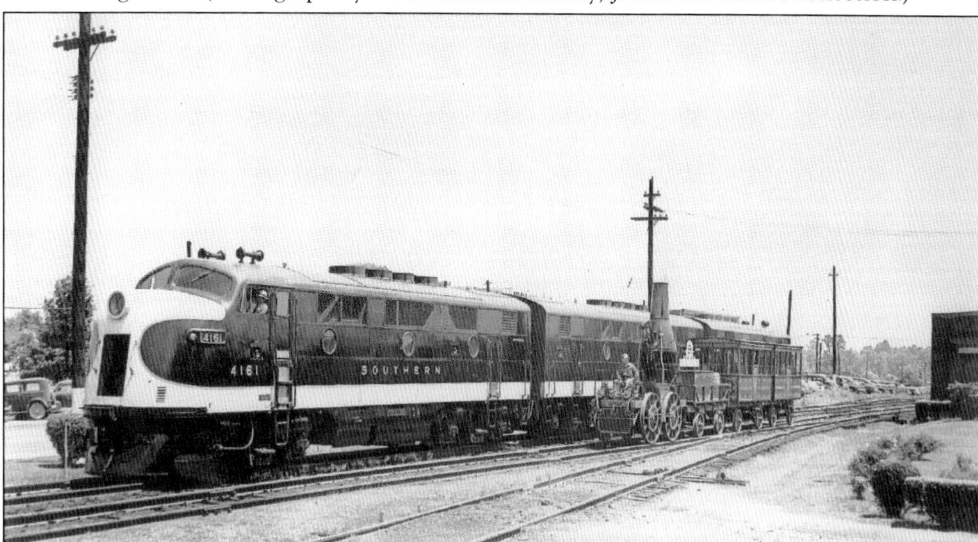

The Southern Railway built an exact replica of the South Carolina Canal and Railroad Company *Best Friend of Charleston* train at the Finley Shop in Birmingham, Alabama, for the 100th anniversary of the SCC&RR in 1930. Through the years, the train toured the Southern Railway system. The train is posed at Spencer Shops near the master mechanic's office with F-3 locomotive 4161 and two other units in the late 1940s. (North Carolina Division of Archives and History.)

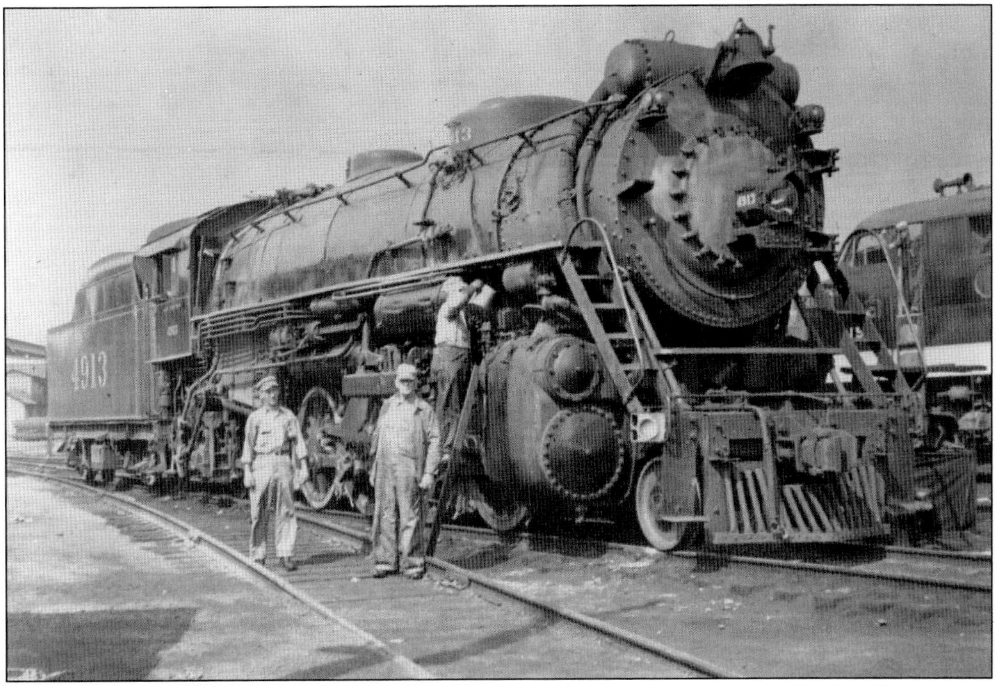

During the transition, crews could be assigned a steam locomotive on one day and a diesel locomotive the next if the engineer was qualified for either locomotive. Posed with Ms-4-class 2-8-2 No. 4913 are, from left to right, W.E. Allen, fireman; W.J. Stadler, engineer; and an unidentified worker on the ladder. To the right of the steam locomotive is FT 4115 with a crewman standing in the doorway. (Photograph by David Driscoll; collection of North Carolina State Archives.)

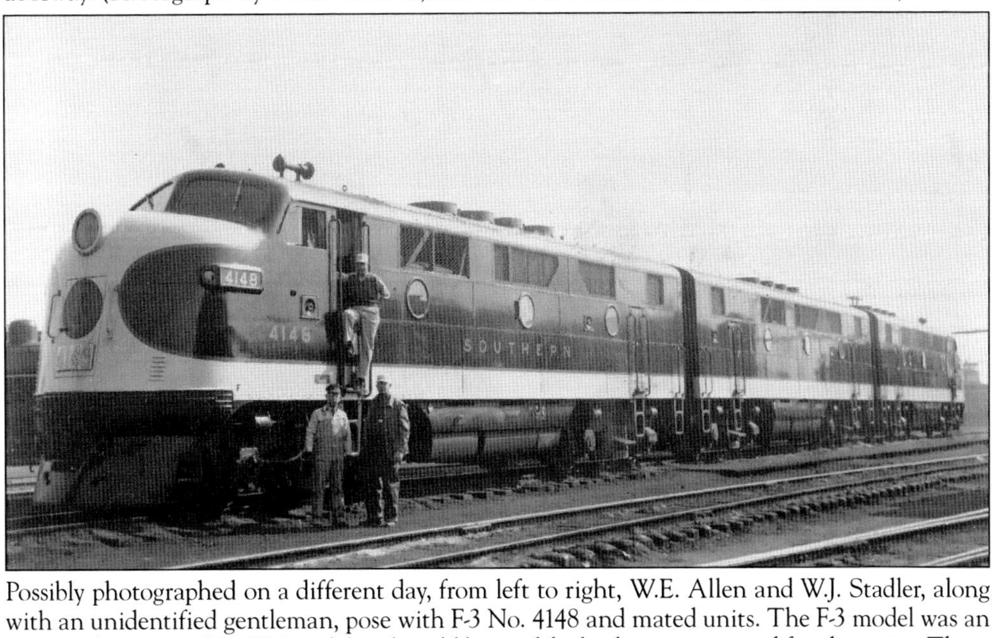

Possibly photographed on a different day, from left to right, W.E. Allen and W.J. Stadler, along with an unidentified gentleman, pose with F-3 No. 4148 and mated units. The F-3 model was an improved version of the FT model and could be used for both passenger and freight trains. These locomotives would soon be repainted in the double-stripe scheme that the Southern Railway used for passenger locomotives until the early 1950s. (North Carolina State Archives.)

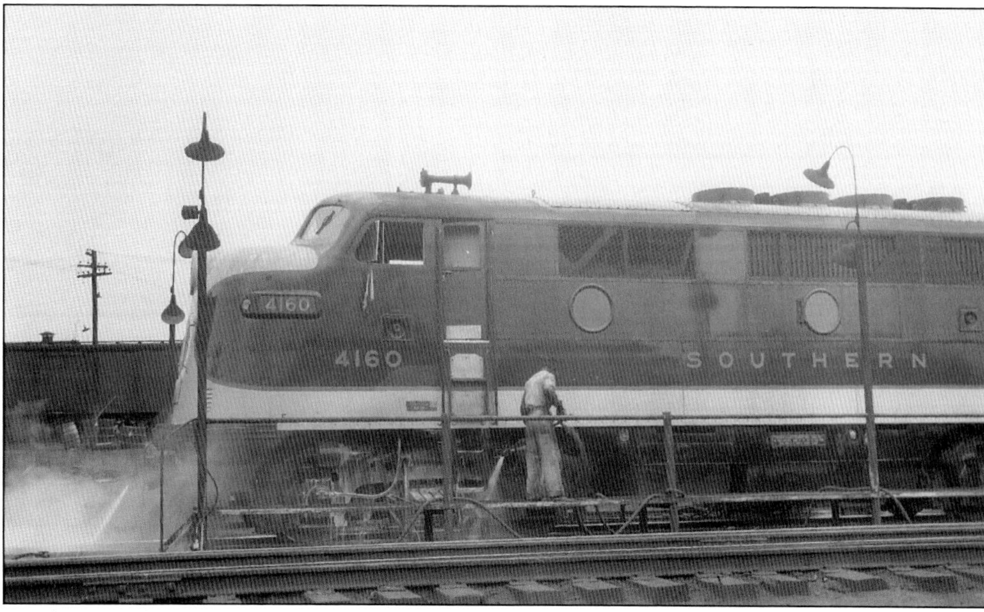

Southern Railway F-3 4160 is seen at the wash tracks in Spencer on August 24, 1947, six months after it was delivered from Electro-Motive Division of General Motors (EMD). The F-3 was a dual-purpose locomotive, able to pull freight or passenger trains, thanks to the installation of a steam generator to heat the passenger cars. Diesels used on passenger trains received regular washes to maintain a clean appearance. (Photograph by David Driscoll; J. Marvin Black's collection.)

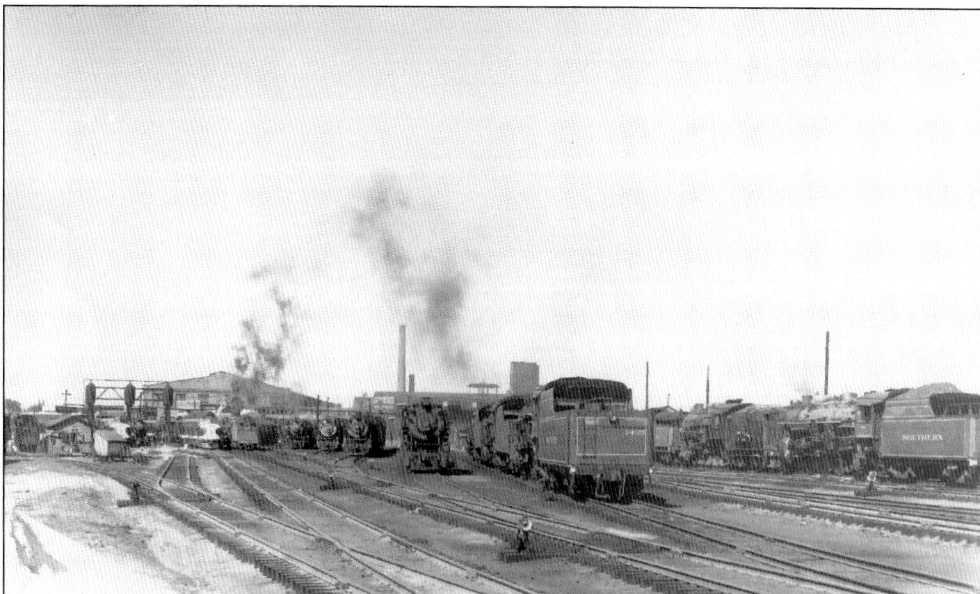

During the transition period from steam to diesel, it was common to see different locomotive types in the fuel tracks. This photograph from the late 1940s shows the beginning of service divisions in the yard. The new fuel and sand towers, which could service several locomotives at once, are located just behind the diesel on the left. The steam locomotives still had their coaling tower, not visible in this photograph. This view was taken near the sand tower, as evident by the large amount of sand near the tracks. (Photograph by David Driscoll; J. Marvin Black's collection.)

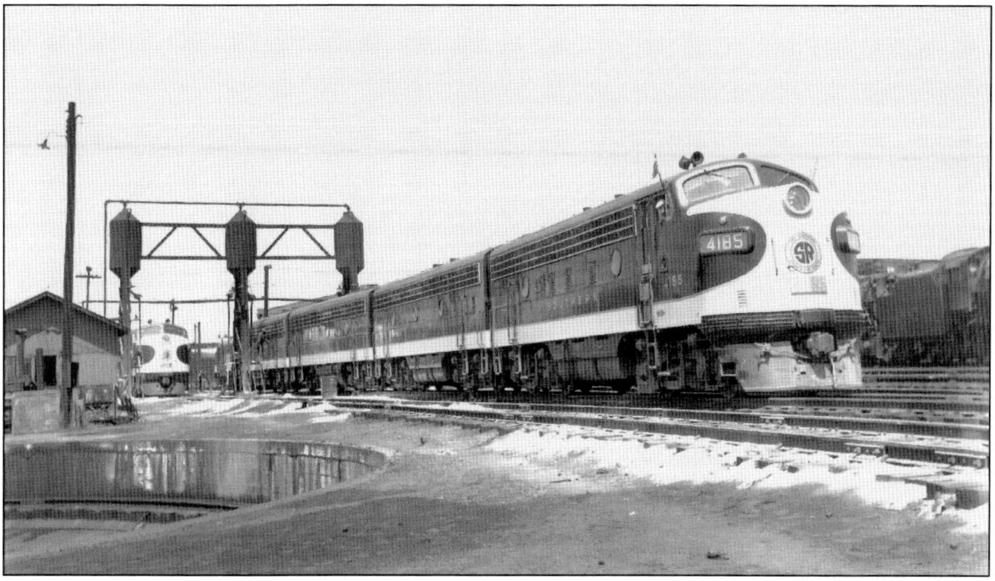

A brand new A-B-B-A four-unit F-3 diesel locomotive set is being refueled at Spencer on May 29, 1949. A brand new service area was constructed near the oil house for diesels, allowing locomotives to receive diesel fuel and sand in the same area. The second turntable pit was still in use to turn steam locomotives, though it was removed by the early 1950s. (Photograph by David Driscoll; J. Marvin Black's collection.)

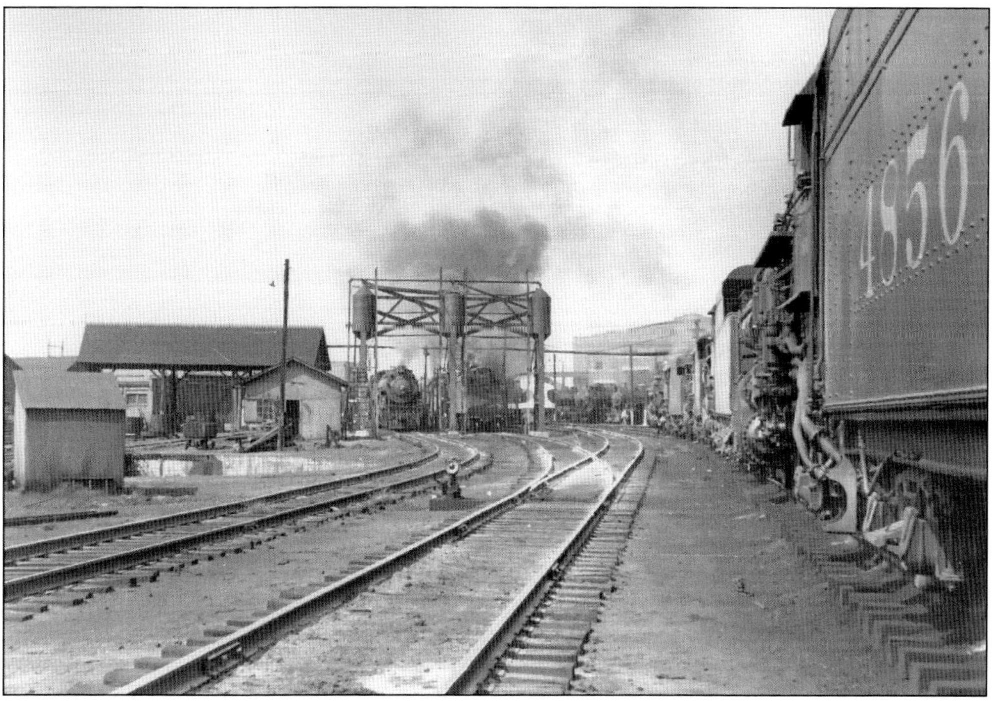

Another 1949 view illustrates the transition taking place during this time. Steam locomotives are lined up, stored out of service awaiting their fate. In the background are some of the garden tracks near the roundhouse, and other steam locomotives are awaiting the next train. (Photograph by David Driscoll; J. Marvin Black's collection.)

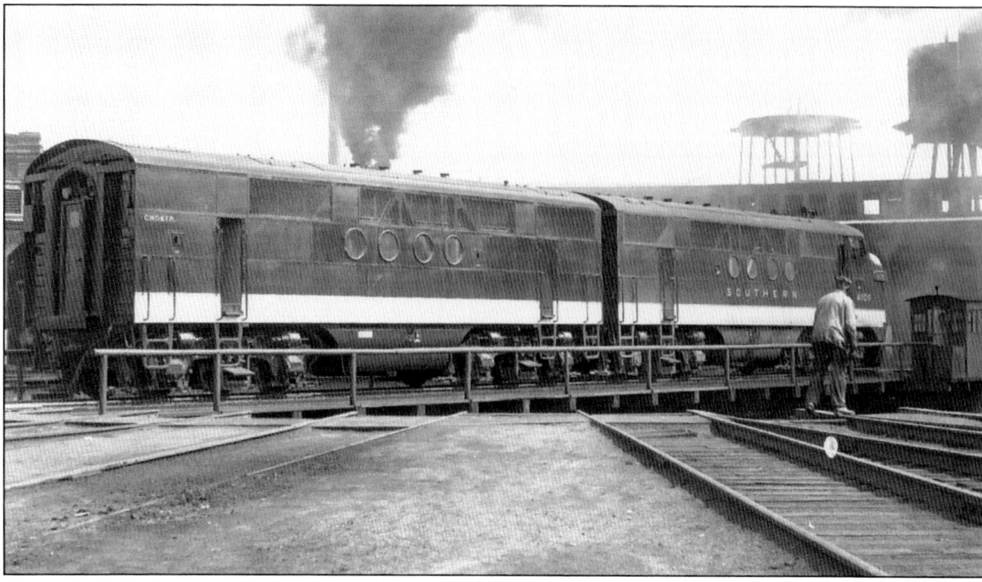

Southern FT diesels 4105 A and B units are lined up on the turntable to enter the roundhouse in 1949. The smoke is not coming from the diesels but from a steam locomotive already inside the building. One of the two wooden water tanks behind the roundhouse, no longer needed, is being dismantled. (Photograph by R.D. Sharpless; J. Marvin Black's collection.)

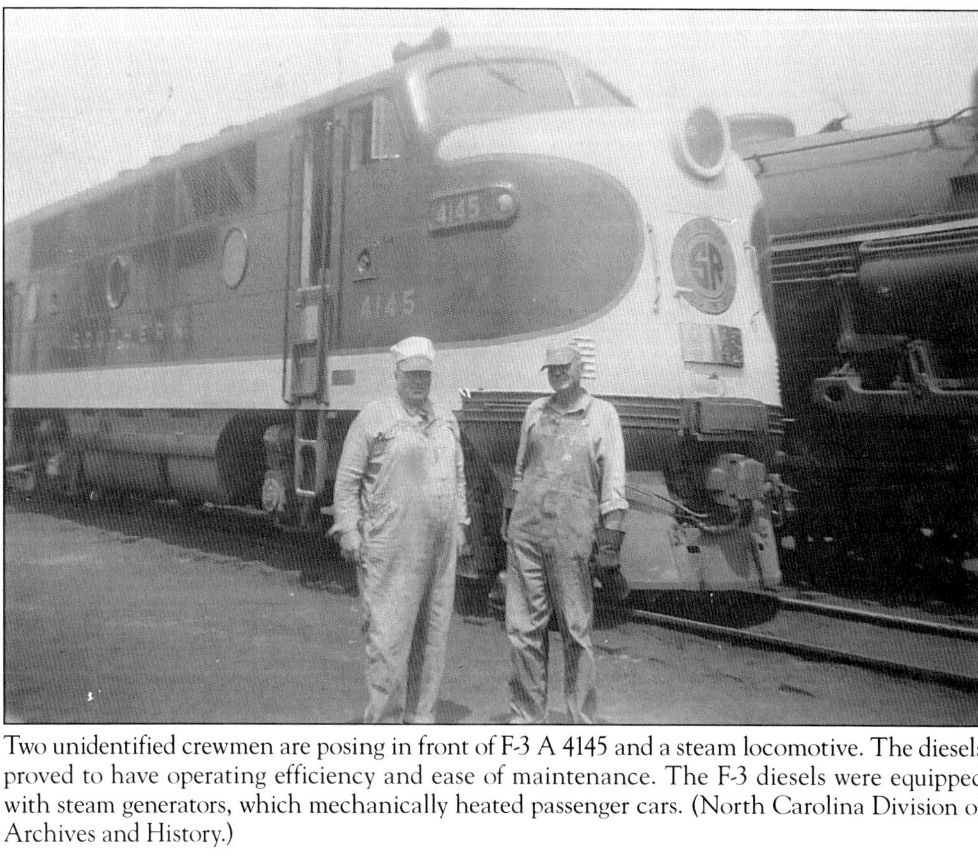

Two unidentified crewmen are posing in front of F-3 A 4145 and a steam locomotive. The diesels proved to have operating efficiency and ease of maintenance. The F-3 diesels were equipped with steam generators, which mechanically heated passenger cars. (North Carolina Division of Archives and History.)

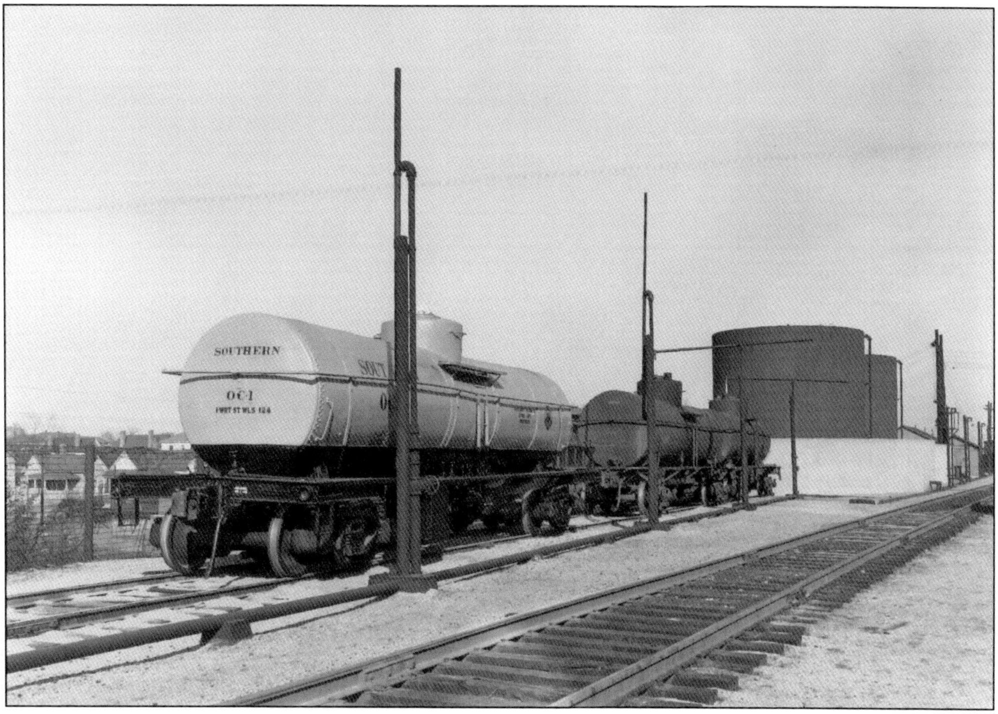

New storage tanks and service tracks were built at Spencer to store diesel fuel at the shops. The largest was a one-million-gallon tank built on the north end of the property in 1950. Tank cars labeled for company service moved the fuel throughout the Southern Railway system. The lettering along the side of car OC-1 states, "When Empty Return To Stores Dept Spencer NC." (Photograph by David Driscoll; J. Marvin Black's collection.)

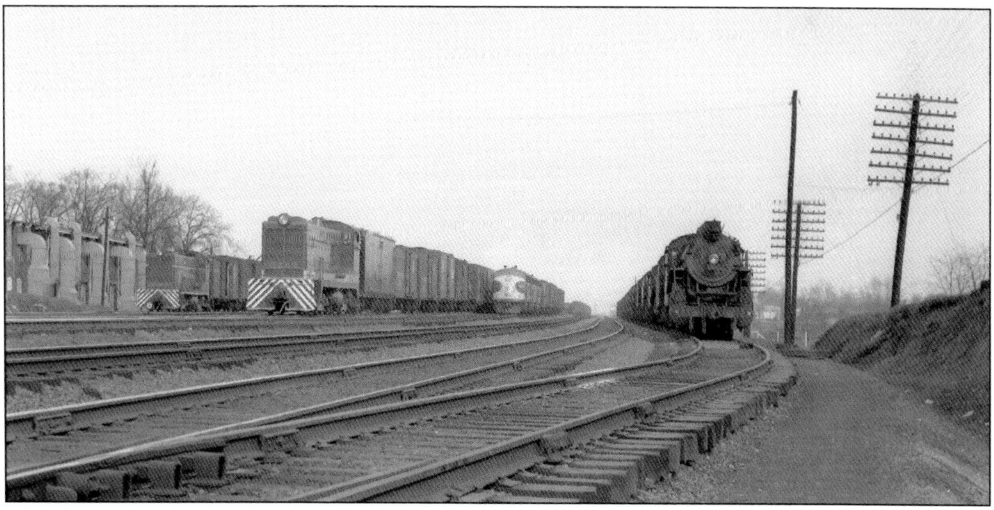

The changes occurring to the Southern Railway and Spencer Shops during the transition from steam to diesel are evident in this view at Eleventh Street in Salisbury, taken on January 15, 1950. From left to right, two Baldwin DS-4-4-1000 switchers—2288 in black paint and 2289 in the new green paint scheme—switch freight for the transfer sheds. F-7 No. 4223, built in May 1949, leads a freight train onto the main line, while a row of out-of -service steam locomotives awaits the trip to the scrap yard on the right. (Photograph by R.B. Carneal; Bob Graham's collection.)

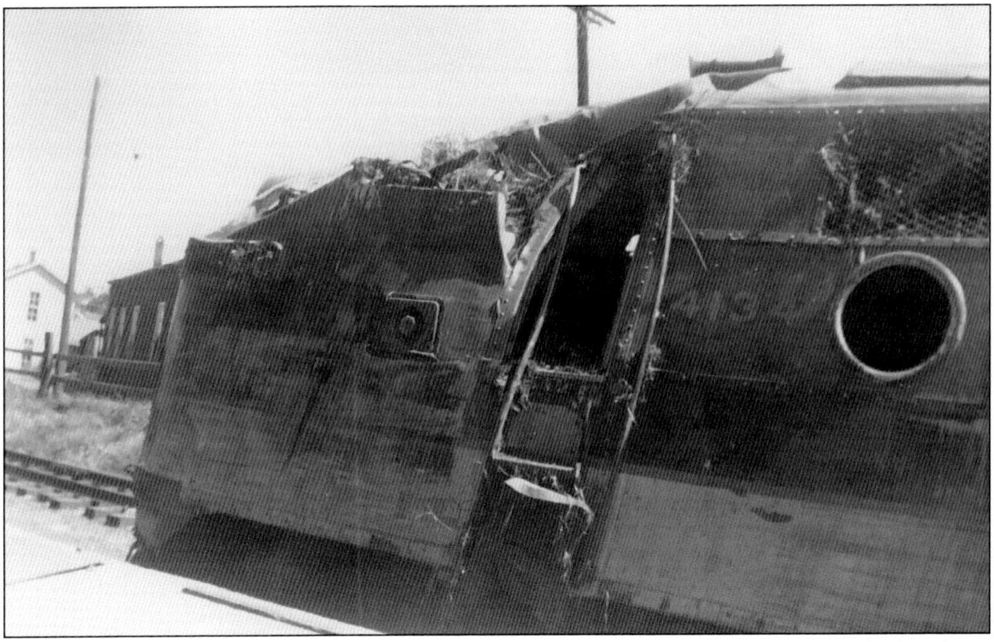

On September 9, 1949, F-3 locomotives 4134 and 4352 derailed at Newton, North Carolina, while pulling a 10-car passenger train. The locomotives were rerailed and brought to Spencer for rebuilding. (Photograph by David Driscoll; J. Marvin Black's collection.)

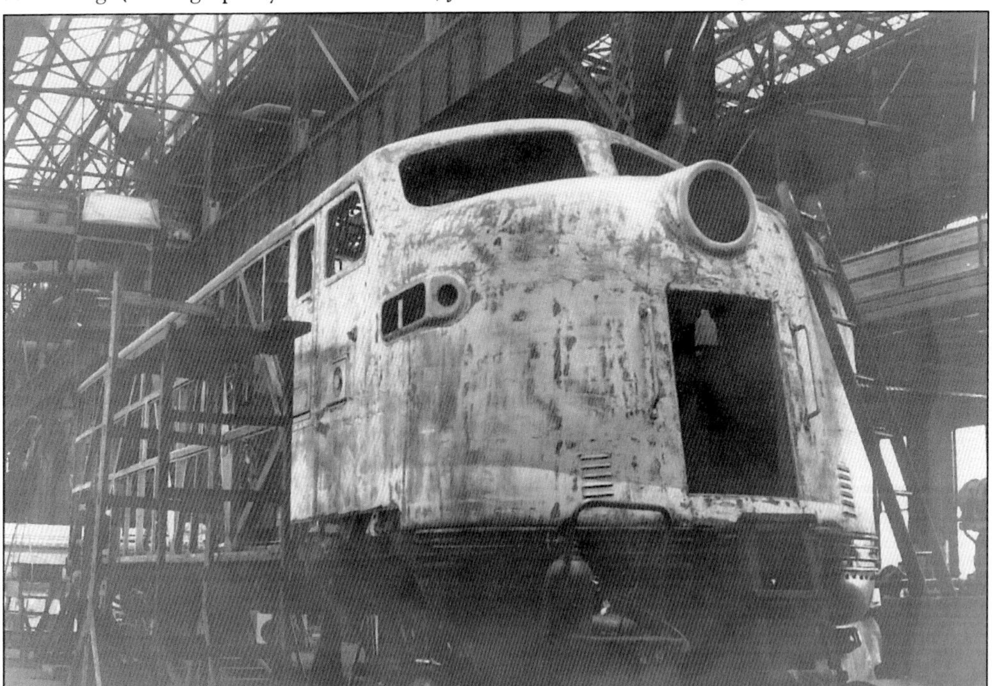

Locomotive 4134 is seen in the Spencer back shop on October 16, 1949, with a rebuilt nose and car body. The locomotive was upgraded to F-7 specifications on November 21, 1950. Further modifications were performed at Spencer in 1954, and it was retired in 1972. (Photograph by David Driscoll; J. Marvin Black's collection.)

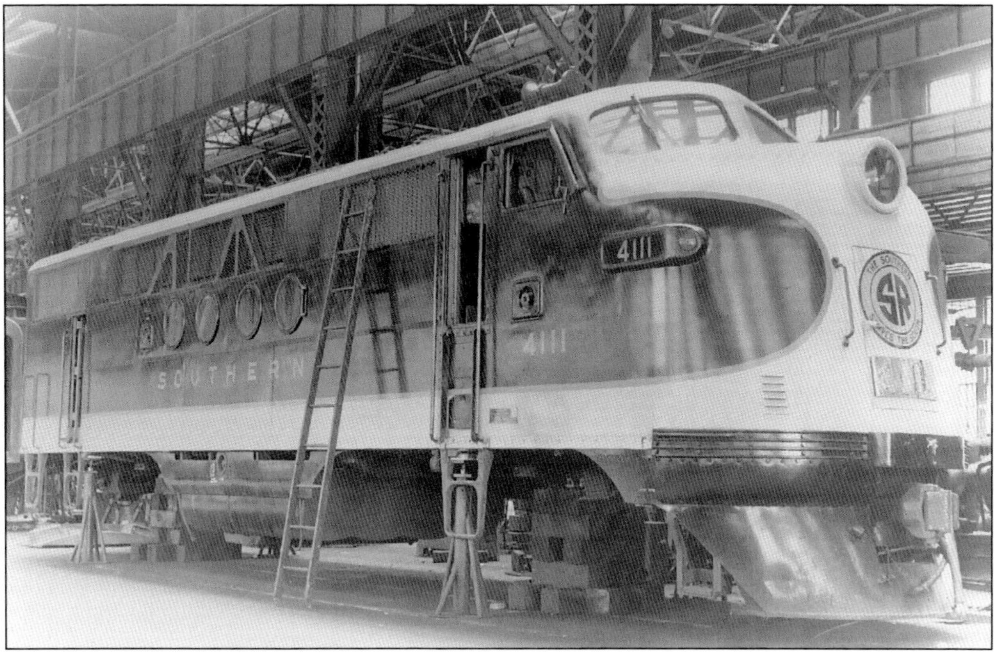

The shop force at Spencer worked hard to convert the back shop and roundhouse for diesel locomotive work between 1947 and 1953. Spencer was modified to perform rebuilds and mechanical upgrades to diesel locomotives. FT 4111, built in 1943, is having its diesel prime mover rebuilt along with traction motor replacement in the trucks. Technically, all diesels are diesel-electric, with an electric generator creating power to turn electric-traction motors around the axles. (North Carolina Division of Archives and History.)

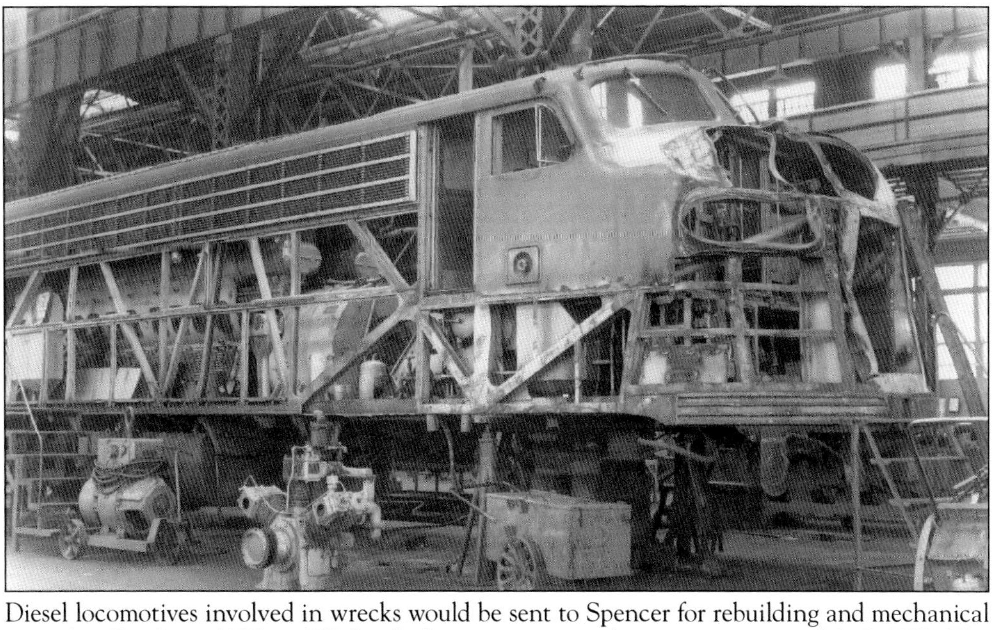

Diesel locomotives involved in wrecks would be sent to Spencer for rebuilding and mechanical upgrades. Southern 4235, an F-7 freight locomotive, is undergoing service on July 9, 1950. The locomotive was involved in a rear-end collision on June 30, 1950, with a Chesapeake & Ohio train in Remington, Virginia. (Photograph by David Driscoll; J. Marvin Black's collection.)

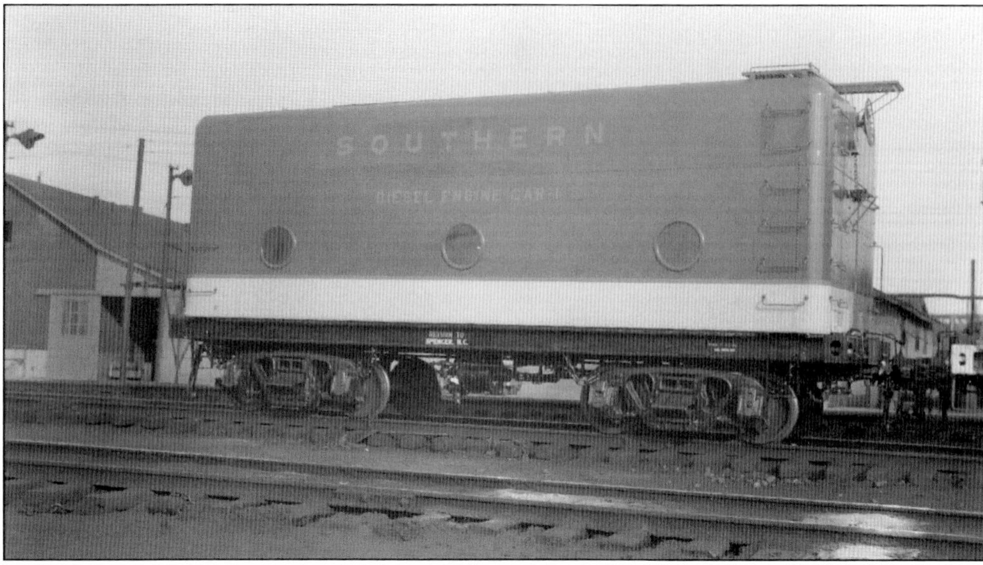

The shop force at Spencer developed the diesel-engine car to transport prime movers to other shops before the back shop was converted over to diesel repair. This special car was converted from the tender of 4802, a Ms-4-class 2-8-2 that was scrapped in 1952. It was painted to match the locomotive paint scheme of the early 1950s and could not be operated off Southern Railway lines due to the absence of required reporting data. (Photograph by David Driscoll; J. Marvin Black's collection.)

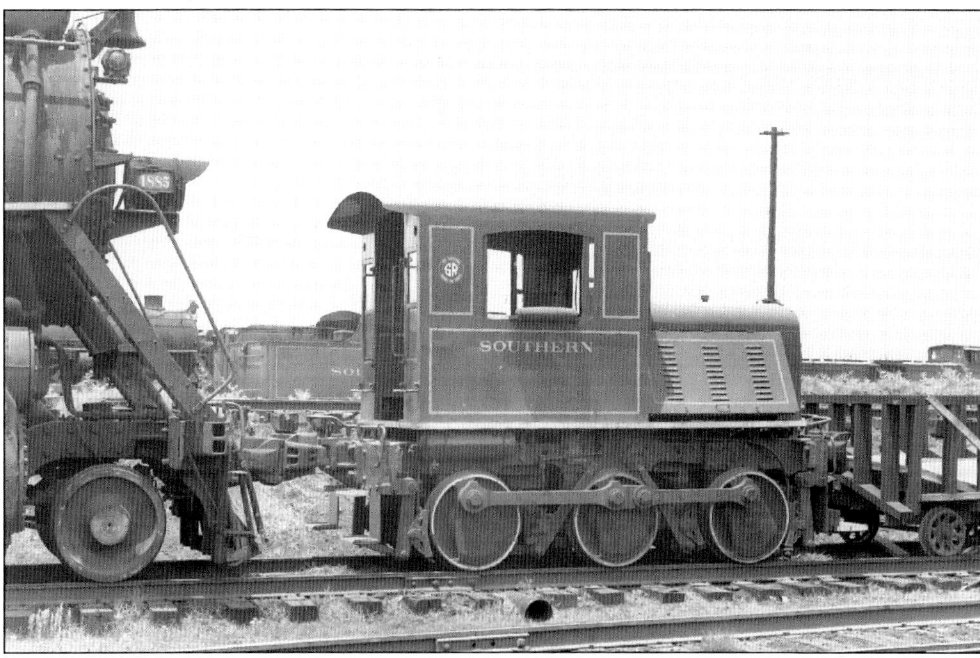

This unnumbered switch locomotive was modified at Spencer to move steam locomotives around the site for scrapping. Shown here in 1953, it had a small diesel engine for power and a homemade cab that resembled a steam locomotive. Unfortunately, it did not perform well and was transferred to Hayne Shop in Spartanburg, South Carolina. (Photograph by Robert L. Drake; J. Marvin Black's collection.)

When a diesel locomotive was overhauled, filters were removed for cleaning and inspection. R.M. Barnett, a general diesel foreman, and Frank Sides are looking over a diesel-engine filter during the cleaning proccss. (Photograph by the Southern Railway; collection of North Carolina State Archives.)

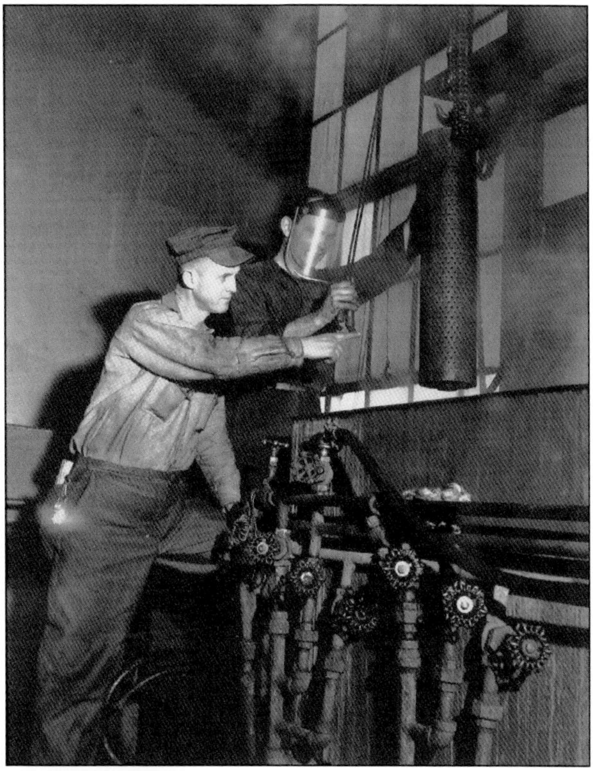

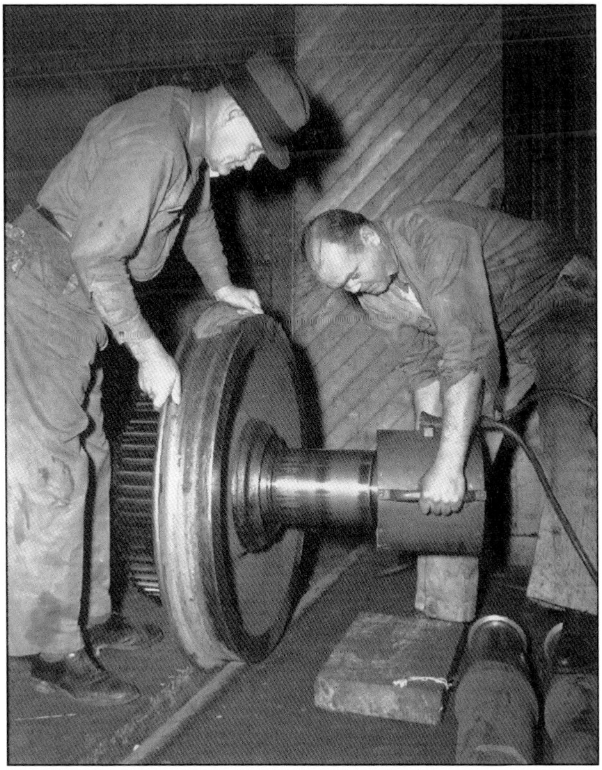

Spencer Shops employees developed technological advancements for the maintenance of diesel locomotives. M.R. Cauble, an electrician, developed an electronic induction heater that could be placed over a diesel locomotive's axle to remove the inner bearing race. He is demonstrating the device to his father, E.M. Cauble, a wheel shop foreman. A ball bearing has an outer and inner ring called a race, which holds the bearings in place. (Photograph by the Southern Railway; collection of North Carolina State Archives.)

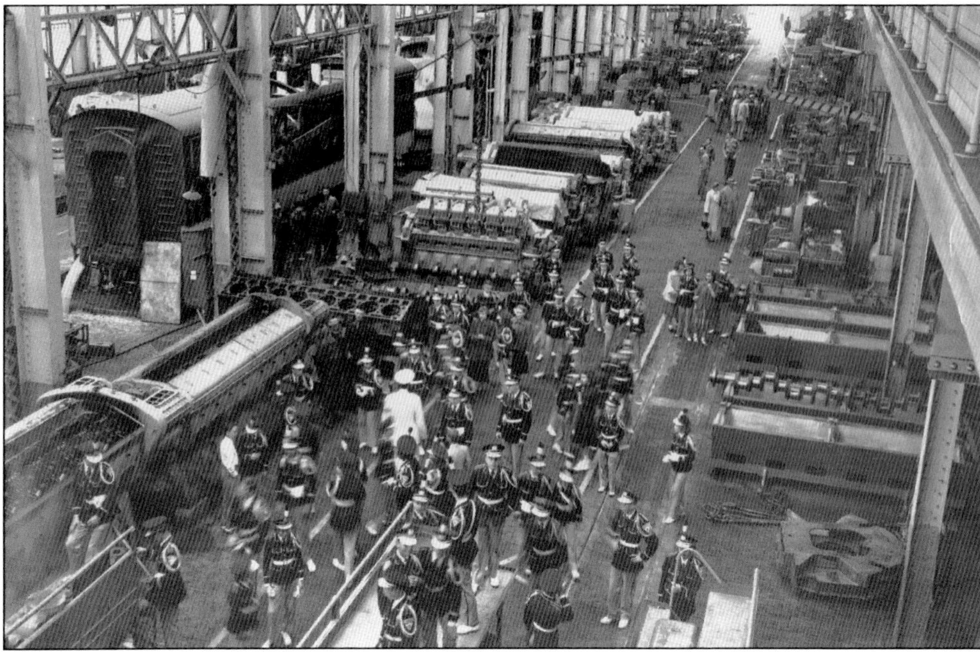

Rowan County celebrated its 200th anniversary in April 1953. As part of the event, members of the Spencer School band took a tour of the back shop. By this date, the shops had completed the modifications to service diesel locomotives. An assembly line was created to take the diesel prime movers through stages to disassembly, overhaul, and reassembly, while the diesel body received work along the building's other side. (North Carolina Division of Archives and History.)

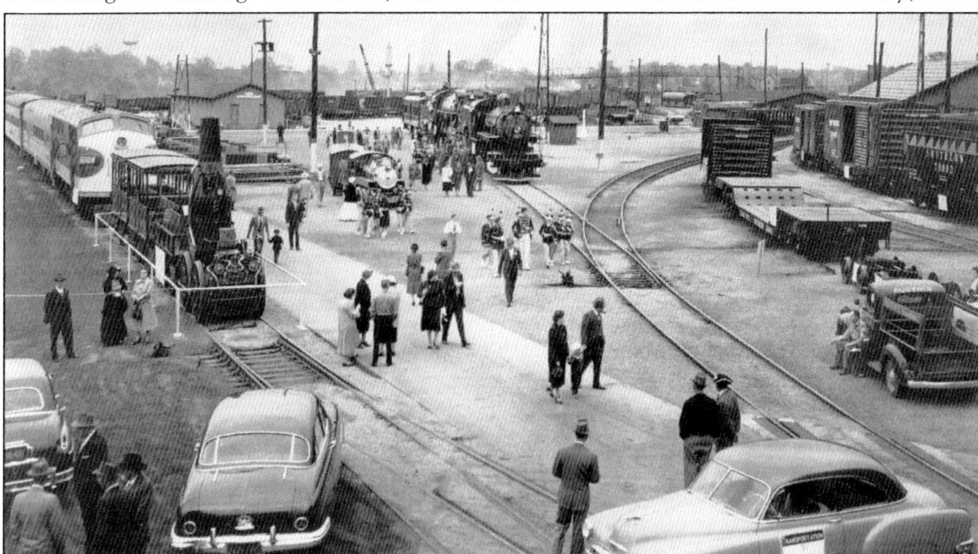

Rowan County, North Carolina, celebrated its 200th anniversary with several activities, including an open house at Spencer Shops. As part of the celebration, many of the employees grew beards to participate in the "Brothers of the Brush." The display included the *Best Friend of Charleston*, the 40&8 Society's locomotive and boxcar, steam locomotives, and a diesel-powered passenger train headed by newly rebuilt 6104. This FT locomotive was rebuilt to F-7 standards at Spencer Shops. (North Carolina Division of Archives and History.)

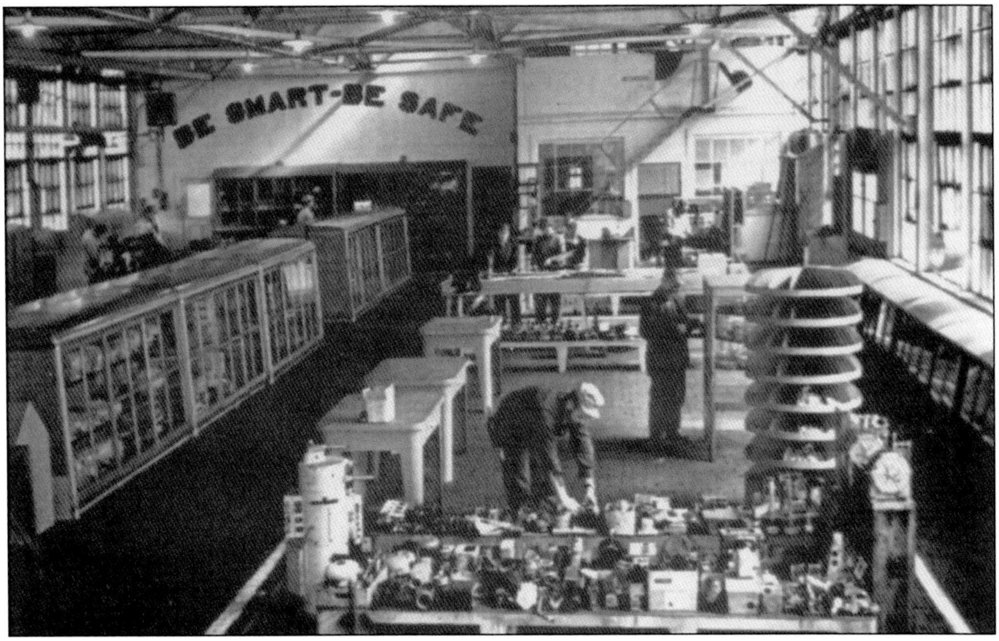

The flue shop building was totally redesigned for the servicing of diesel locomotives. This 1953 view shows the cabinets and equipment installed to create the new electrical shop. (Photograph by the Southern Railway; collection of North Carolina Division of Archives and History.)

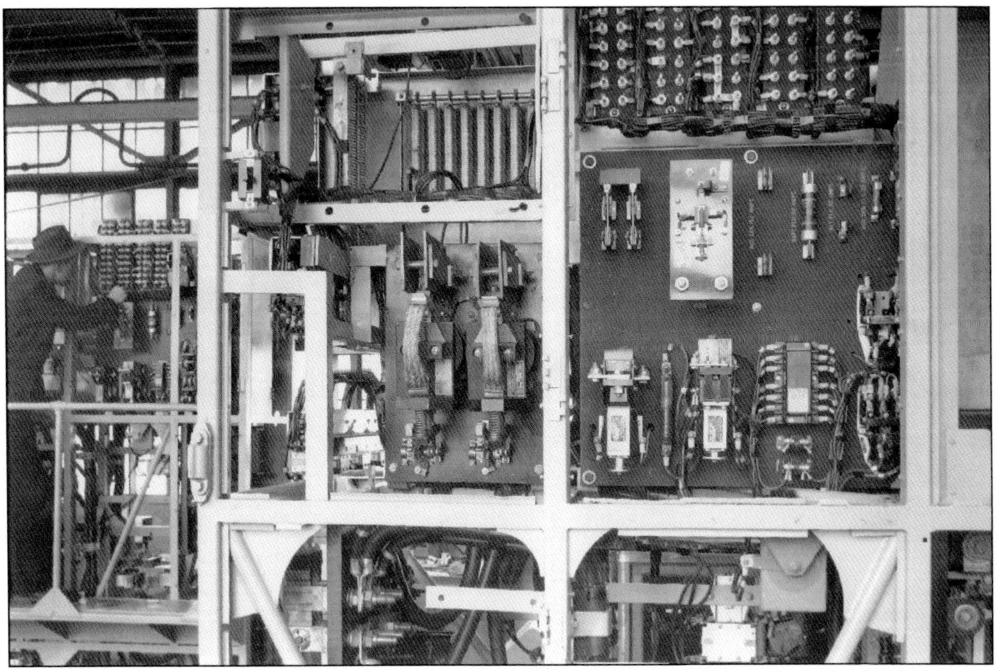

Electrical parts from diesel locomotives were brought to the electrical shop from the back shop on special powered dolly trucks for servicing. Here, they could be tested and, if necessary, completely rebuilt. All electrical components, except large devices like traction motors (to power drive axles) or generators, could be serviced at Spencer Shops. (Photograph by the Southern Railway; collection of North Carolina Division of Archives and History.)

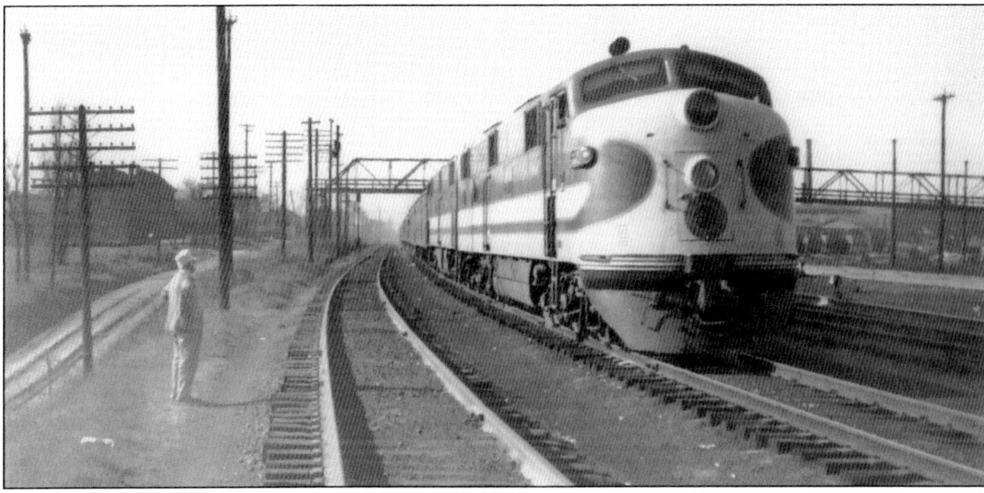

The Spencer station was a busy passenger stop through the 1930s, with several trains stopping each day. As railroad passenger traffic declined through the 1950s, Spencer hosted one or two trains a day, only stopping as needed. Passenger traffic ceased by 1970, and the depot was eventually torn down. An E-7 passenger locomotive passes the Spencer station some time during the late 1940s. It is painted in the double-stripe passenger scheme worn until the early 1950s. (North Carolina Division of Archives and History.)

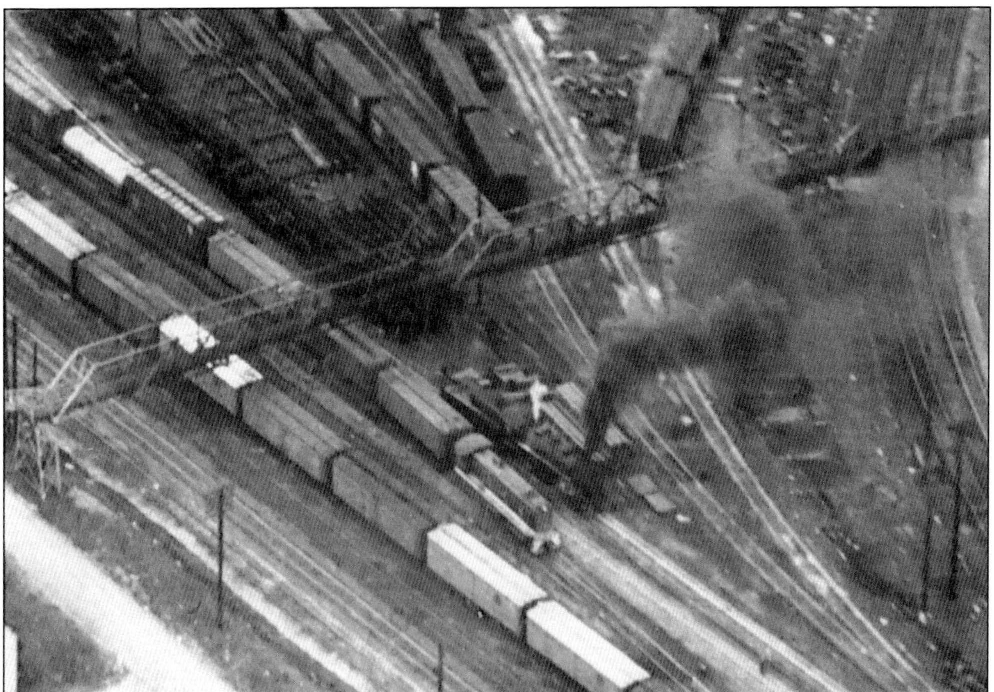

The transition from steam to diesel was evident in the freight classification yard. Moving freight cars around the property, steam and diesel switch locomotives worked side by side. On the north end of the shops, under the pedestrian walk bridge, an ALCO S-2 diesel in the green scheme is working beside an 0-8-0 steam locomotive in 1951. Over the next two years, the Southern Railway phased out all steam in the entire system. (North Carolina Division of Archives and History.)

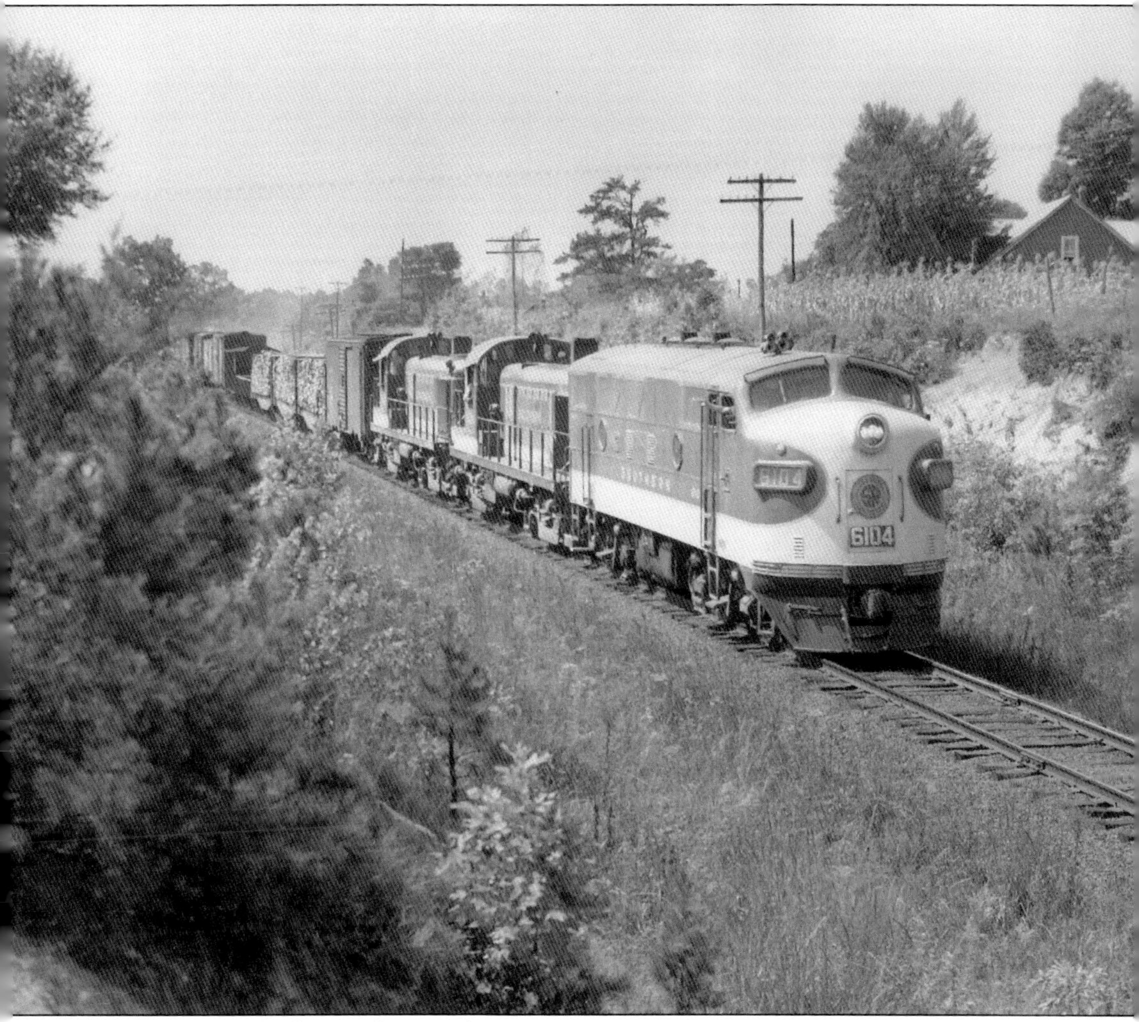

The rebuilt FT 6104 leads two Alco RS-3 locomotives on a test run on train 154 through Graham, North Carolina, in 1953. Mechanical upgrades to the 6104 included new horns, new exhaust fans, sealed beam headlight, changes to the side portholes and vents, the 1,500-horsepower prime mover, and a new green paint scheme. It was common practice for rebuilt Spencer diesel locomotives to run a freight train between Spencer and Selma to check for any problems. The Southern Railway chose Spencer Shops to perform most of the mechanical upgrading to older FT and F-3 locomotives over other shops around the system. These older locomotives were upgraded to specifications similar to F-7 locomotives with more horsepower and larger traction motors. Most of this work was performed between 1950 and 1953, though some locomotives received continued work through the 1950s. (Photograph by J. Marvin Black.)

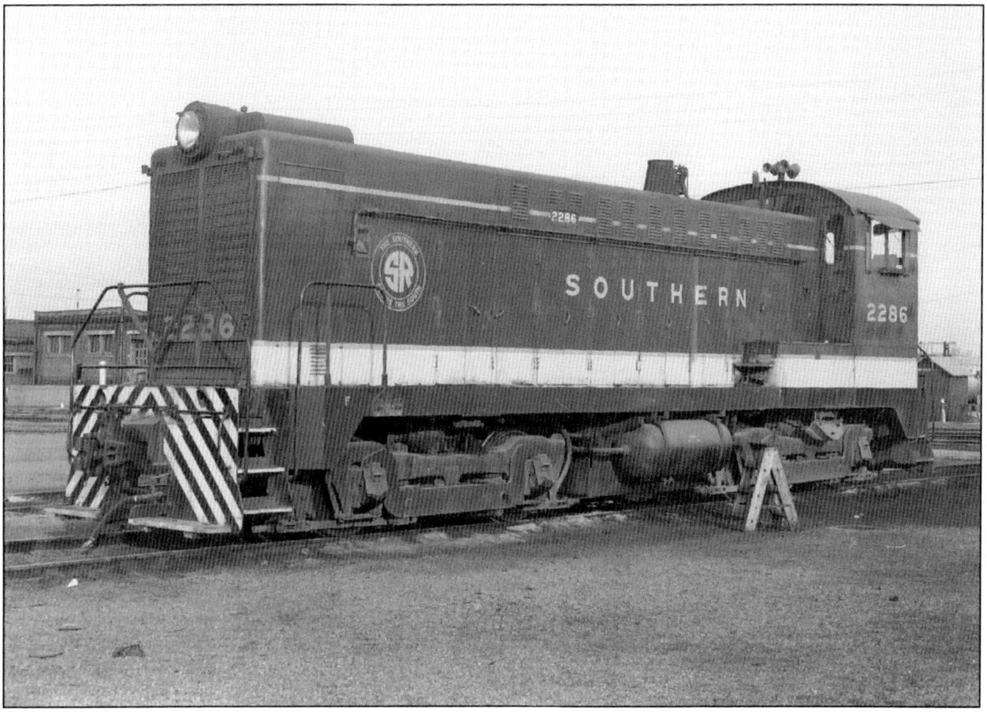

Southern 2286, seen at Spencer in 1956, was built by the Baldwin Locomotive Works in 1941. It was a 1,000-horsepower switcher, model DS-4-4-1000. These early diesel switchers brought the first use of diesels at Spencer Shops. (Marvin Rogers's collection.)

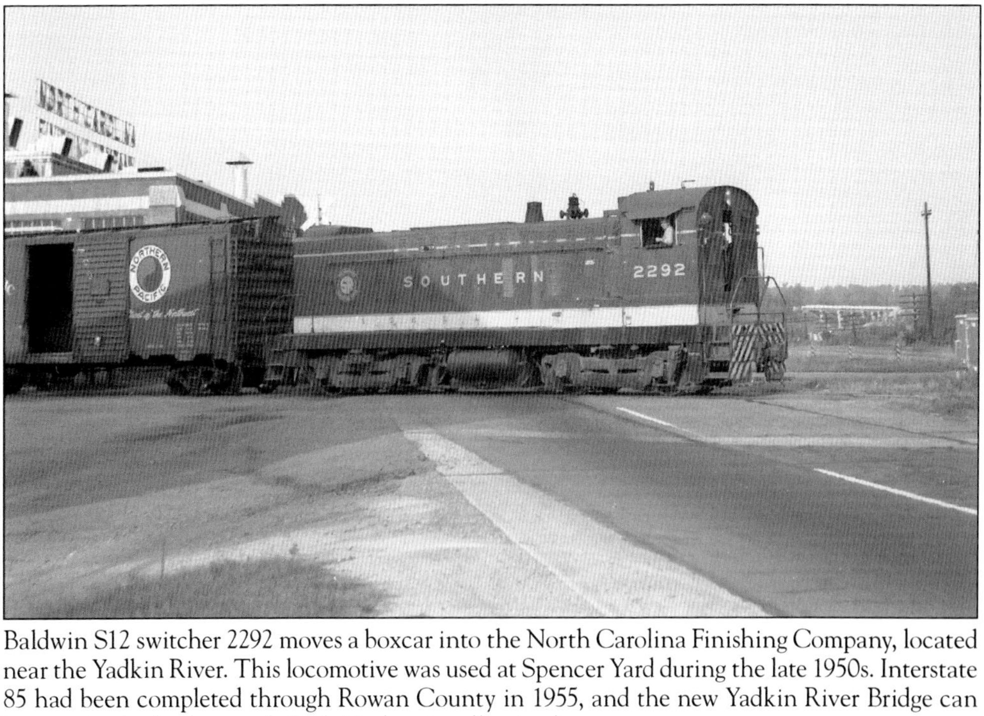

Baldwin S12 switcher 2292 moves a boxcar into the North Carolina Finishing Company, located near the Yadkin River. This locomotive was used at Spencer Yard during the late 1950s. Interstate 85 had been completed through Rowan County in 1955, and the new Yadkin River Bridge can be seen in the background. (Bob Graham's collection.)

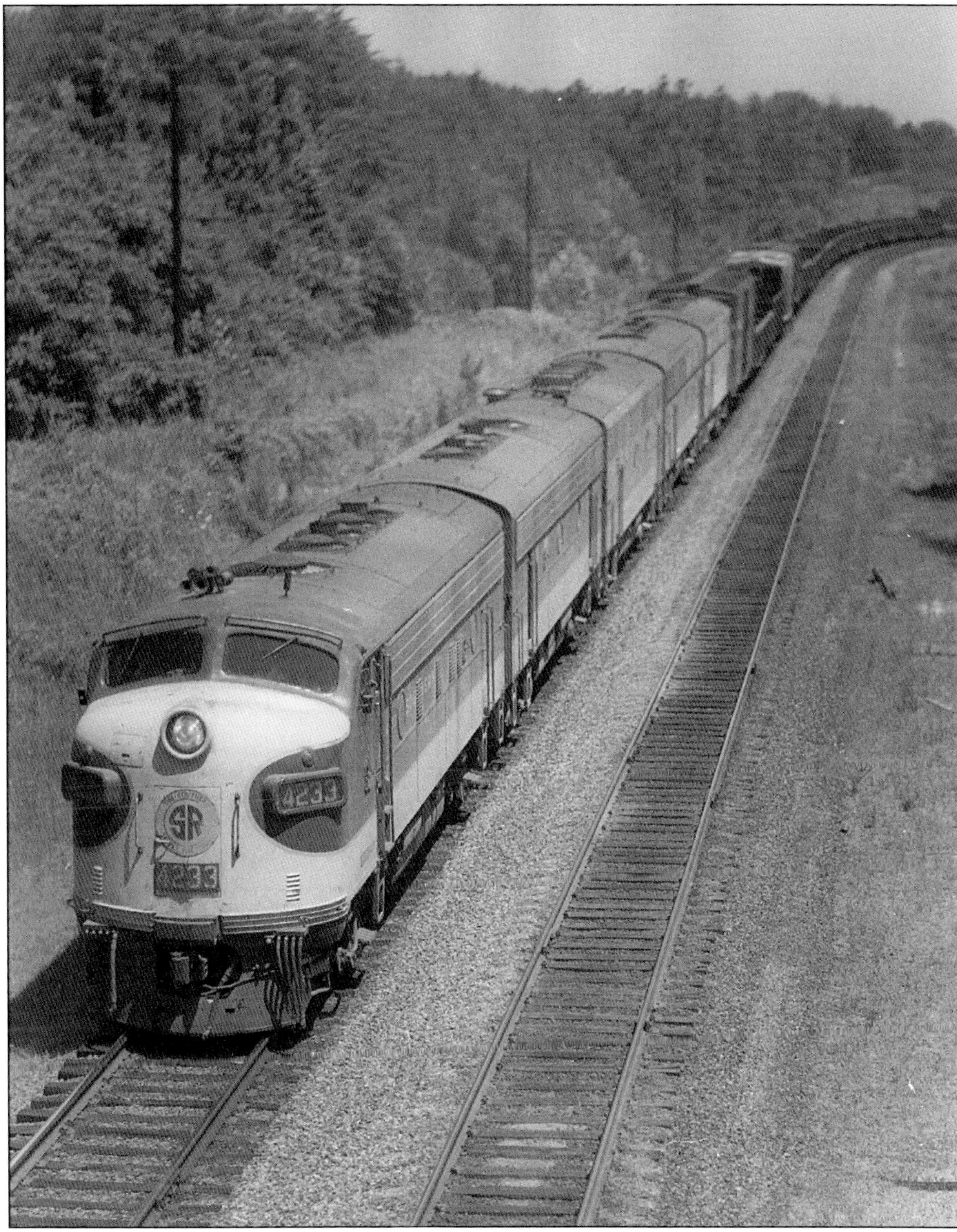

A quintet of Spencer-maintained F units leads a freight train, with 197 freight cars, south of Reidsville, North Carolina, on July 10, 1956. The locomotives are F-7 No. 4233, F-3 B No. 4383, F-3 B No. 4326, F-7 B No. 4401, and F-7 No. 4245. (Photograph by J. Marvin Black.)

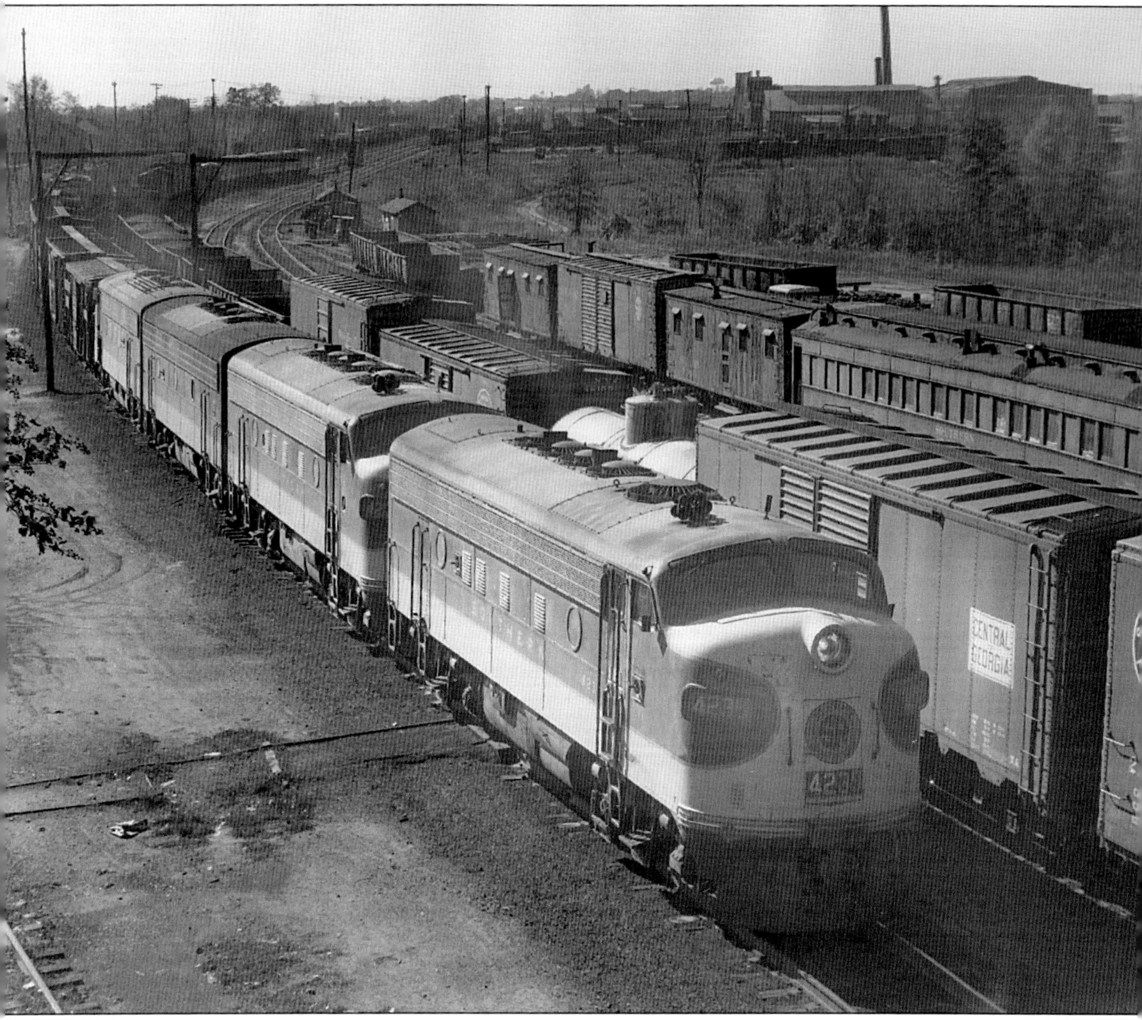

Electro-Motive Division F units continued to be the main locomotives used for freight trains on the Southern Railway through the 1950s. The freight classification yard at Spencer could receive trains from the north, south, east (via Greensboro), and west. Freight cars would be sorted for other trains or switched through the transfer sheds at the south end of the yard. Shown above, a northbound freight is leaving Spencer on November 18, 1956, with 4239, 4200, 4405, and 4229. It is passing a southbound freight entering the yard and the wreck train equipment. The wreck train would respond to any derailments on the Danville Division. The shop buildings are in the background, and the Spencer depot track is visible in the left corner. (Photograph by J. Marvin Black.)

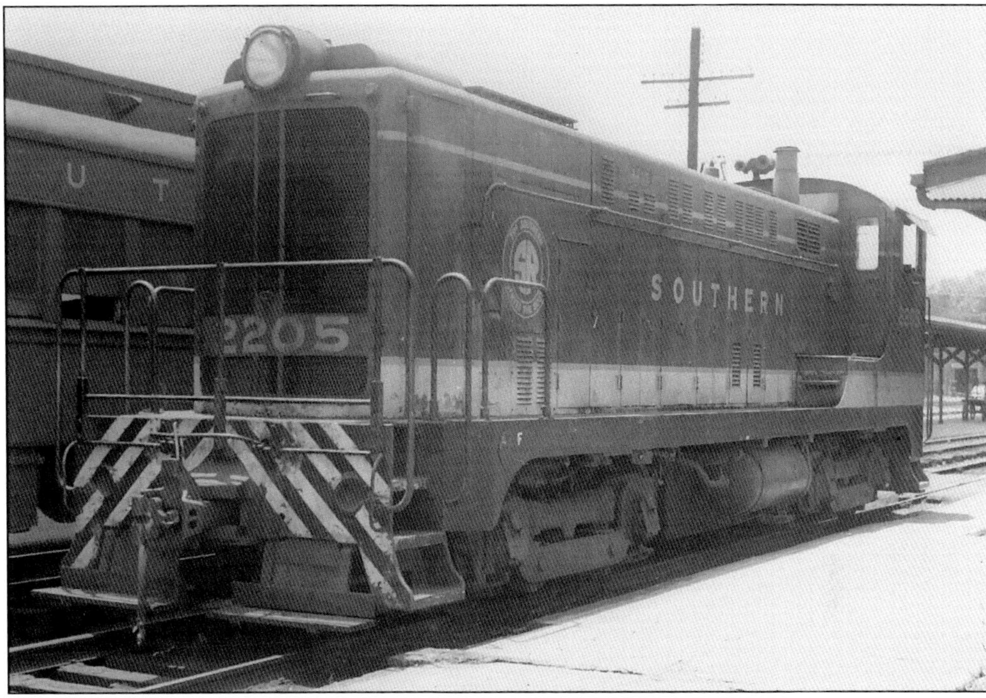

Locomotive 2205 was built by the Baldwin Locomotive Works in 1941 and was the only VO 1000 on the Southern Railway's diesel roster. It was photographed at Salisbury on July 8, 1959, performing passenger train switch duties. (Photograph by J. Marvin Black.)

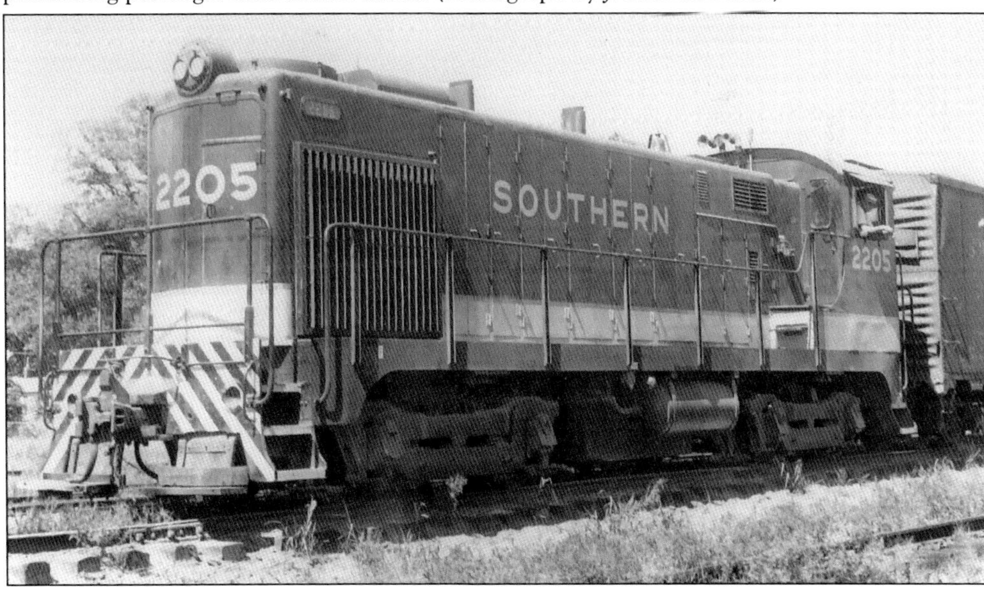

The 2205 received a new lease on life at Spencer during the early 1960s. Instead of transferring to Atlanta for scrapping, this unit became the last to be rebuilt at Spencer Shops. The shop force used an EMD 1,500-horsepower prime mover, EMD traction motors, generator and electric fan, and other parts to completely rebuild the unit inside and out. The rebuilt unit continued to serve Spencer Yard until the new EMD SW-1500s arrived in 1967. (Photograph by James H. Wade Jr.; J. Marvin Black's collection.)

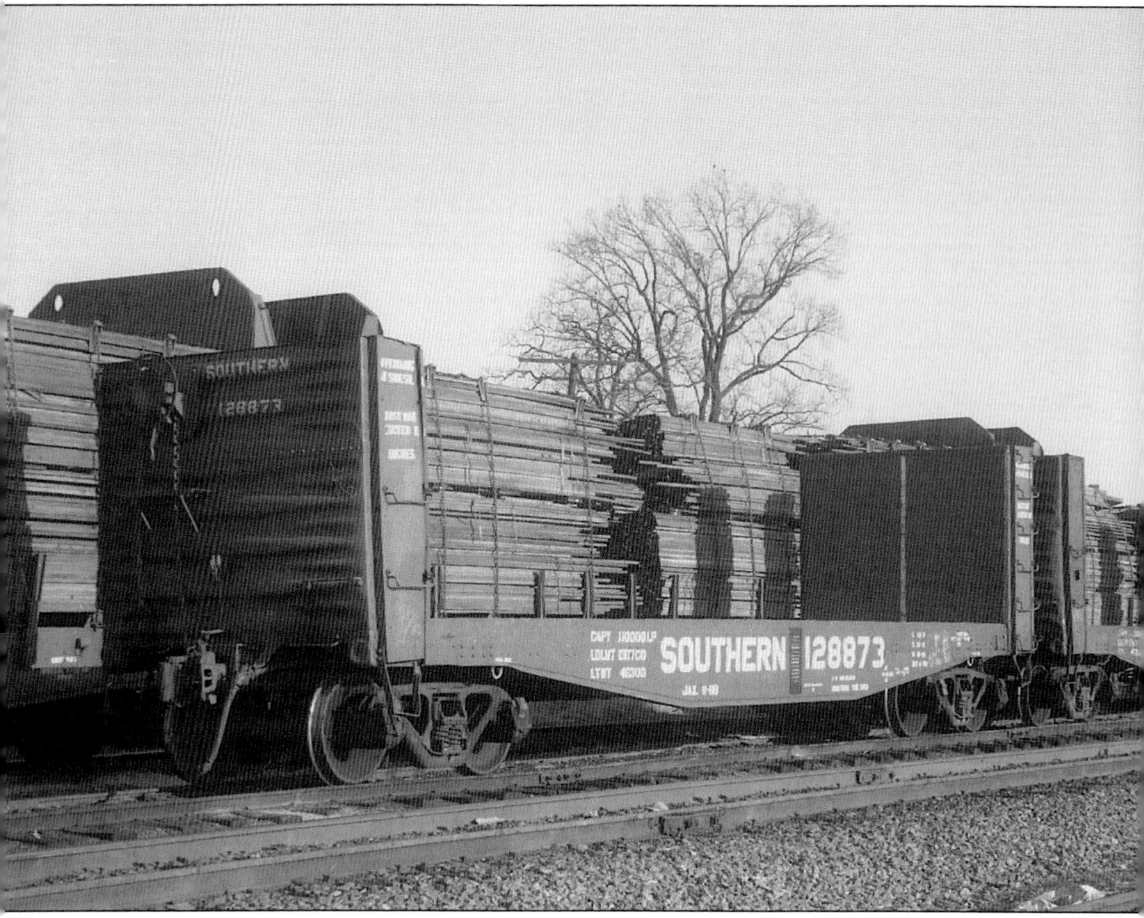

The Spencer Shops' car department was assigned the task of converting old 40-foot boxcars into pulpwood cars in 1951. The old boxcars were stripped down to the underframe, center sill, side sills, and steel ends. The ends were cut to the appropriate height, and steel was added to create the sides and floor. A new handbrake and 50-ton trucks completed the rebuild. This pulpwood rebuild was photographed in Burlington, North Carolina, on January 2, 1970, and was still in service after 19 years. (Photograph by Bob Graham.)

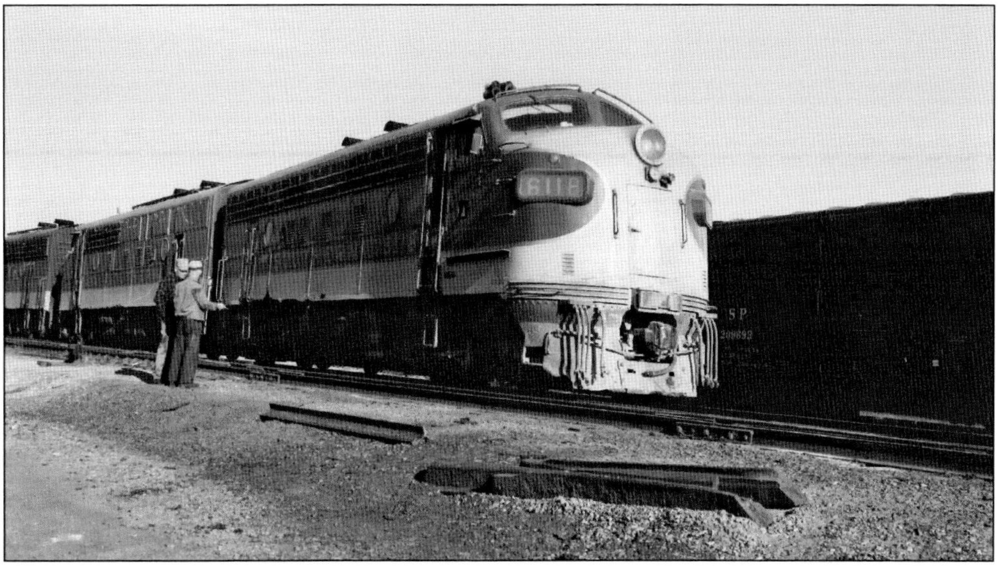

Locomotives 6118 and 4264 and an unidentified unit appear ready for another freight run at Spencer in 1969. The second unit has received some damage to the radiator grill, as evident by the large section removed, exposing the openings underneath. Both of these locomotives were retired by 1974. (Photograph by J. Marvin Black.)

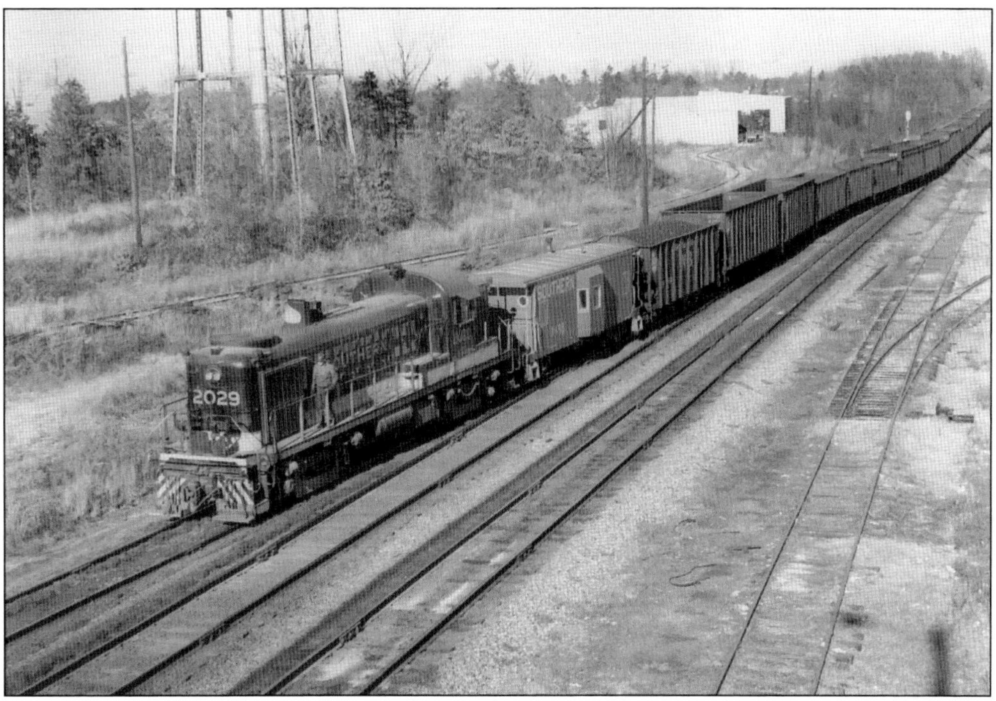

Locomotive 2029 and crew are switching the Dukeville train, taking coal to the Duke Power Plant on the Yadkin River. This switch run was the responsibility of Spencer Yard until the opening of Linwood Terminal. This locomotive was retired in 1976 and rebuilt into road slug 937 for hump yard service. (Marvin Rogers's collection.)

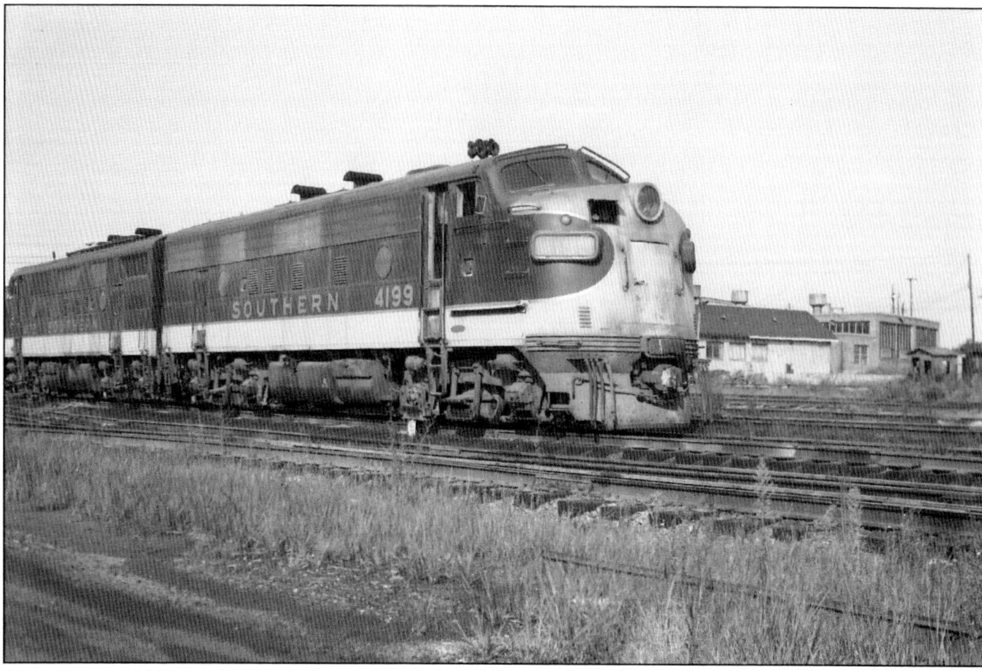

Locomotive 4199, an EMD F-3, was one of the last F-3s purchased by the Southern before EMD started producing the F-7 in 1949. Photographed in 1969 with the Spencer roundhouse in the background, it shows several modifications performed over the years to keep the older F units in operation. All of the F units, except four FP-7s, would be retired by 1979, traded to EMD for newer power. (Photograph by J. Marvin Black.)

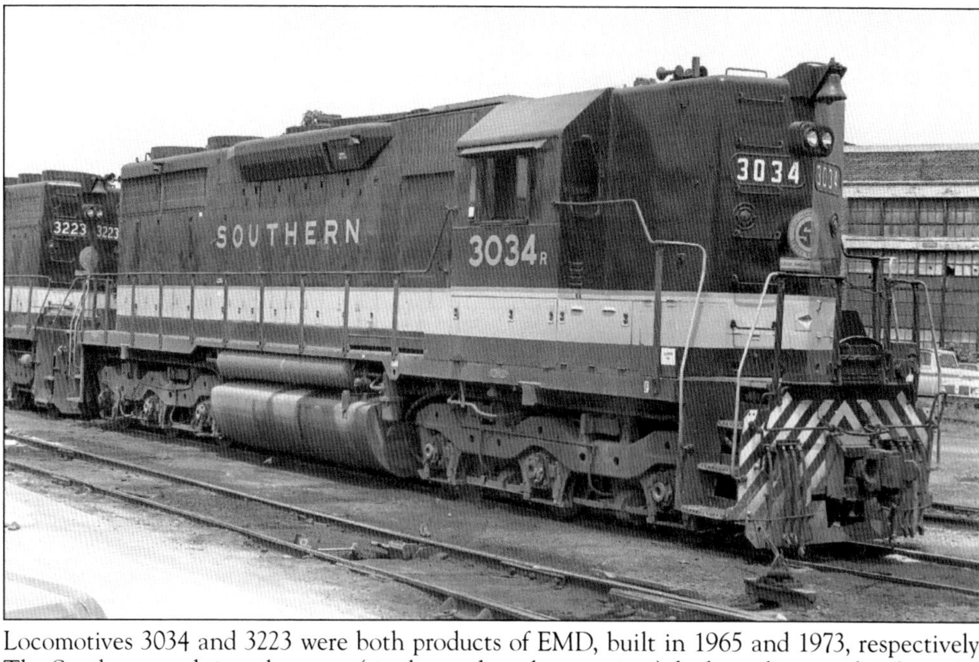

Locomotives 3034 and 3223 were both products of EMD, built in 1965 and 1973, respectively. The Southern used six-axle power (similar to these locomotives) for long-distance freight trains between Washington, DC, and Atlanta. (Photograph by Marvin Rogers.)

Four

THE PEOPLE OF SPENCER SHOPS

When the Southern Railway began constructing Spencer Shops in 1896, everything, including the labor force, had to be brought to Rowan County. The town of Spencer grew from a few hundred residents to 4,000 people by the 1920s. As Spencer grew, professional photographers documented the operation and workers.

The photographs of Spencer workers during the 1910s and 1920s illustrate working conditions and work attire, as well as the different crafts stationed around the property. The photographs show the rough nature of railroad work while also showing the pride of the workers, as evident in their poses and facial expressions.

Through the years, railroad employees took photographs at the shops to remember friends, job assignments, or special occasions. Through these images, the history of Spencer Shops unfolds—steam locomotive maintenance, transition to diesel locomotives, and the final days during the 1970s.

These photographs are presented as a tribute to the workers of Spencer Shops from the beginning in 1896 to the final Southern Railway operations in 1979.

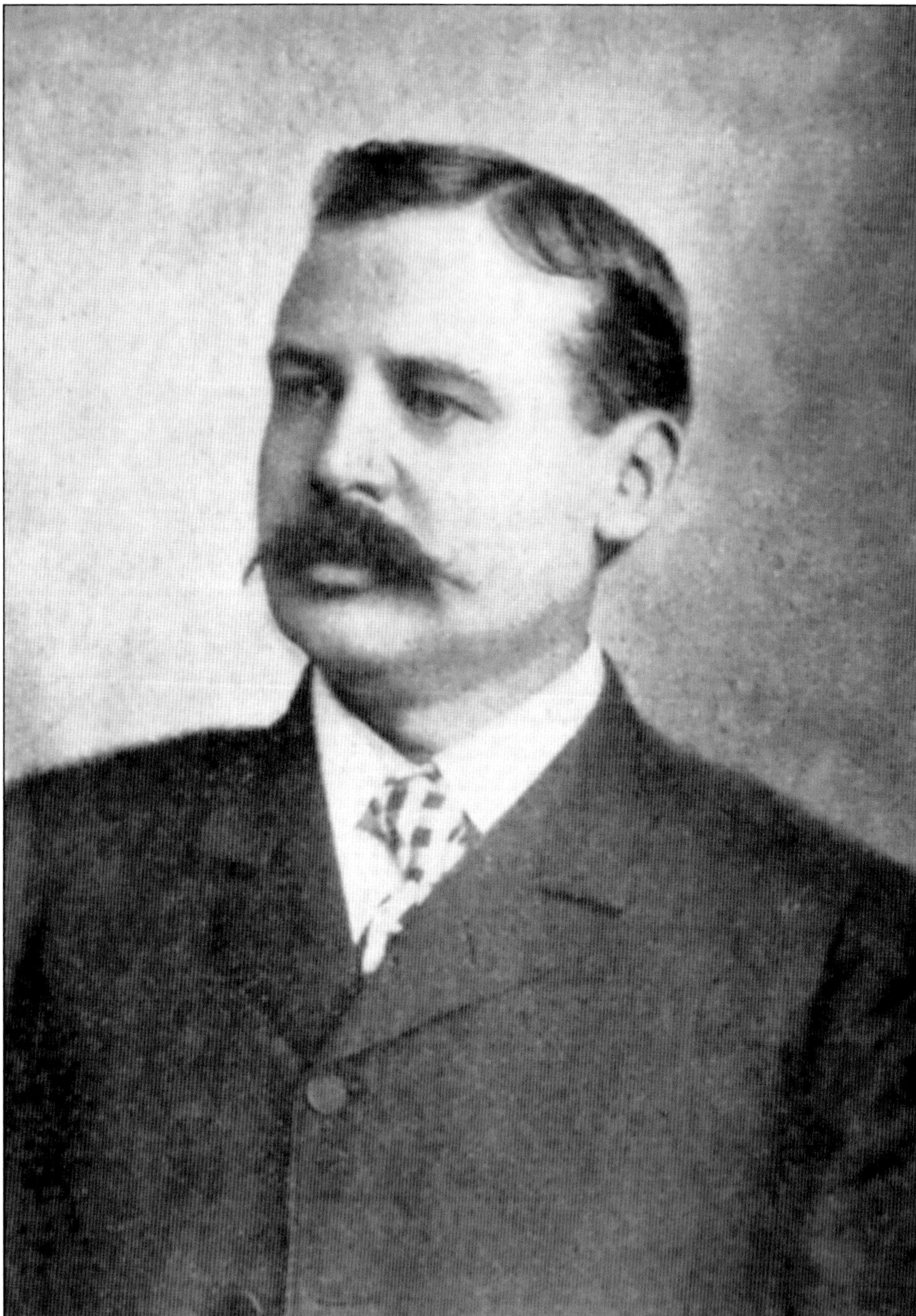

J.T. Robinson was the second master mechanic at Spencer Shops, serving from October 1, 1900, to June 15, 1903. He superseded W.H. Hudson, the first master mechanic, who started on October 19, 1896, the date the shops officially opened. (North Carolina State Archives.)

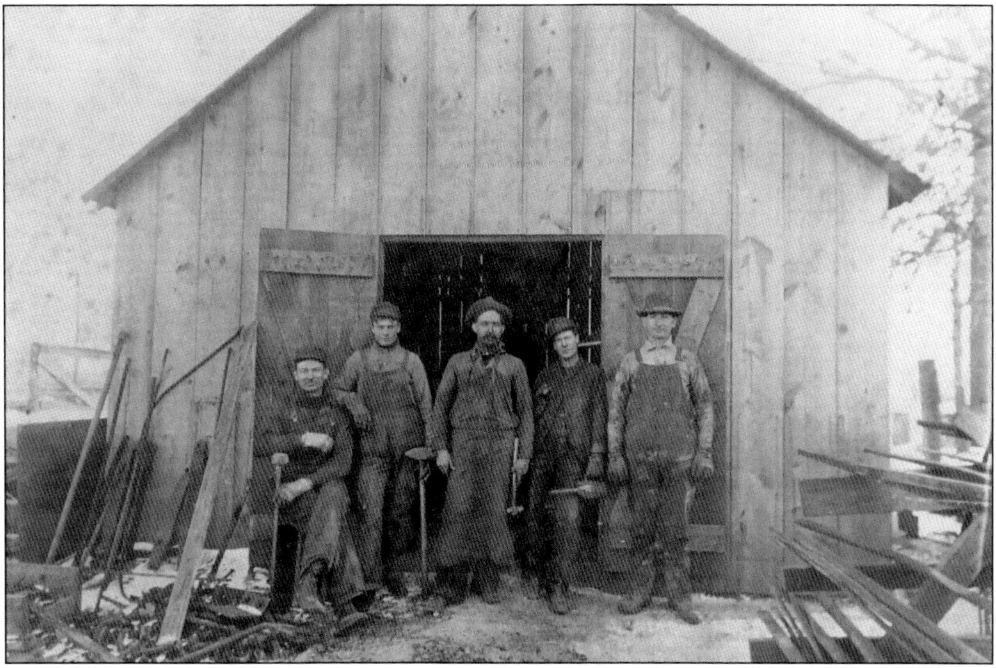

The blacksmiths at Spencer were used for metalwork repair and construction. These workers were moved in 1911 to the machine shop building, which included a transfer table for moving locomotive wheelsets or other parts into the building. (Both, North Carolina Division of Archives and History.)

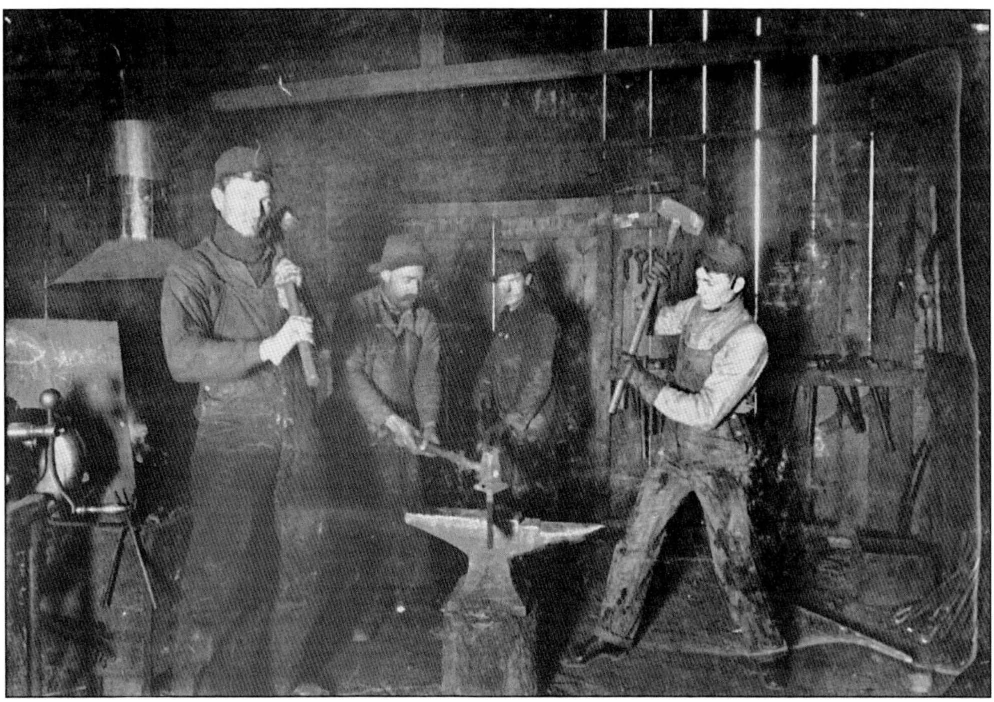

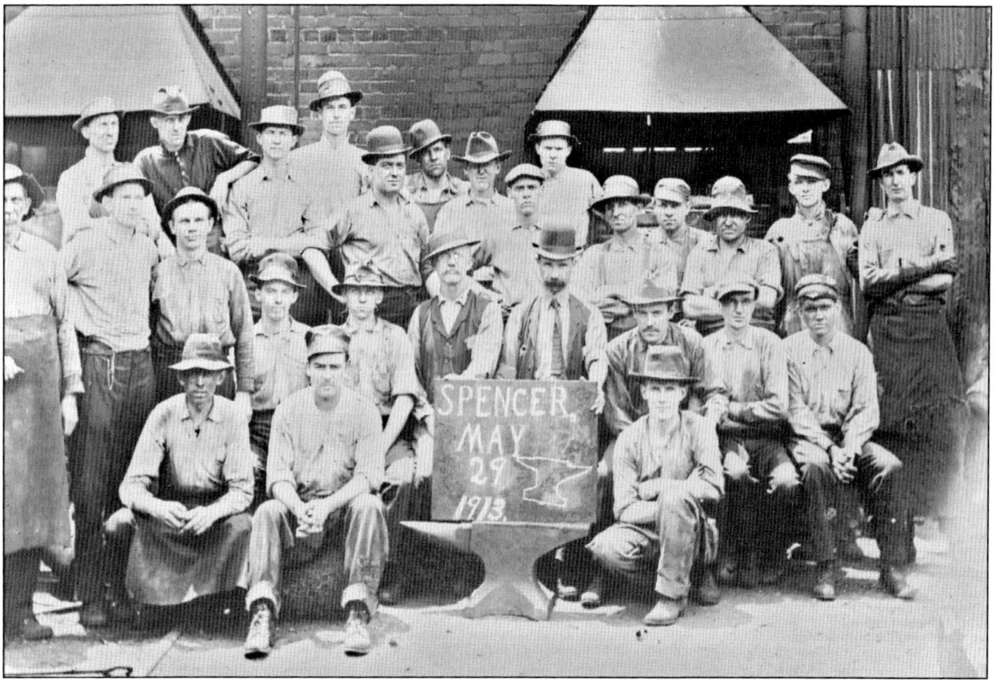

The blacksmiths pose beside their building on May 29, 1913. Those pictured, are, from left to right, (first row) Harry Rimer, R.P. Thompson, and David Geekie; (second row) R.E. Knox, J.C. McDaniel, R.U. Goodman, Jim Overman, H.A. Safrit, J.M. Cox, T.E. Conley, G.O. Coberth, R.A. McCall, and R.B. Wright; (third row) A.A. Safrit, J.A. Wiggins, L.A. Alsobrooks, Francis Goodman, H.C. Ware, D.G. Parks, A.J. Gillespie, Otis Ervers, J.F. Hess, L.B. Shuler, A.H. Heilig, J.A. Horton, Mason Owens, and Bailey Tucker. (North Carolina Division of Archives and History.)

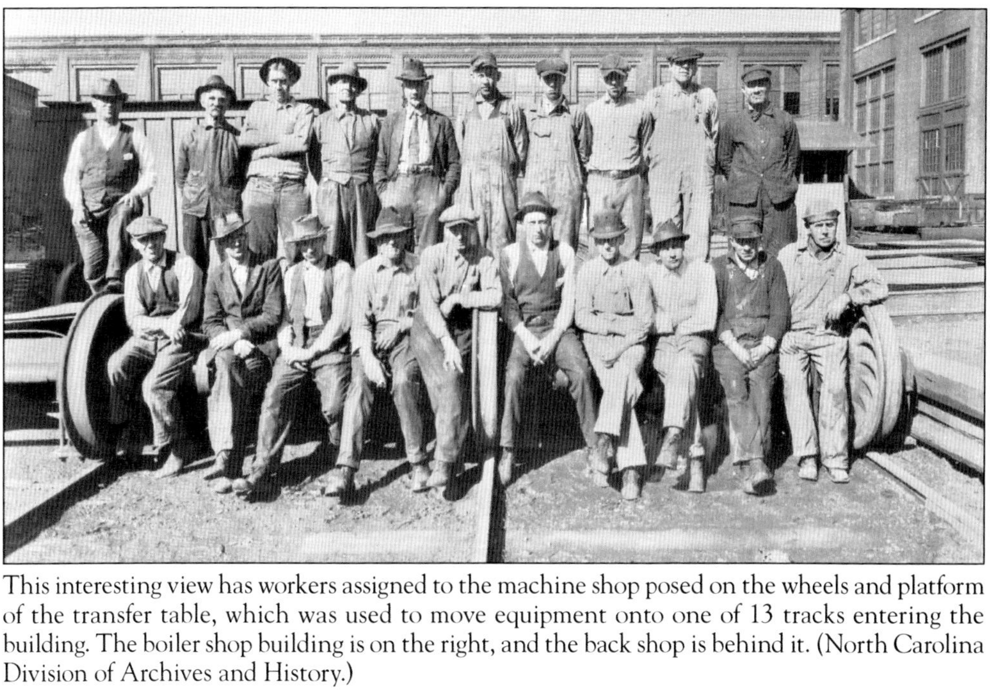

This interesting view has workers assigned to the machine shop posed on the wheels and platform of the transfer table, which was used to move equipment onto one of 13 tracks entering the building. The boiler shop building is on the right, and the back shop is behind it. (North Carolina Division of Archives and History.)

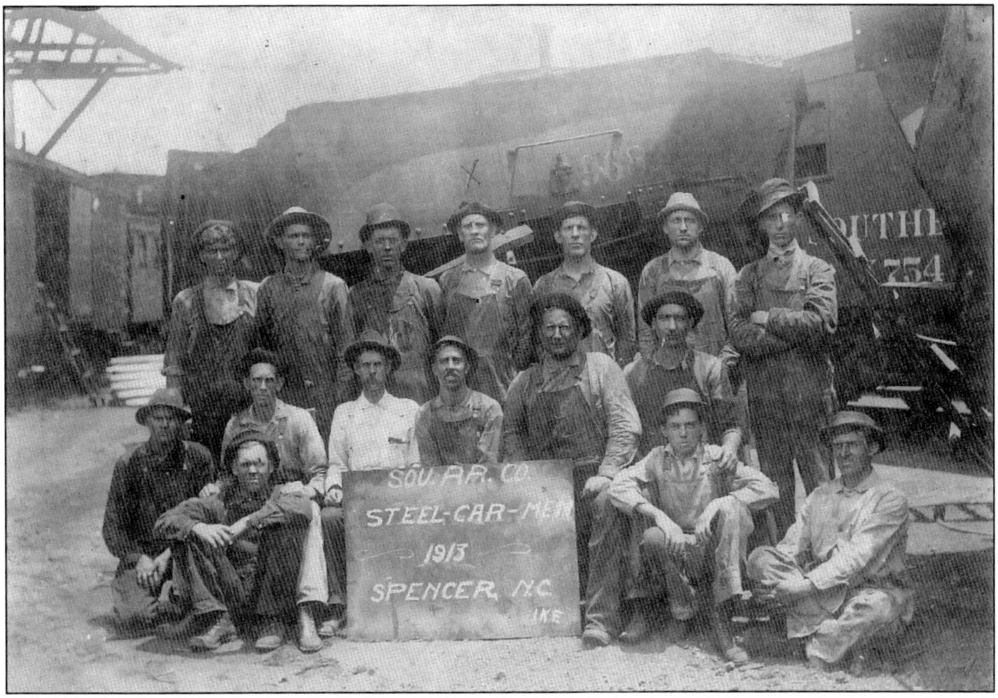

A professional photographer, only known by his initials IKE, visited Spencer Shops during 1913 and took several photographs of different work trades around the site. Groups of workers were posed near their work location with a similar sign. The photographs show men assigned to the machine shop, which had several different positions, such as the drill press men. (Both, North Carolina Division of Archives and History.)

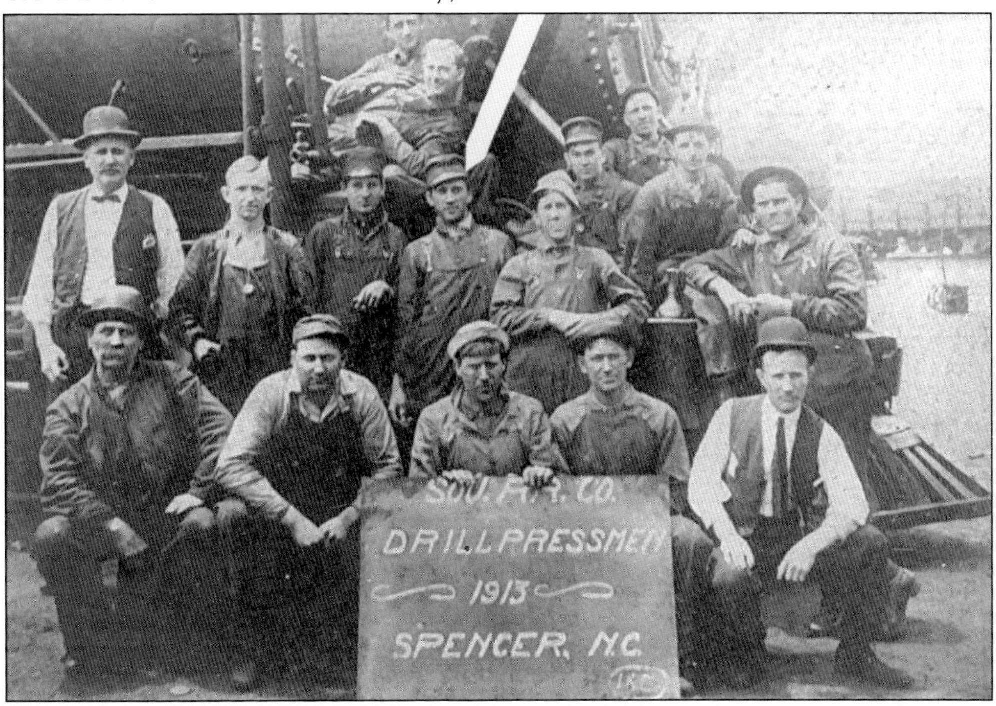

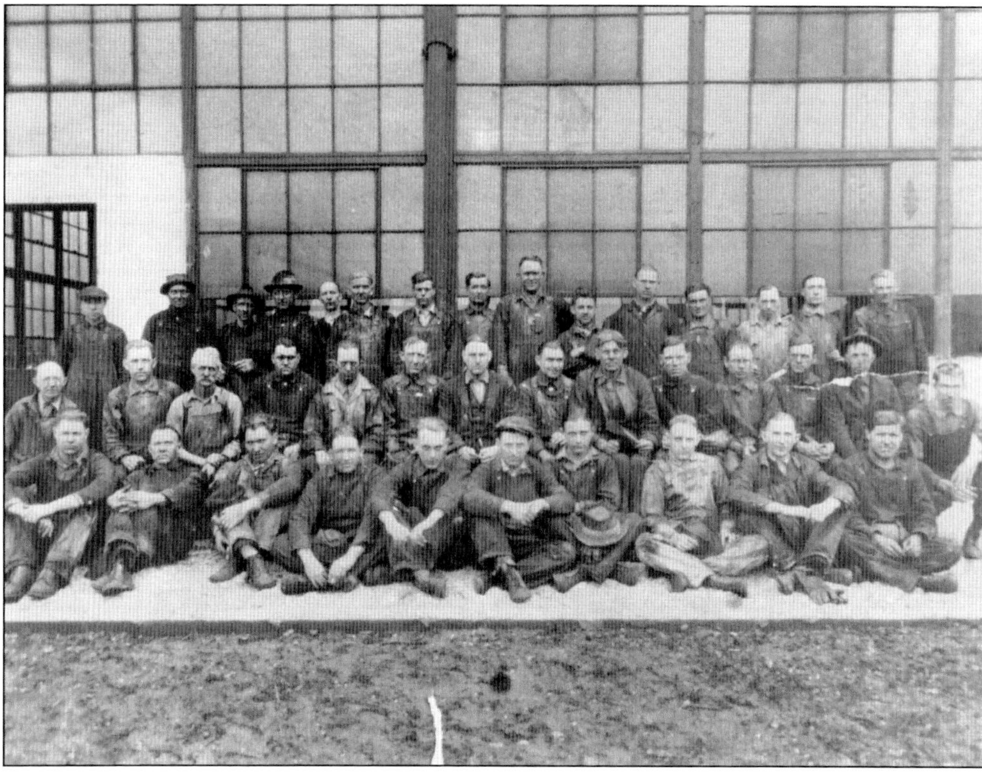

The flue shop was used to maintain and repair the boiler tubes used in steam locomotives. The building was constructed in 1924 and divided in two as a flue repair and a tin-and-babbit shop. (Both, North Carolina Division of Archives and History.)

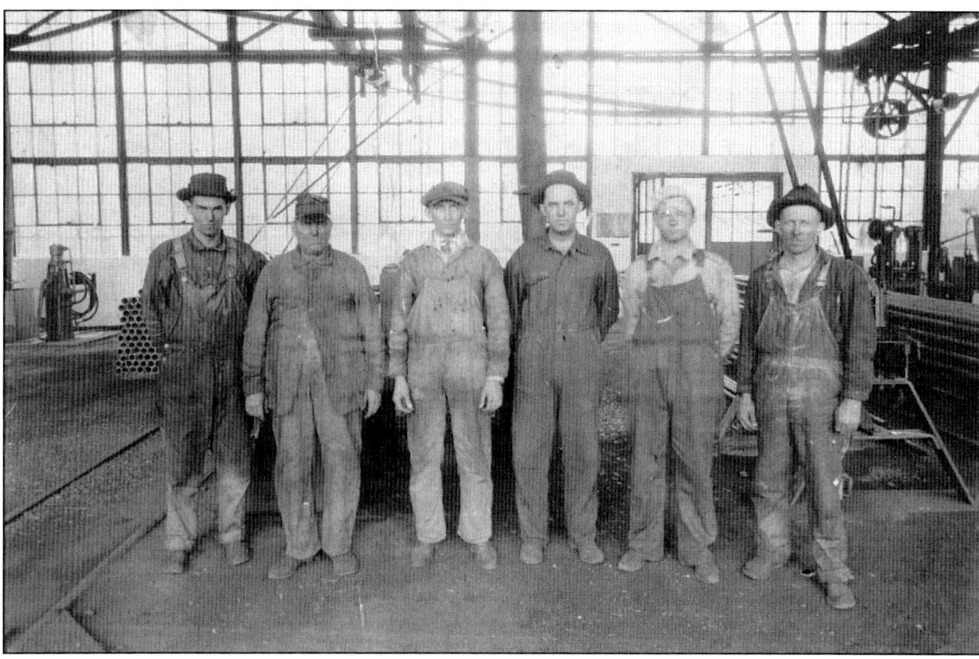

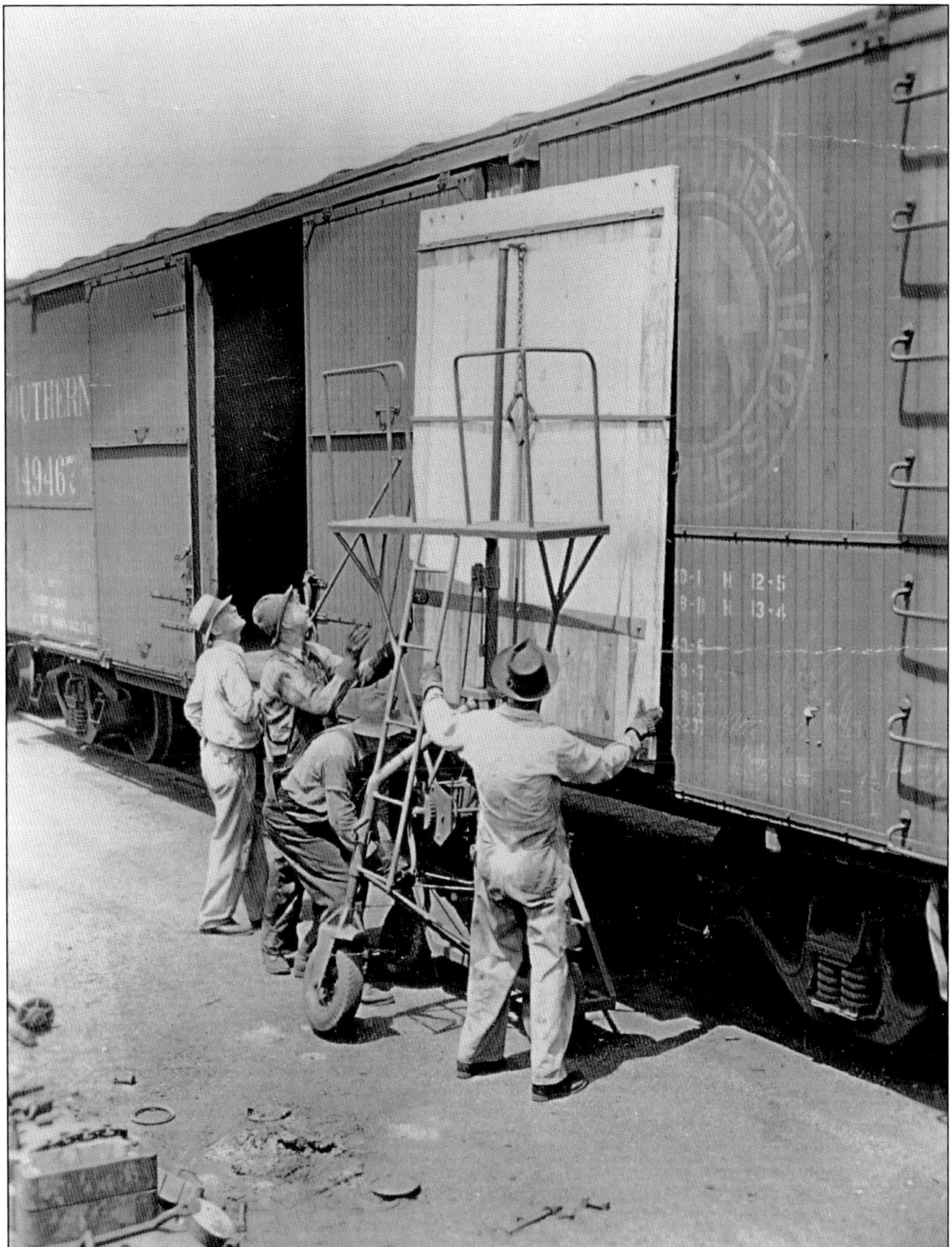

The car department was located in a long covered building containing five tracks and almost 600 feet in length. This department performed routine maintenance and minor repairs to freight cars operating through Spencer Shops. In this view, Southern Railway wooden boxcar 149467, built in 1930, receives work. Workers performed routine maintenance that allowed freight cars like these, to remain in service over 30 years. (North Carolina Division of Archives and History.)

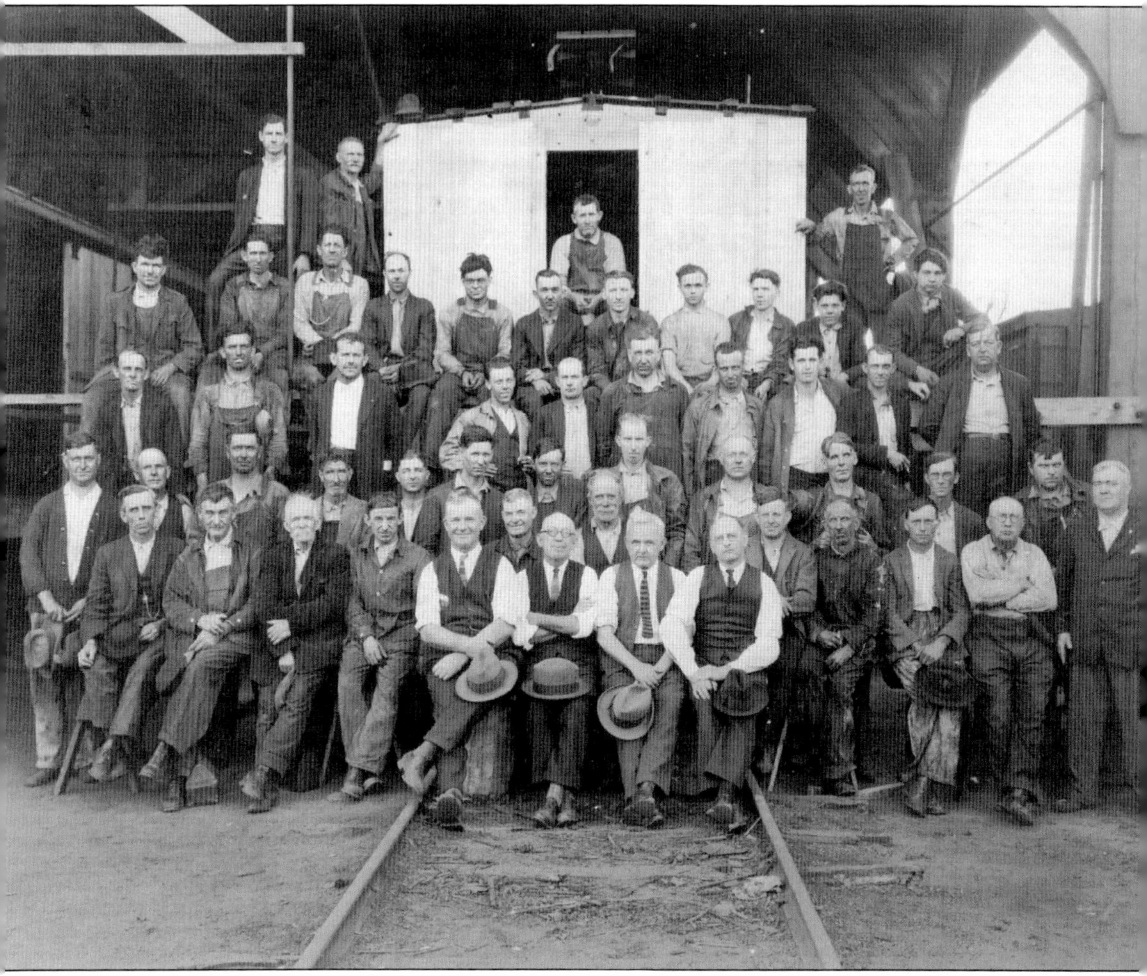

Here is another view of the car department, which is posed at one end of the long shed. Only the roof was covered, leaving the sides and ends open. The car shed was located behind the roundhouse, adjacent to the main freight classification yard. Its tracks stretched from one end of the yard to the other. (North Carolina Division of Archives and History.)

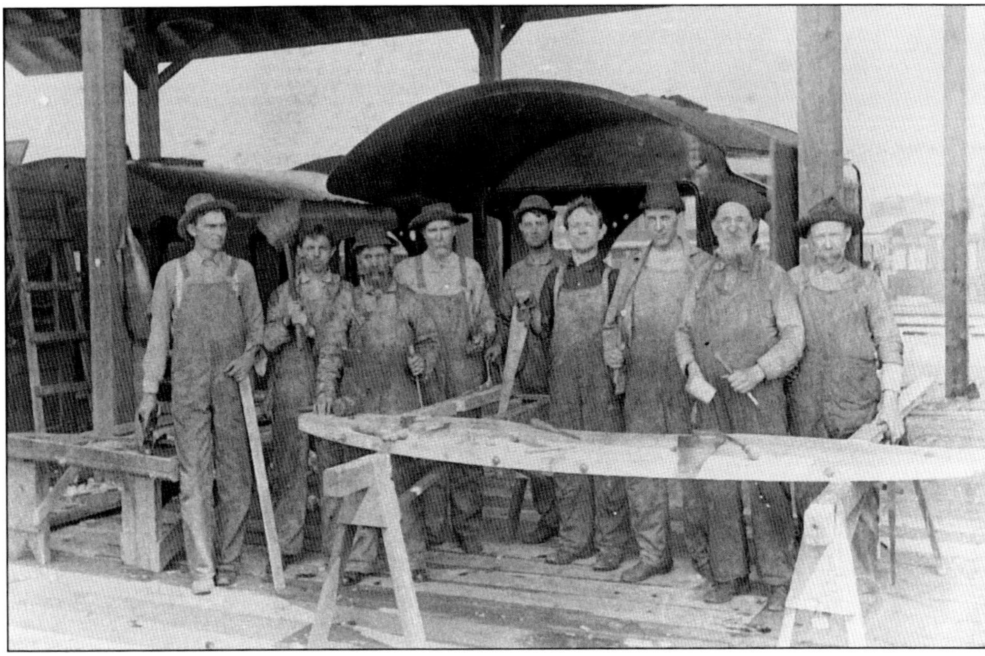

Similar in operation to the car department was the steam locomotive cab shop. When a steam locomotive entered the back shop, the cab was removed and taken to the adjacent cab shop to have the interior wood sheathing replaced or to repair sheet metal. (North Carolina Division of Archives and History.)

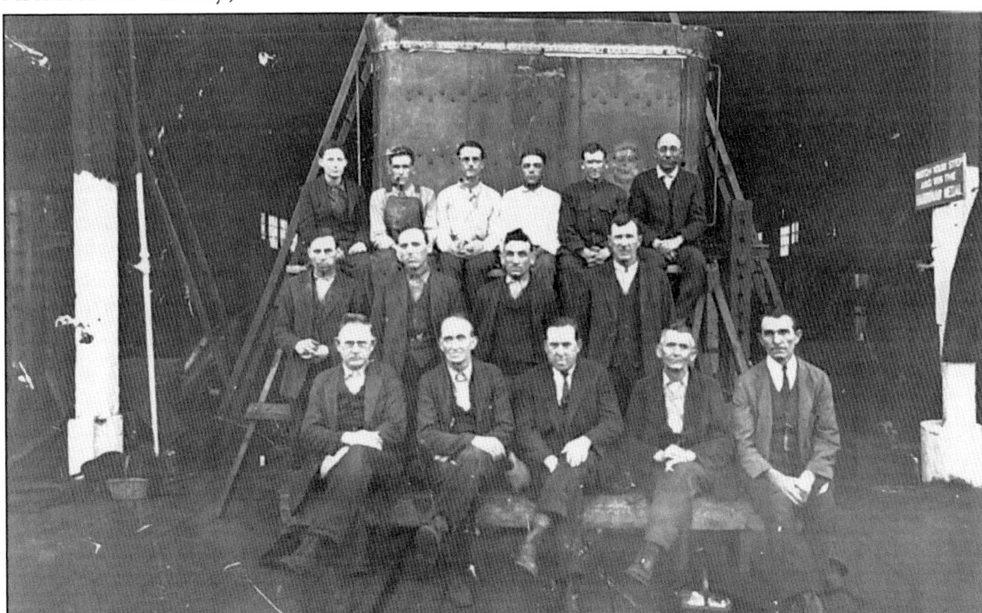

The steam locomotive tender repair facility was located in an open pole building north of the back shop, beside the firing-up shed. Tenders were separated from steam locomotives before entering the back shop and brought here for repair work or routine maintenance. Once the locomotive exited the back shop, it was mated with its tender at the firing-up shed. This building was later converted into a paint shop in 1950. (North Carolina Division of Archives and History.)

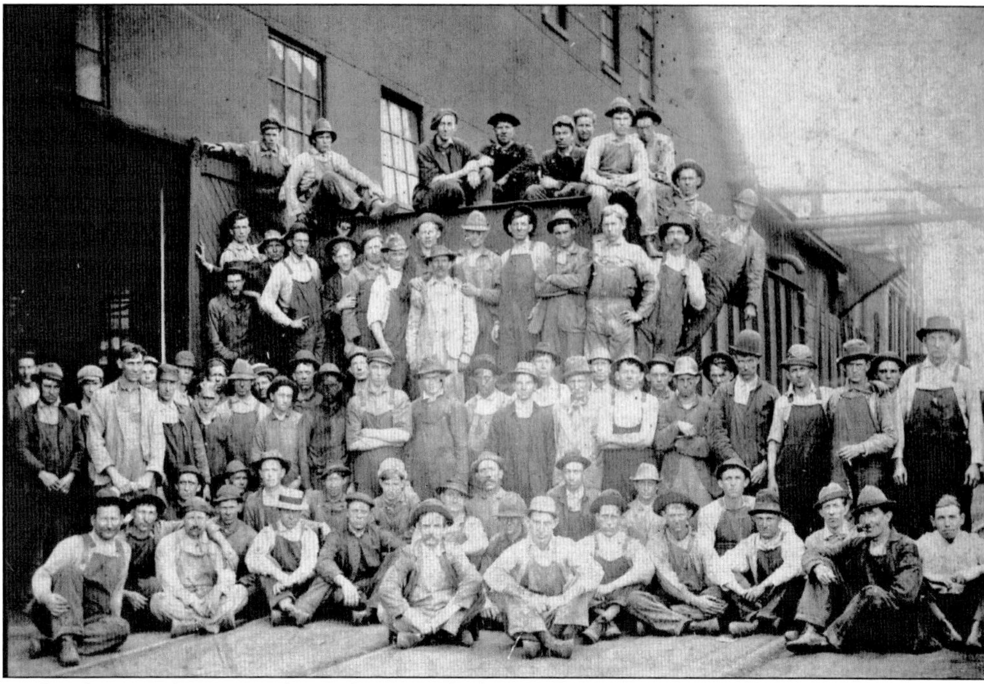

Boiler shop workers pose for a photograph during the 1910s or 1920s. The boiler shop was constructed in 1911 to replace an existing blacksmith shop. Boilermakers and machinists occupied the building, repairing or fabricating items from sheet steel. (North Carolina Division of Archives and History.)

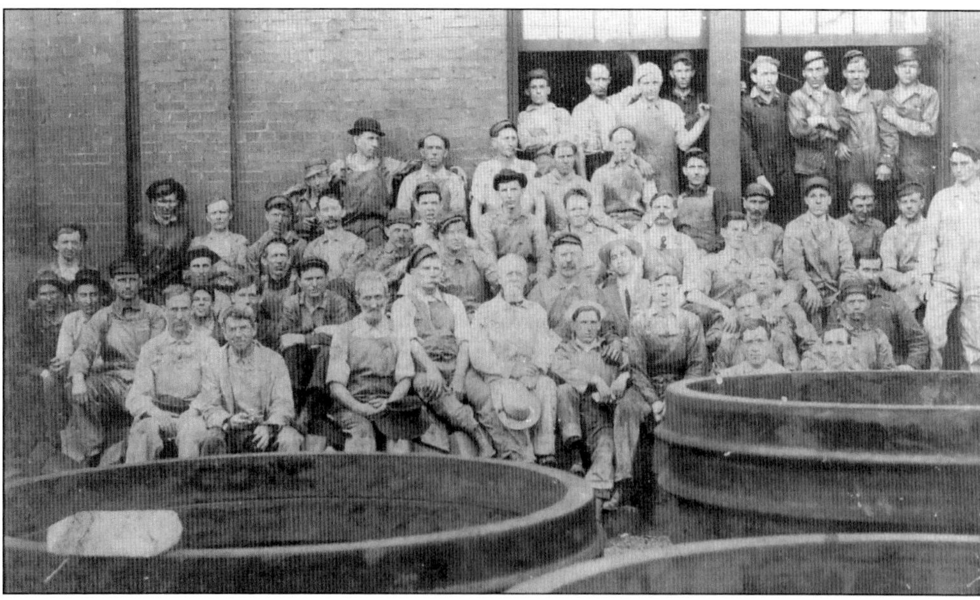

Blacksmith shop employees are captured posing behind stacks of steam locomotive drive tires. Steam locomotive drive wheels had a center rim and a tire, similar to an automobile. These tires were replaced by heating up the old tire until it expanded and pulled from the rim. Then the new tire, also heated, was pressed onto the rim. Once cooled, it would be locked in place. (North Carolina Division of Archives and History.)

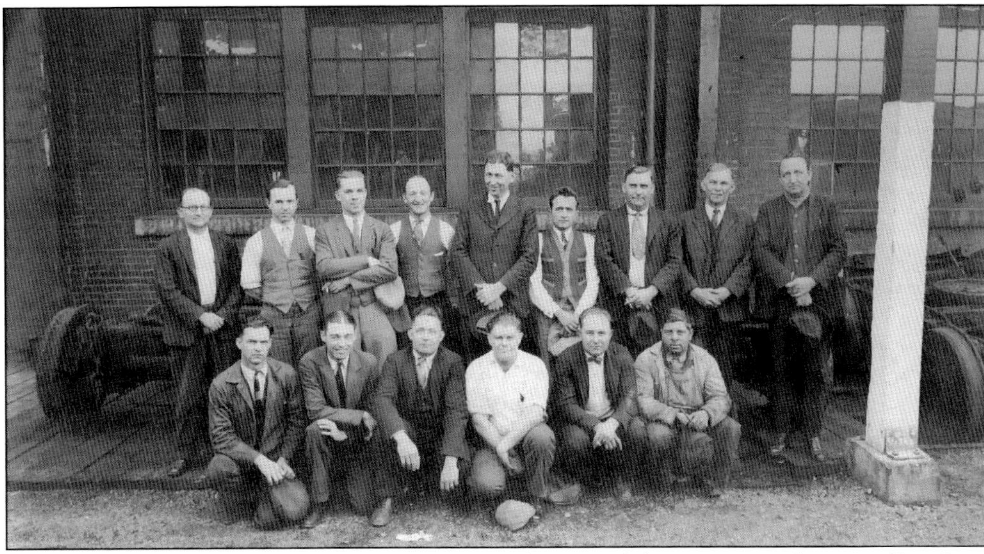

The storehouse at Spencer Shops was located in the rear of the master mechanic's office. Parts were stored in both the first and second stories, with a firewall separating the clerk's offices from the storehouse. This photograph shows the foremen of the storehouse during 1927, posed along the exterior wall of the back shop. Those pictured are, from left to right, (first row) Monk Lomax, Walt Folger, H.D. Stuttz, Henry Owens, Harlie Frick, and Joe Hodge; (second row) Murray Mesimer, Ray Earnhardt, Clarence Rickman, Red Earnhardt, J.W. Bean, Doc Young, Boone Wagoner, Bob Finger, and Alvin Baucom. The next five photographs were also taken during 1927. (North Carolina Division of Archives and History.)

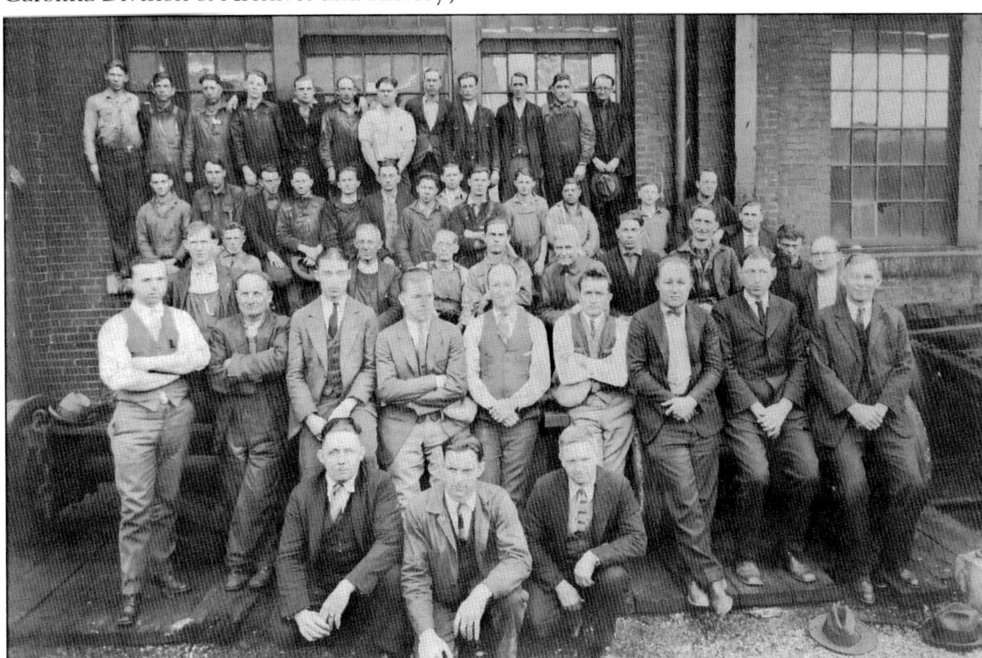

This view is of the employees and foremen of the storehouse. The only known worker seen above is Thomas Lee Coughnour, who is located second from left on third row. (Bill Rabon's collection.)

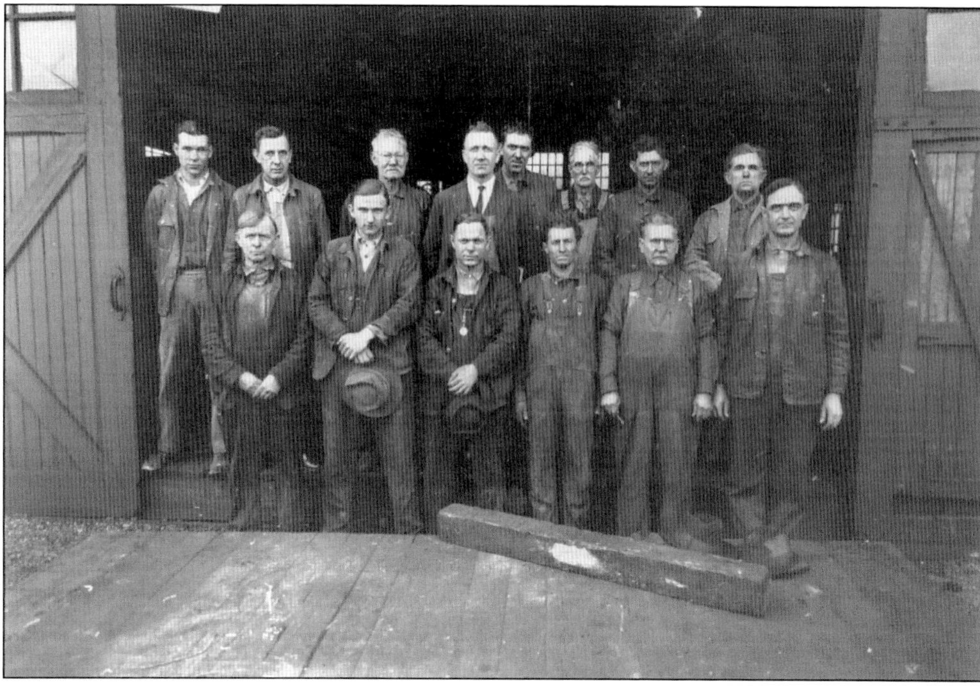

E.F. Kluttz, foreman of engine carpenters, poses with employees at their building. The woodworking shop was located between the powerhouse and tender repair building. (North Carolina Division of Archives and History.)

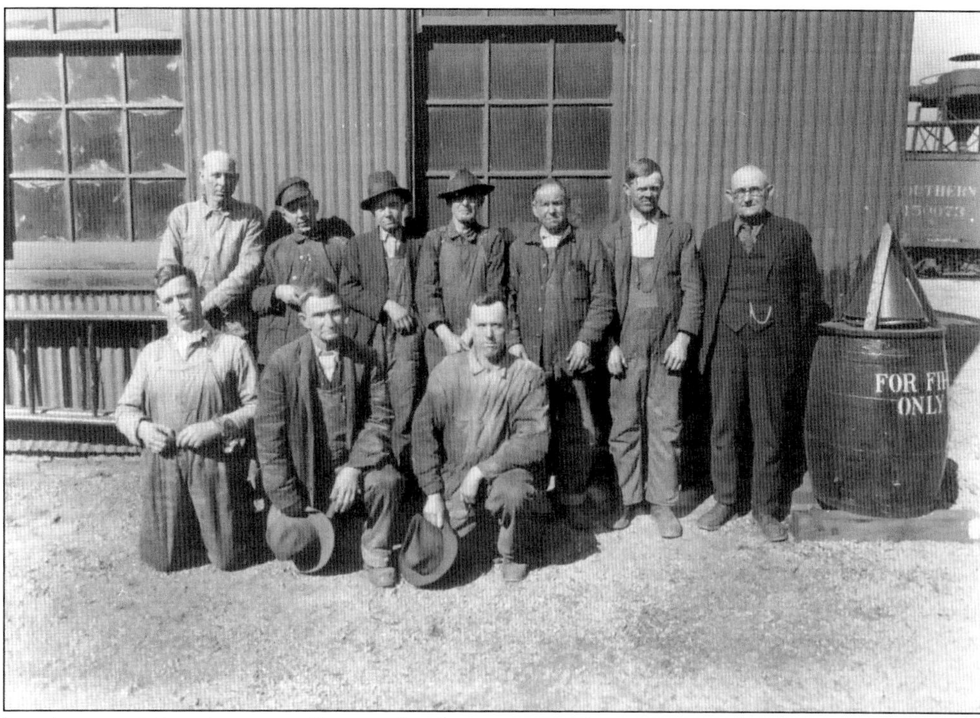

Employees of the planing mill pose for the camera. These men worked in a section of the woodworking shop. (North Carolina Division of Archives and History.)

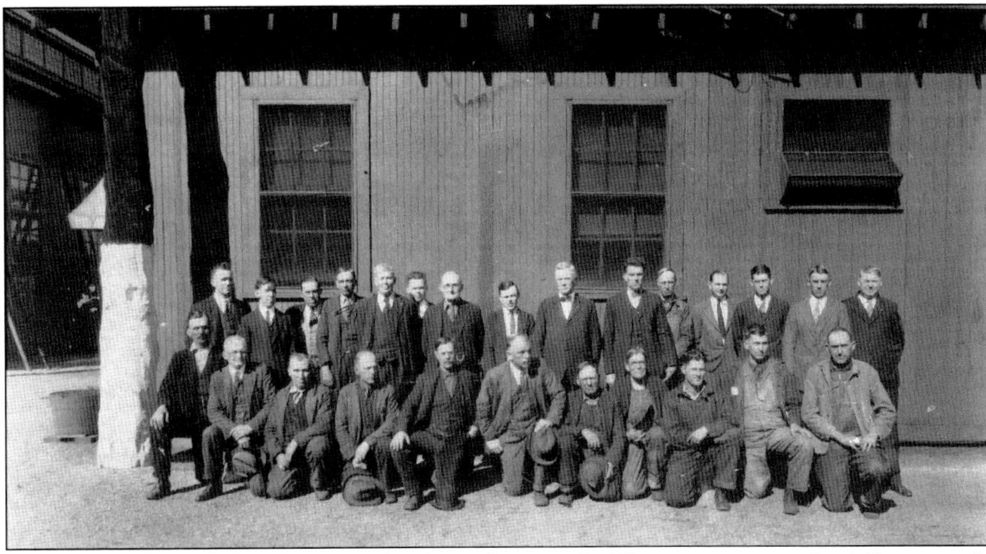

Shop supervisors and foremen pose for their photograph. The men oversaw the different crafts divided among the shop buildings. Union rules at the time strictly delegated which craftsmen were allowed to perform repairs or work in certain buildings. (North Carolina State Archives.)

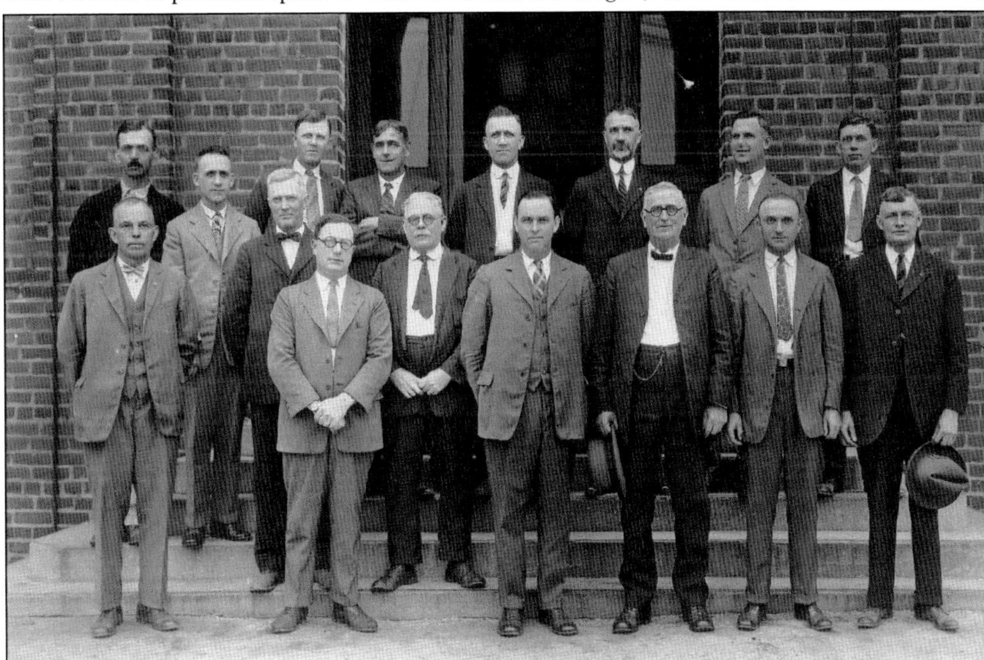

Here are Spencer Shops foremen. Those pictured are, from left to right, (first row) Charles A. Sides, car repairers; K. A. Lentz, erecting shop (back shop); R.N. Porter, pipe shop; E.L. Heilig, machine shop; H.C. Trexler, shop superintendent; and J.L. Cantwell, master mechanic; (second row) R.J. Overton, general foreman and car repairers; and W.S. Sweet, chief electrician; (third row) W.H. Thompson, derrick foreman; and V.B. Dewey Webb, night roundhouse foreman; (fourth row) H.T. McCubbins, paint shop; Robert L. Julian, general roundhouse foreman; E.F. Kluttz, engine carpenters; T.E. Conely, blacksmith shop; P.P. Surratt, boiler shop; and J.E. Connell, chief clerk master mechanic's office. (North Carolina State Archives.)

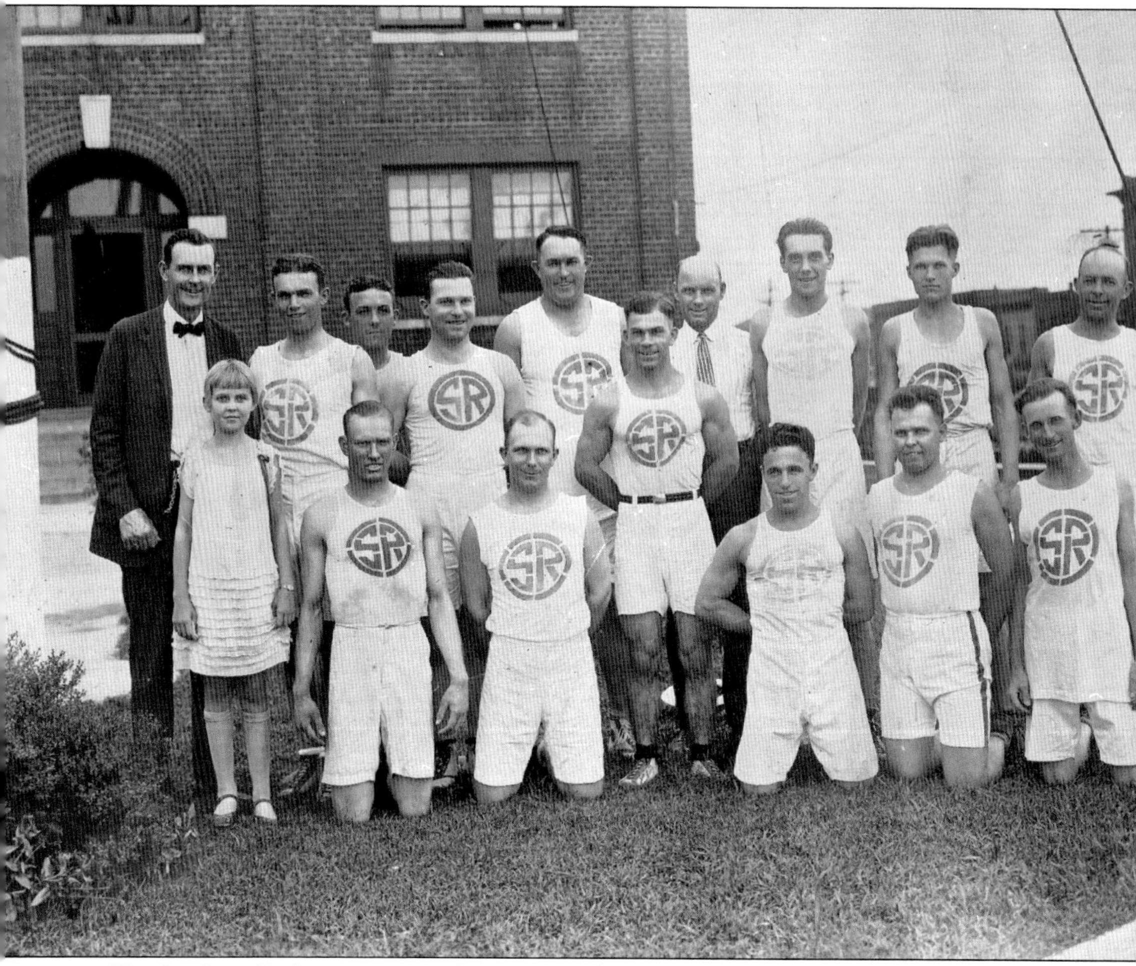

The Southern Railway encouraged competition between the repair shops across the system. One sport was hose reel cart teams, which pulled the hose carts used for fire suppression. Hose carts were stationed across the shops in small sheds, and workers were assigned to a specific cart in case of fire. At the 1926 North Carolina State Fireman's Tournament, held in Morehead City, the team from Spencer ran the 100-yard hose reel race in 17.6 seconds, breaking their own past record of 18 seconds flat. The team had to run 100 yards, unreel 98 feet of hose, attach the hose to a hydrant, and run water. Spencer hose reel teams held the record from 1906 through the 1920s. Those pictured are, from left to right, (standing) Spencer Shops fire chief W.P. Neister and daughter Margaret; J. L. Rimer, Jack Wright, H.L. Suggs, J.L. Safrit, W.F. Barker, E.M. Cauble, E.L. Weber, J.H. W. Miller, and G.L. Miller, captain; (kneeling) "Red" Talbert, G.R. Kluttz, T.C. Calhoun, W.D. Spake, and T.L. Benton. (North Carolina State Archives.)

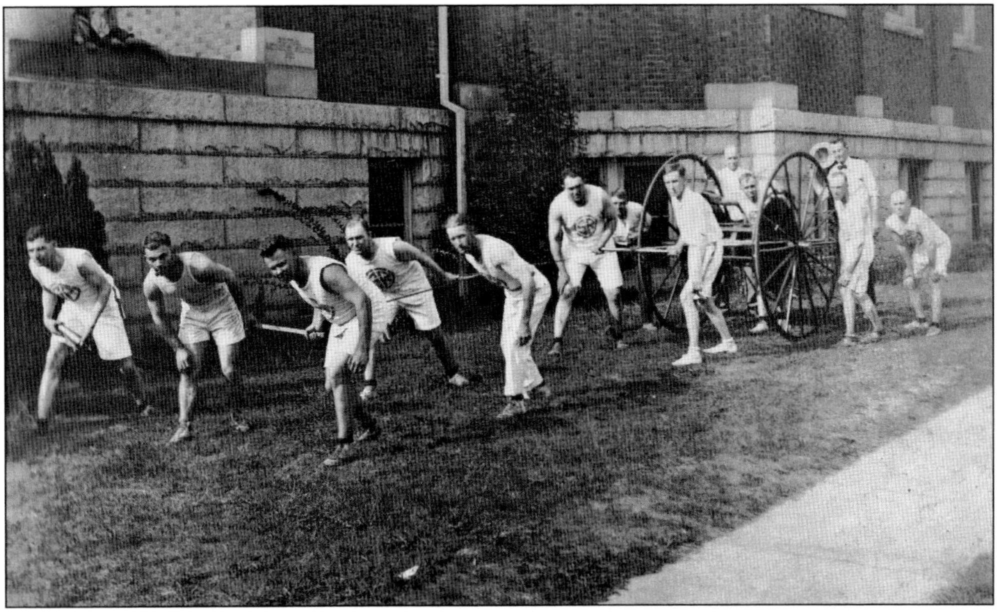

Members of the Spencer Shops hose reel team pose beside the Methodist church on the corner of Fourth Street and Yadkin Avenue in 1924. According to the November 1920 issue of *Southern News Bulletin*, the Spencer Shops Fire Company could run water in 45 seconds at any time to any shop building on a surprise alarm. They often assisted the Spencer and East Spencer departments during fire emergencies. (North Carolina State Archives.)

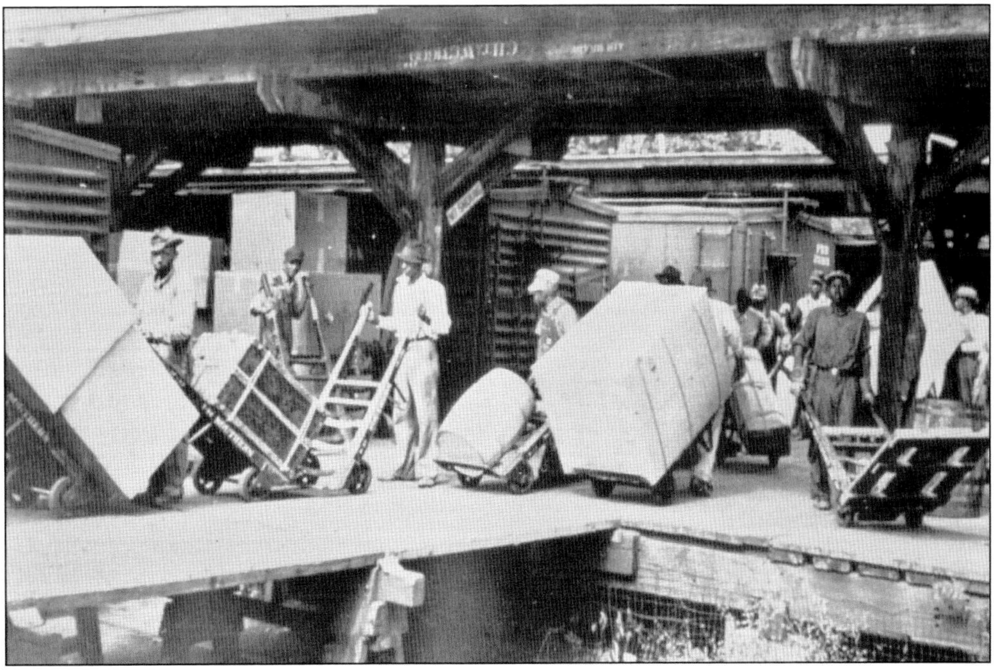

African American workers staffed the transfer sheds, located to the south of Spencer Shops, until it closed in the 1960s. The transfer facility at Spencer was the largest one on the Southern Railway north of Atlanta. During the 1930s and 1940s, 250 to 300 freight cars could be serviced every day at the facility. (North Carolina Division of Archives and History.)

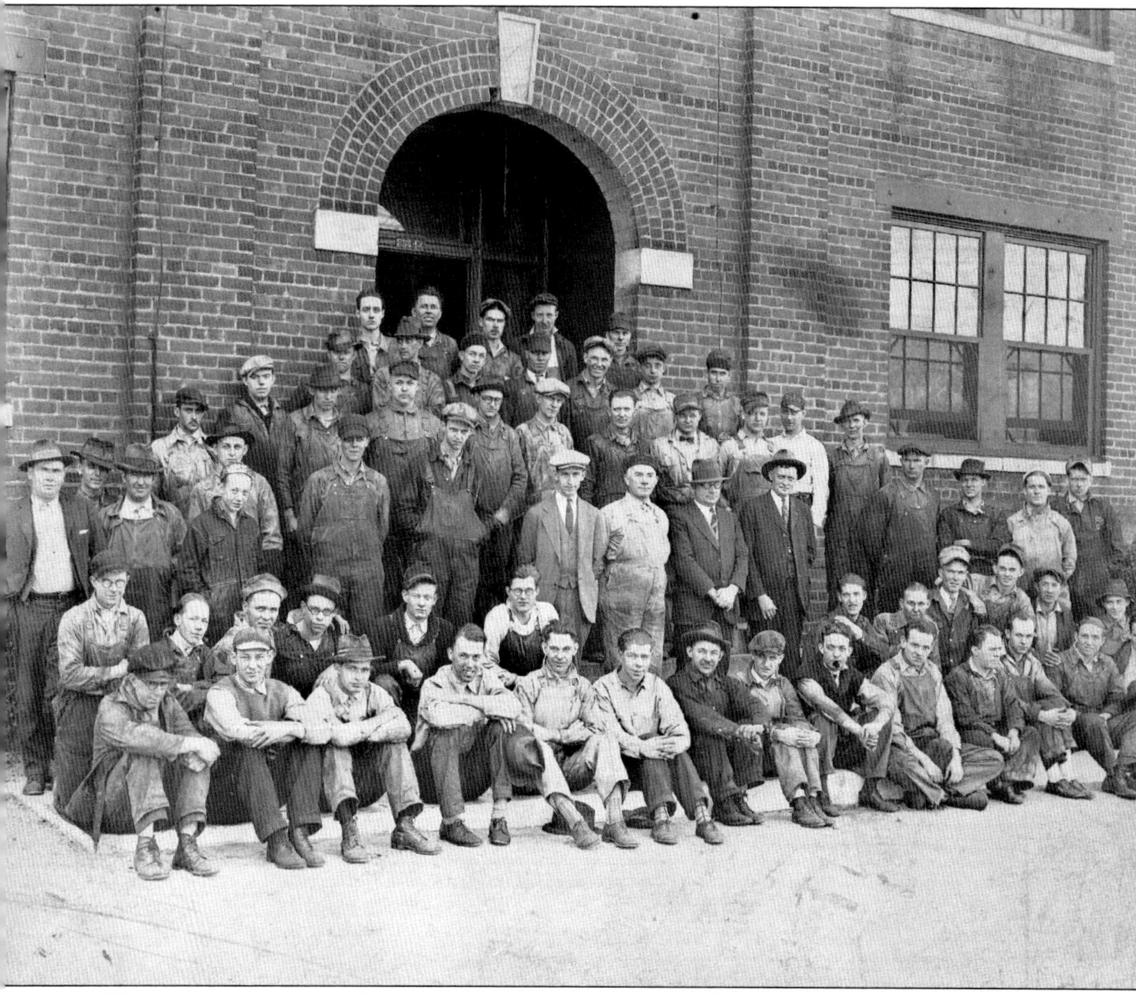

Here are apprentices at Spencer Shops in January 1927. Those pictured are, from left to right, (first row) Bill Kester, W.B. Harrison, Walter Hall Jr., Kermit Klapp, T.J. Johnson, B.B. Surratt, Mr. Young, R.L. Rusher, Jack Wright, Tom McAllon, Thomas Calhoun, W.M. Brown, Robert Bickett, and T. Otis Feamster; (second row) Robert Clark, Leo Trexler, Floyd Miller, Oars R. Wagner, Hugo Talbert, John Henry Miller, Clyde Wilson, Ervin Tutterow, Howard Harrison, Kenneth Barber, Walter Hinson, and J.B. Yarborough Jr; (third row) Jeff Winter, Mr. Patton, Red Reynolds, Ralph Huff, Luther Pace, J.W. Style, Bill Shuping, Carl Lentz, J.L. Cantwell (master mechanic), M.B. Sapp, Paul Misenheimer, Gerald Hawkins, and John Connell; (fourth row) R. Lock Julian, Harry Eller, Mr. Goodman, Joel Sheen, J.C. Beck, Glean Pickler, Tracy Thompson, Delmar Wiggis, Dave L. Shuler, and Mr. Freeman; (fifth row) J.B. Jordan, Houston C. Shoaf, Buddy Garvin, Ervin Steel, Lamont Smith, Roy Loman, Mr. Reed, Charlie Beckman, and Claude O. Sebastian; (sixth row) W.C. Bill Feamster, C.L. Hardister, Bill Pickler, Charles Franklin Connor, and Doc Snider. (North Carolina State Archives.)

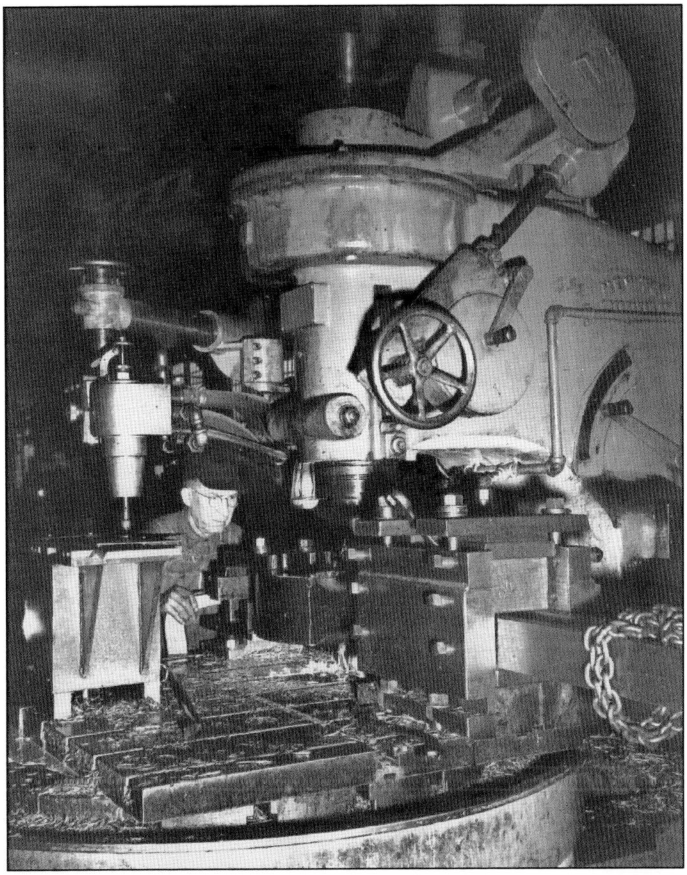

J.C. Moore operates a Newton vertical milling machine with a Turchan follower attachment in this view from 1947. (Photograph by the Southern Railway; collection of North Carolina State Archives.)

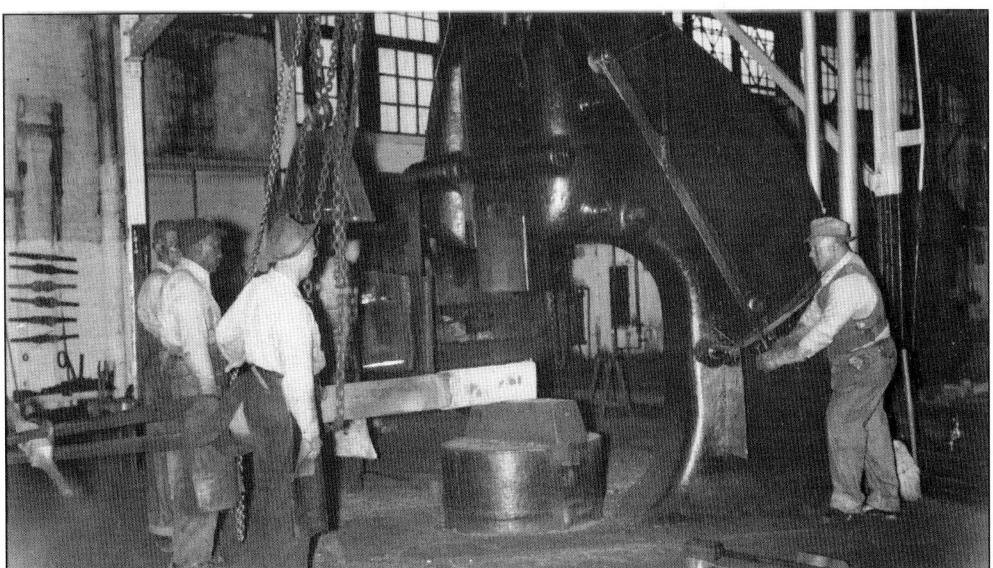

In another scene from the 1940s, men in the blacksmith shop are forging a new steam locomotive drive rod using a large steam-powered hammer to shape the metal. (Photograph by the Southern Railway; collection of North Carolina State Archives.)

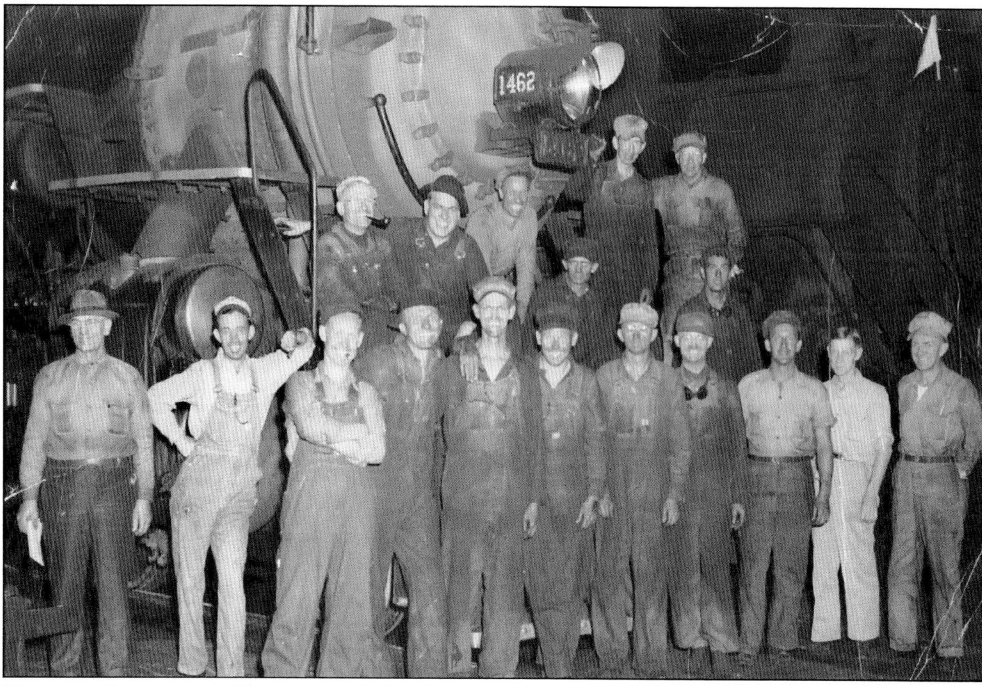

The roundhouse stayed busy around the clock, performing regular maintenance and light repair work. This view from 1944 shows some of the night shift workers posed at locomotive 1462, a Ts-class 4-8-2 locomotive used for passenger service between Salisbury and Asheville. (North Carolina Division of Archives and History.)

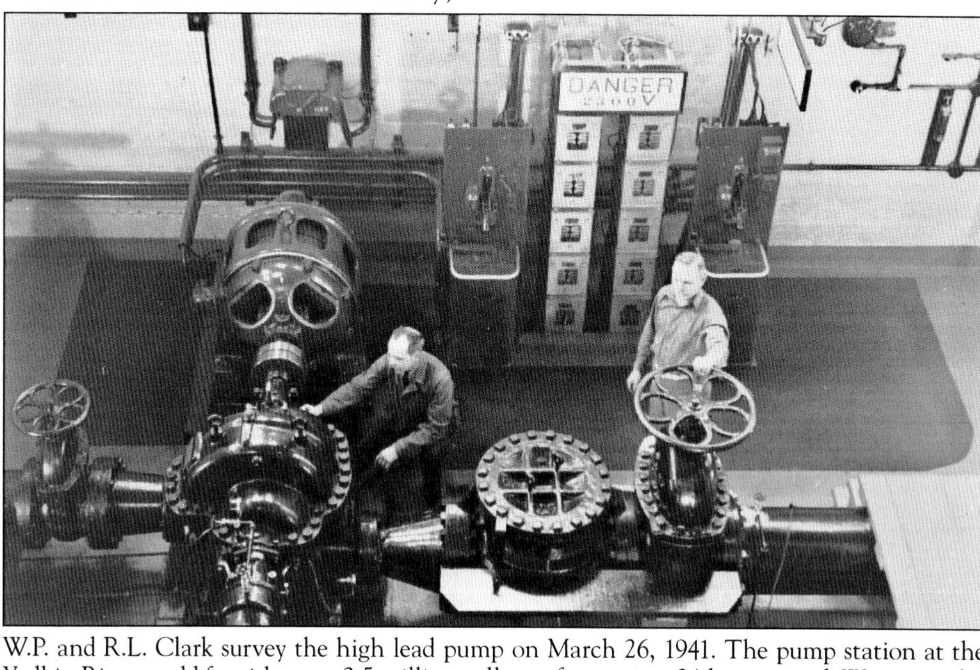

W.P. and R.L. Clark survey the high lead pump on March 26, 1941. The pump station at the Yadkin River could furnish up to 2.5 million gallons of water in a 24-hour period. Water was fed from the river into a 2.5-million-gallon concrete sedimentation basin through an 18-inch pipe and 1,800-gallon-per-minute centrifugal pumps. (North Carolina State Archives.)

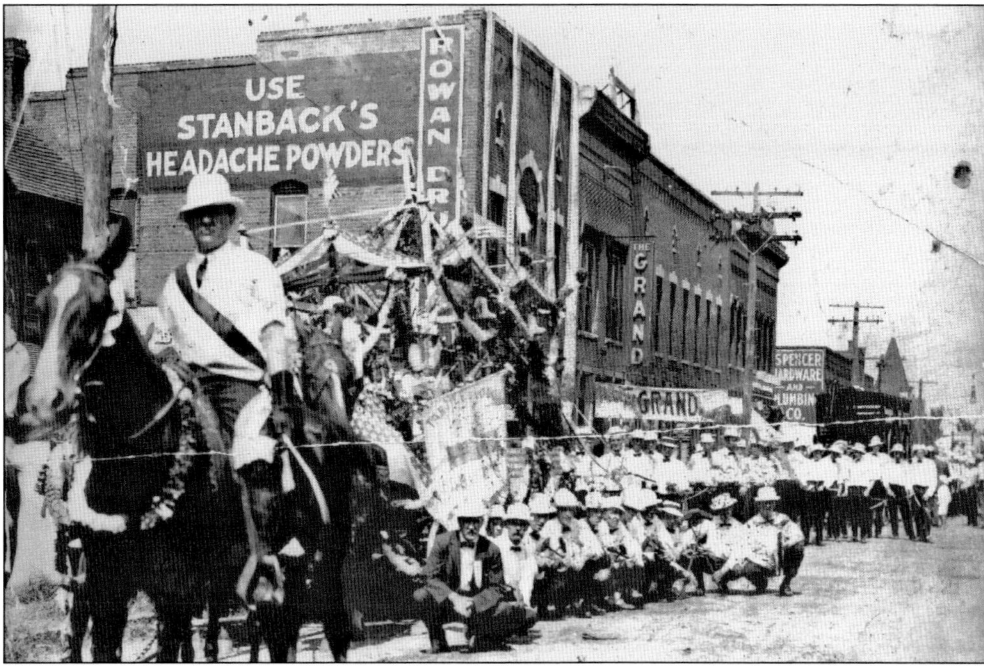

Spencer Shops employees took the Labor Day holiday seriously by organizing parade floats created from the different crafts. The image above shows a parade on Fifth Street, posing in front of Rowan Drug Company. Thomas M. Stanback compounded Stanback Headache Powder (advertised on the building) in Rowan Drug Company in 1911. The photograph below shows a winning float entry by the blacksmiths during the 1920s. (Both, North Carolina Division of Archives and History.)

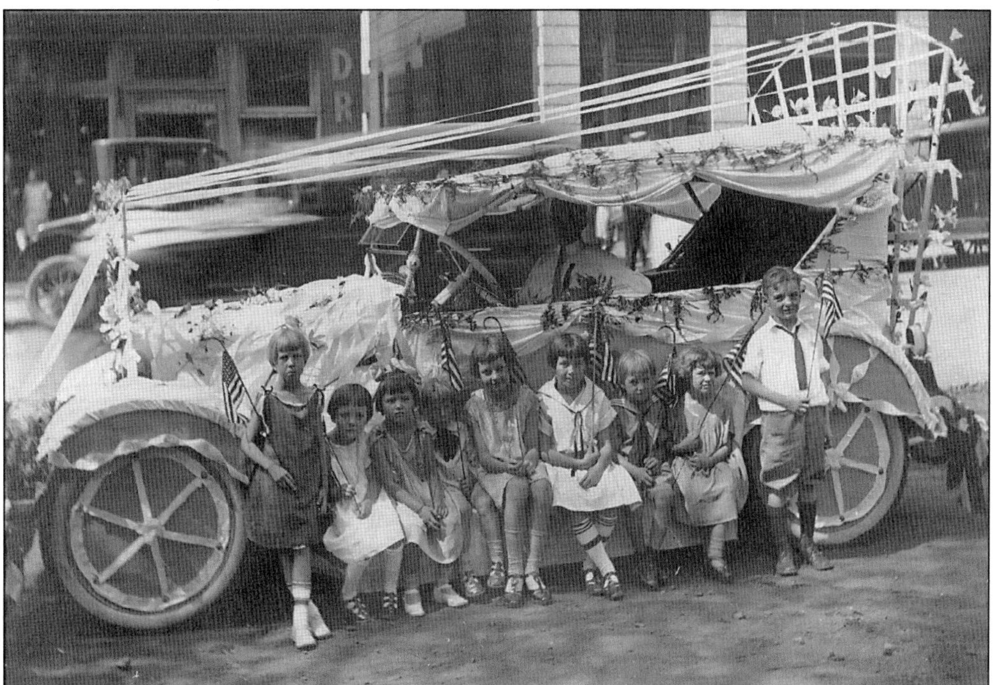

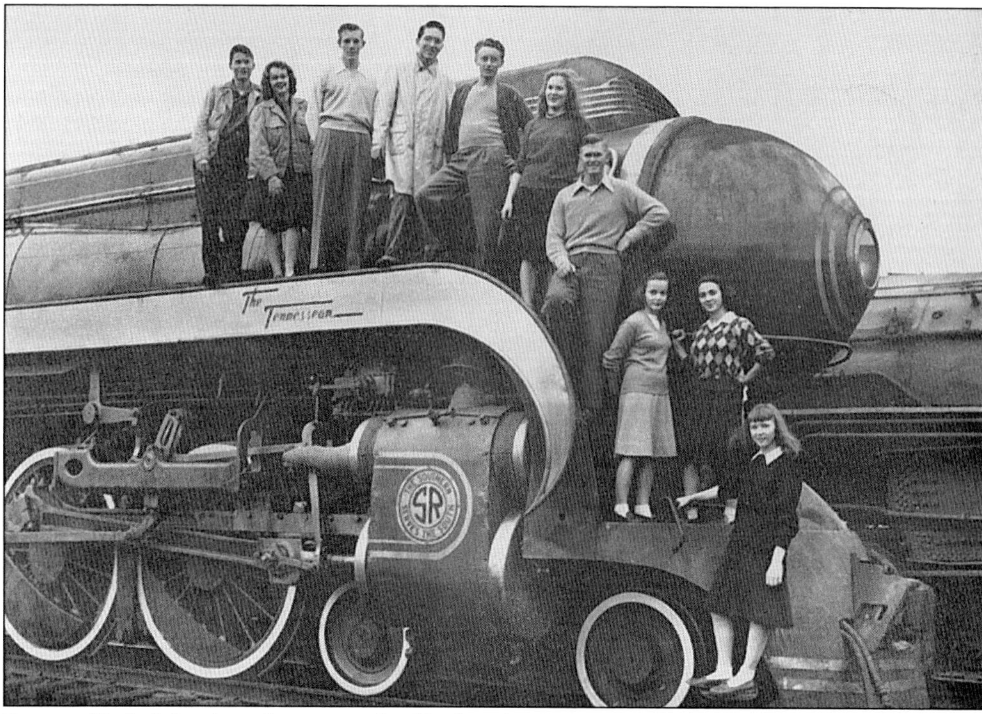

Spencer High School was known as the "Railroaders," so it was appropriate for the yearbook staff to pose with equipment from Spencer Shops. The view above shows the staff with locomotive 1380, still lettered for the *Tennessean* in 1948, while the view below has the staff hanging from a Southern wooden caboose in 1949. (Both, North Carolina State Archives.)

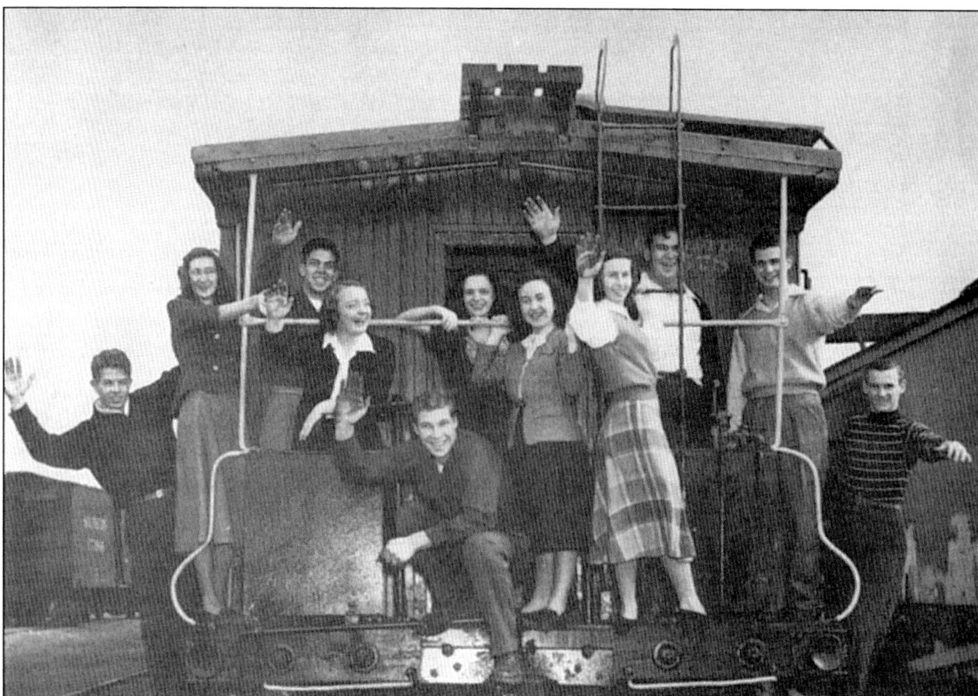

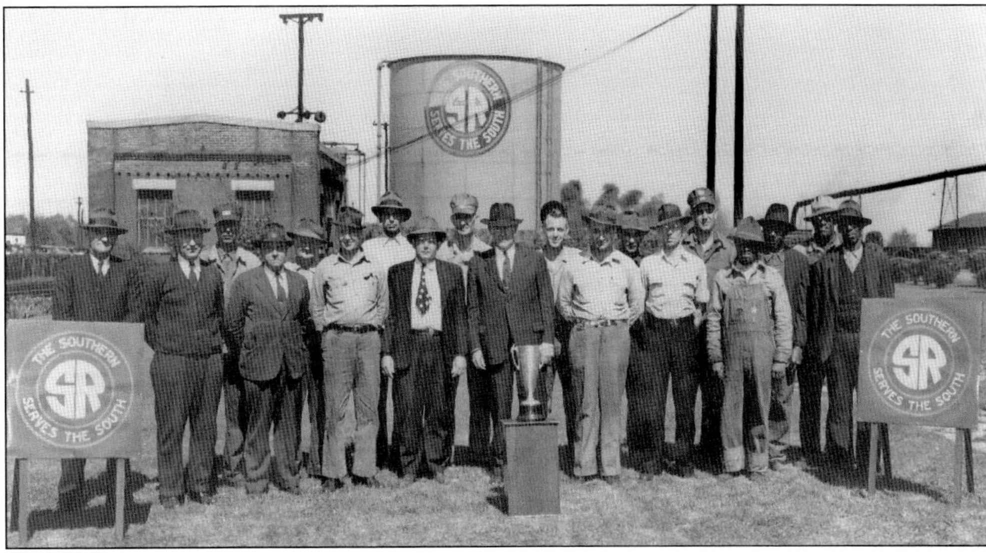

Spencer Shops received several awards through the years for safety, workmanship, and other competitions between different Southern Railway shops. The Storage Department Safety Committee posed for a group photograph in 1957 after receiving a safety award. (North Carolina Division of Archives and History.)

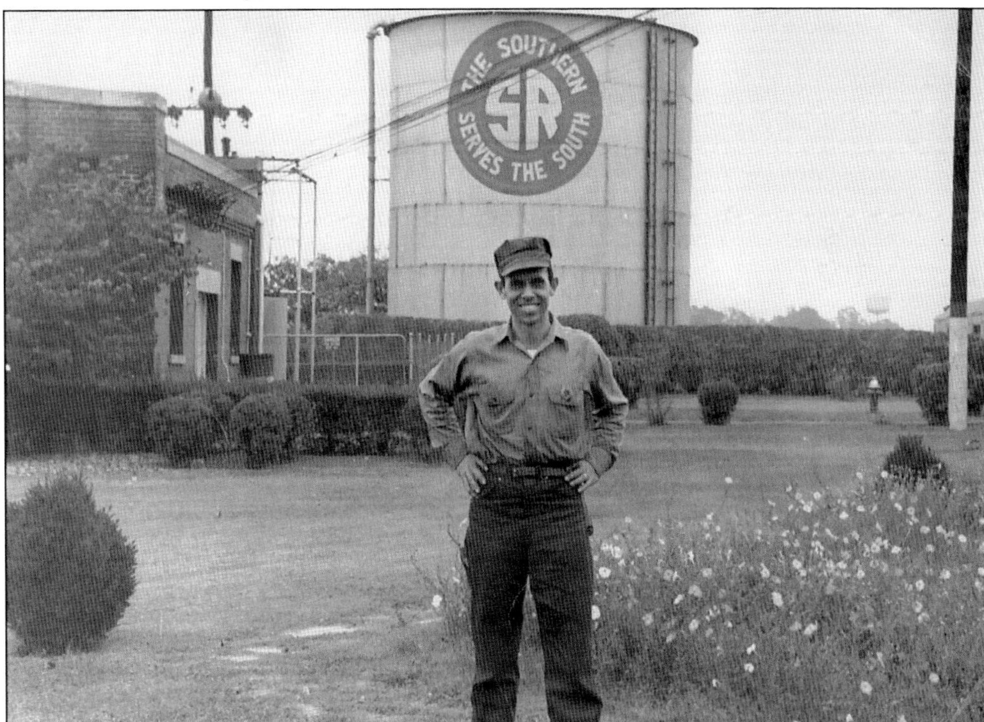

Individuals were also awarded for their ideas in promoting safety or improving work performance. Boilermaker W.J. Rimer won the Safety Slogan of the Month for October 1953. Unfortunately, the winning slogan was not recorded in the records. (North Carolina Division of Archives and History.)

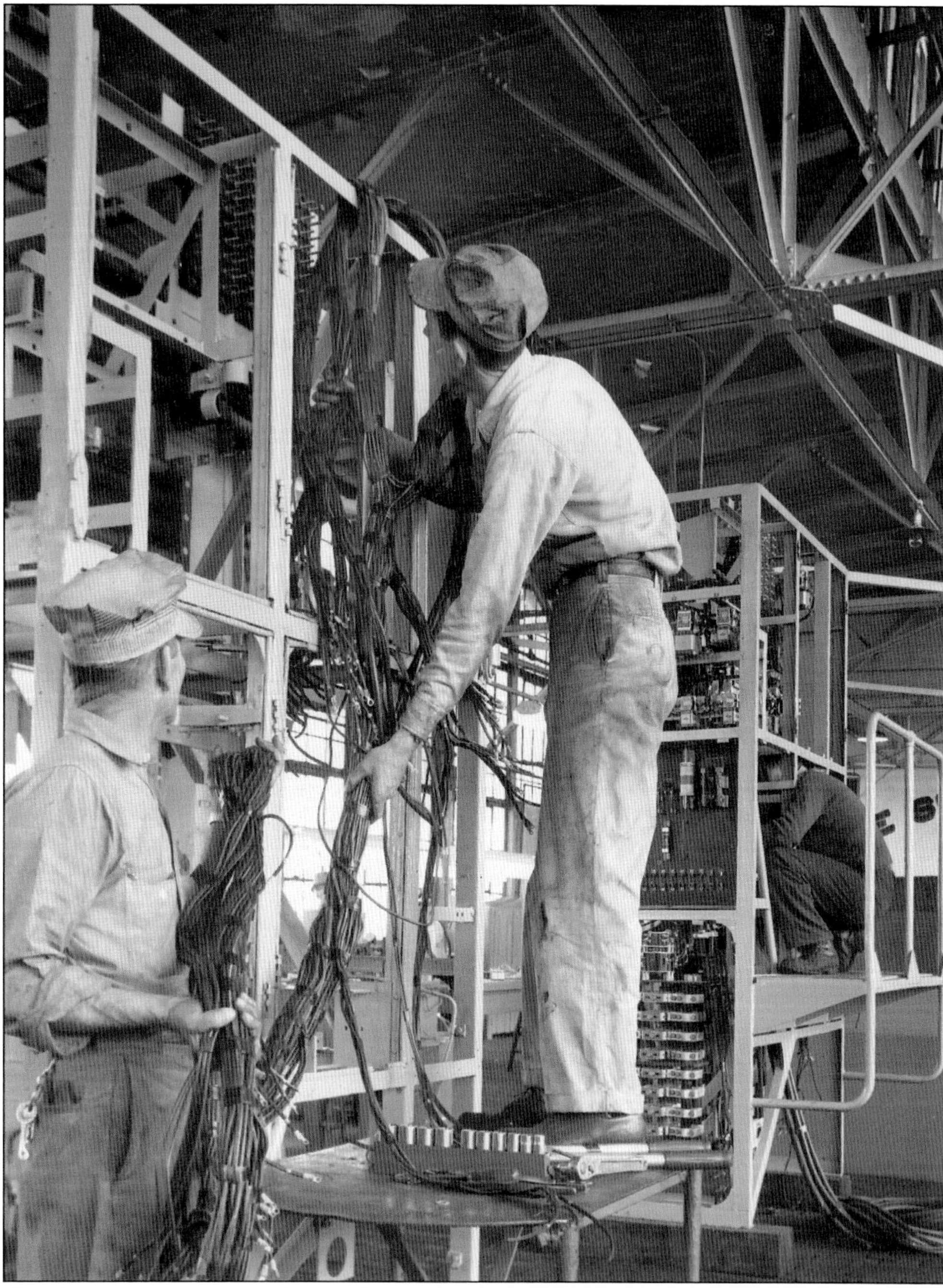

The electricians at Spencer Shops took over the old flue shop building during the conversion from steam to diesel in the early 1950s. This 1952 view shows electricians John Peeler (standing on platform) and W.W. Ott running cables for new electrical equipment. (North Carolina Division of Archives and History.)

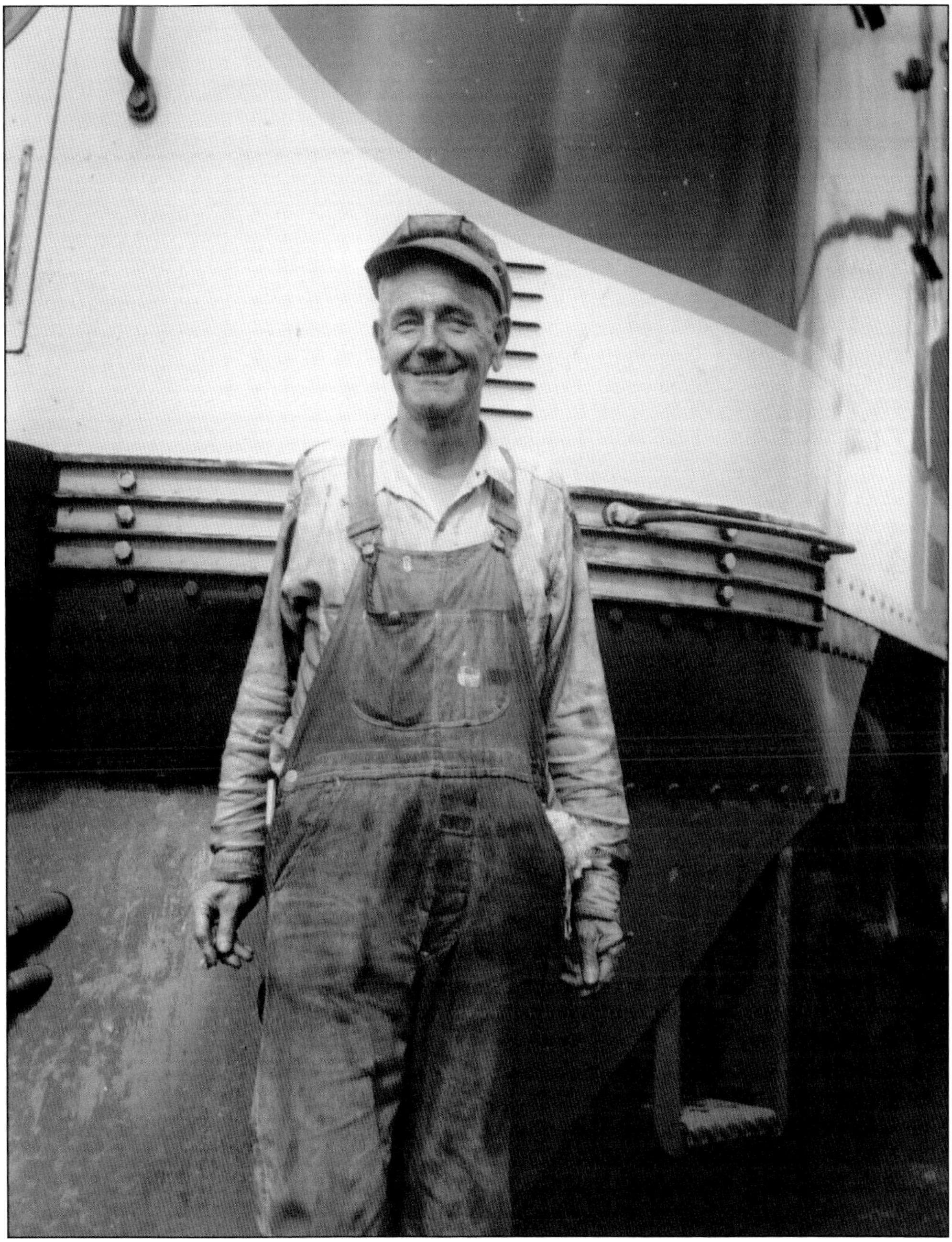

Robert L. "Bob" Julian was one of the first Spencer Shops employees, starting his career with the Southern Railway in 1897 as a pipefitter. He was promoted to machinist in 1901, night roundhouse foreman in 1904, and general roundhouse foreman in 1911. From 1931 to 1936, he again served as a machinist and, in his final years at Spencer, he was the chief locomotive inspector. He retired on July 30, 1949, with 52 years of service. When the roundhouse was completed in 1924, it was named the Bob Julian Roundhouse by Fairfax Harrison, president of the Southern Railway. A special plaque was later affixed to the building with the inscription "Bob Julian 1924." (Photograph by David Driscoll; collection of North Carolina Division of Archives and History.)

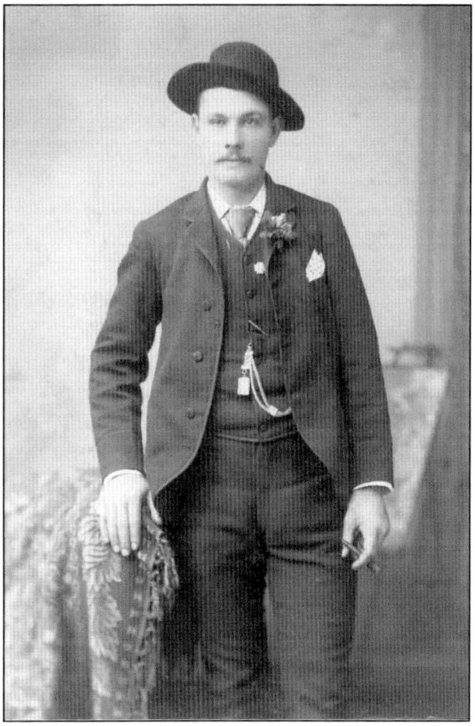

John Wingate was an engineer assigned to the Southern Railway's Danville Division, operating between Salisbury and Monroe, Virginia. He was first employed as a fireman on November 1, 1884, and was promoted to engineer on July 2, 1885. He was killed in a train wreck in 1914 on locomotive 1207 while pulling train 29 through Sadler, North Carolina. (North Carolina Division of Archives and History.)

This iconic railroad view from July 1936 shows engineer H.M. Busha and conductor Frank Marshall comparing the time on their watches before they leave the station. These gentlemen were assigned to the Charlotte Division, which operated from Greenville, South Carolina, to Salisbury. (North Carolina Division of Archives and History.)

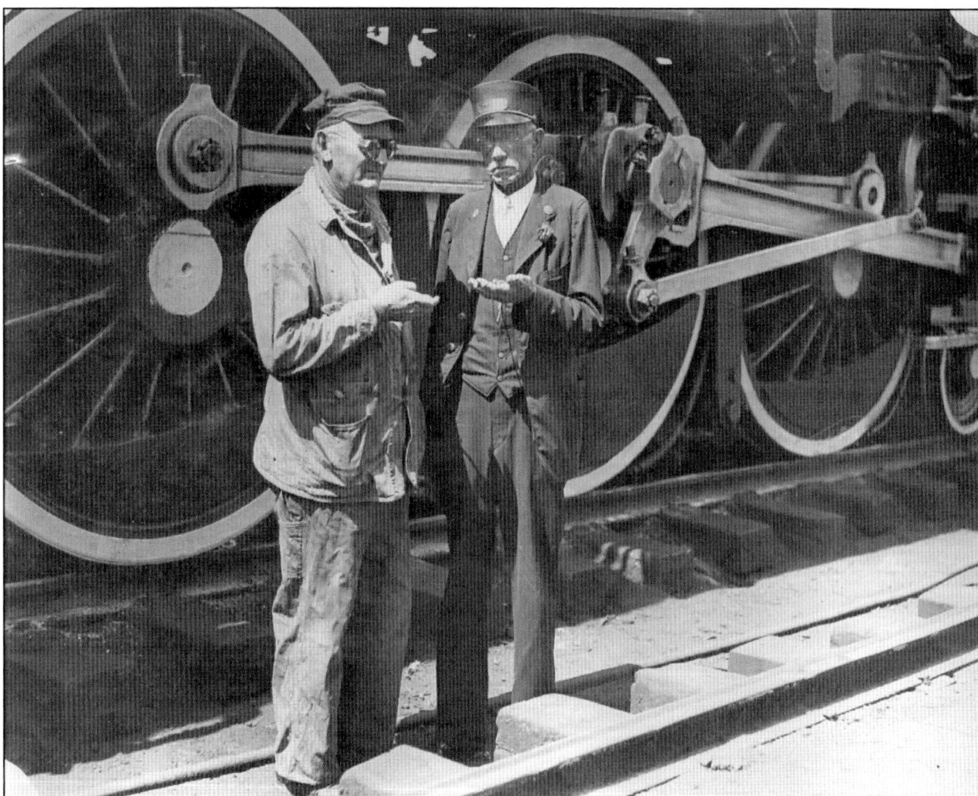

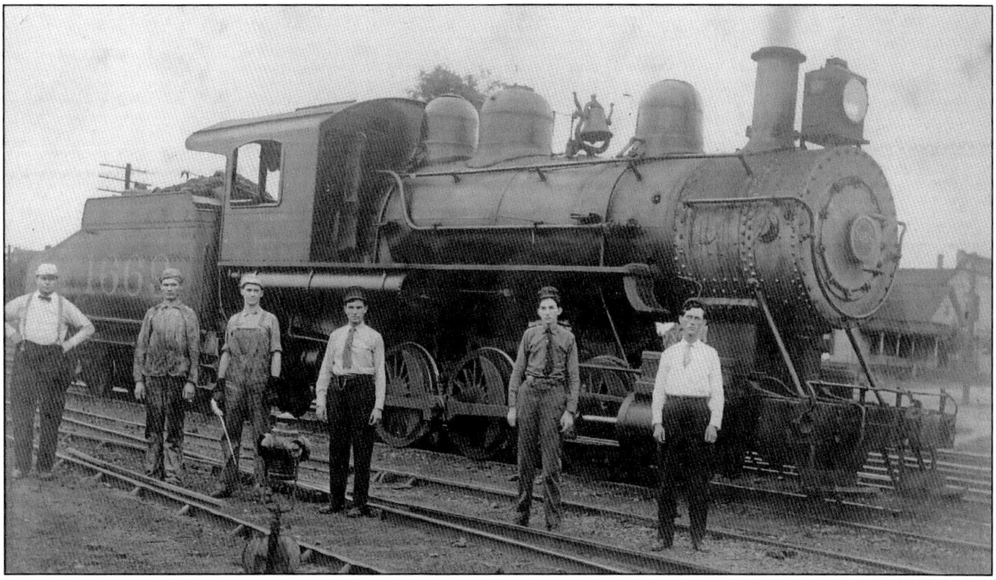

Local photographers loved to take pictures of locomotive crews at Spencer. This switch crew, photographed in the 1910s, was assigned to the main freight classification yard, sometimes called the north yard. Crewmembers are, from left to right, George Perkenson, yardmaster; A.B. Duke, engineer; Jay Ray Freeman, fireman; Robert Waller, conductor; Luther G. Hines, brakeman; and Oscar Mahaley, brakeman. It is interesting to see the photographer's bowler hat posed on the switch stand. (North Carolina Division of Archives and History.)

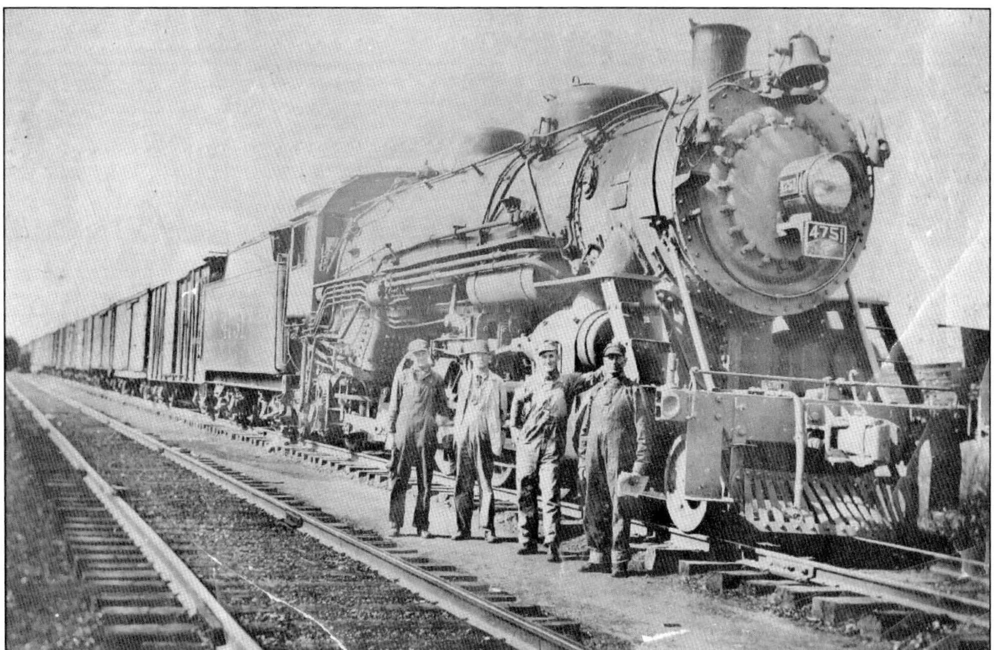

Another locomotive crew poses for a photograph made while waiting to leave the yard with a long freight train. Photographed are, from left to right, Joe Brittain, Ben Waddell, unidentified, and Henry Carr. Built in 1918, locomotive 4751 was based on US Railroad Administration plans for a light Mikado. (North Carolina Division of Archives and History.)

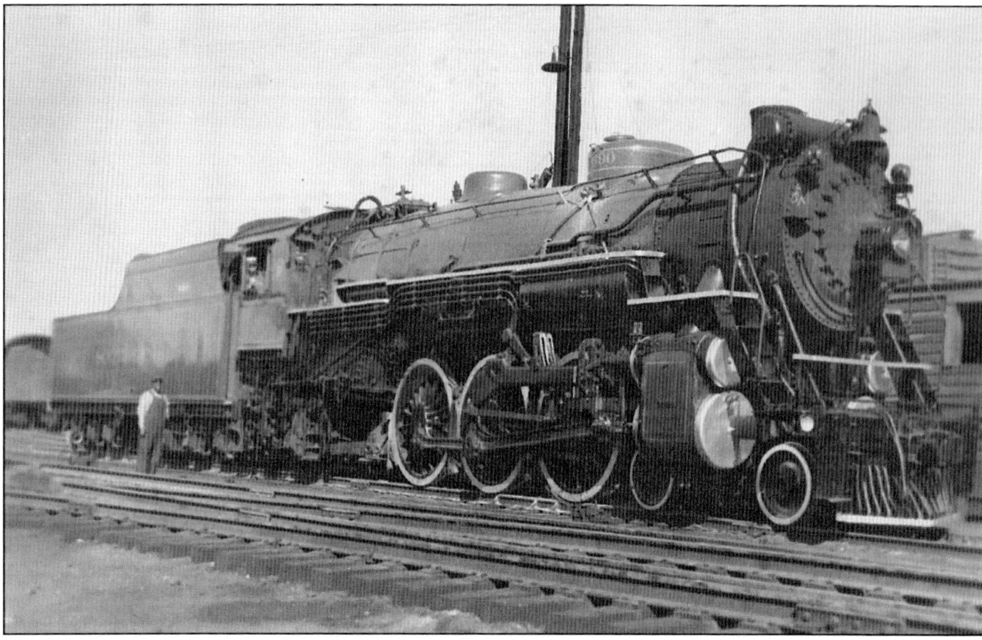

A hostler crew was responsible for moving a locomotive around the shop property or delivering at the Salisbury depot for a locomotive change. In this view from April 17, 1952, engineer George Willis Albright and helper Tom Barber prepare to move No. 6690, a passenger locomotive assigned to the Southern Railway subsidiary Alabama Great Southern. (Patsy McBride's collection.)

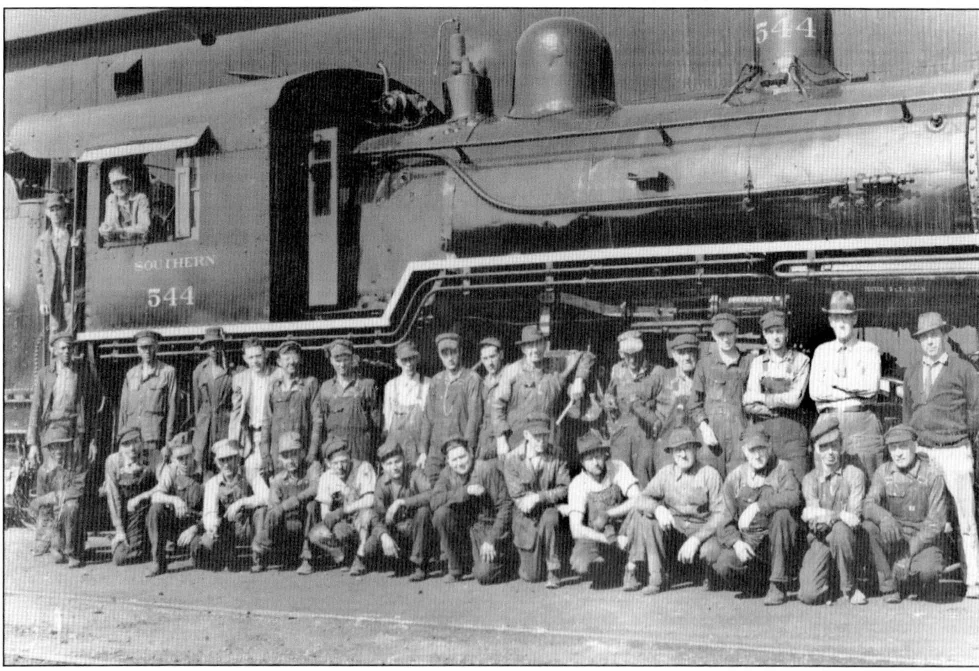

Spencer workers are posing with 544, a 2-8-0 consolidation type locomotive. The Southern Railway used small locomotives like this one to pull freight trains on branch lines and local switching runs. The 544 was built by Baldwin Locomotive Works in 1903 and retired at Spencer Shops in July 1953. (North Carolina Division of Archives and History.)

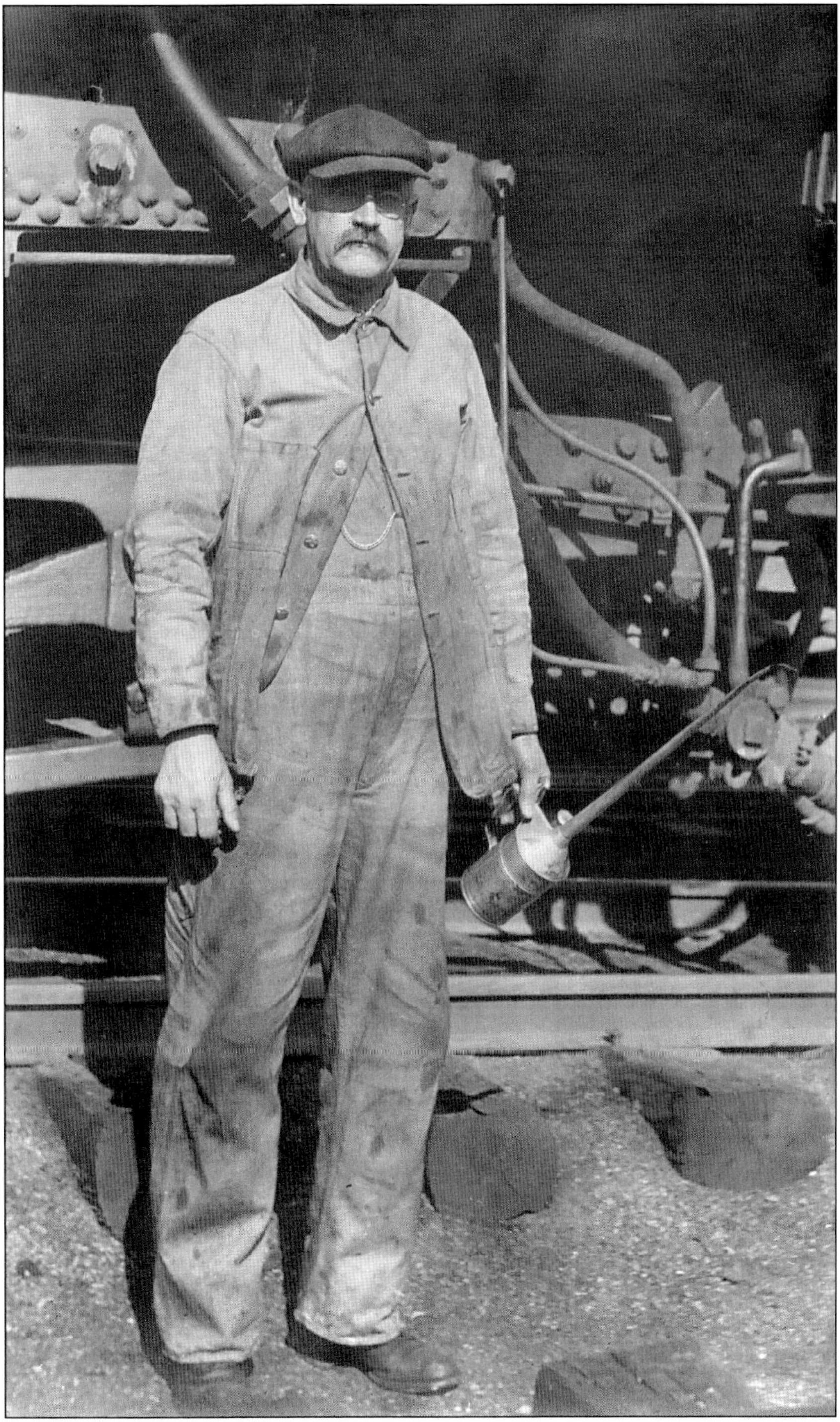

William Alexander Kizziah was either a fireman or engineer for the Southern Railway and retired some time during the 1920s, based on the Danville Division records. He was the father of Eric Fay Kizziah and grandfather of William Emmett "Bill" Andrews, Nancy Andrews Ellis, and Robert Edward Andrews. (North Carolina Division of Archives and History.)

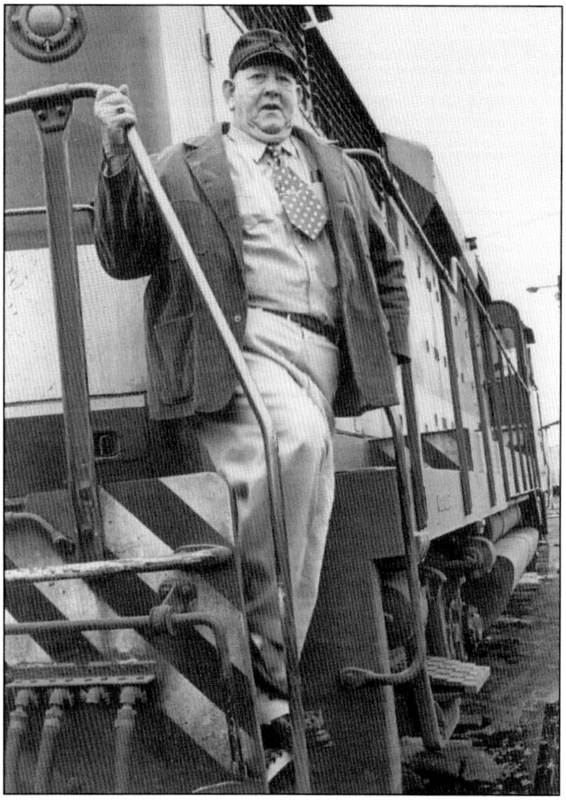

Steele D. "Big John" Myers retired from the Southern Railway as a yard engineer on January 7, 1969, after a 51-year railroad career beginning on March 28, 1918. He started as a steam fireman working on the Danville Division from Salisbury to Monroe, Virginia. He was promoted to yard engineer on May 23, 1941, a position he kept until retirement. He is photographed running GP-30 No. 2540. (Photographs by *Salisbury Post*; both, June Pryor's collection.)

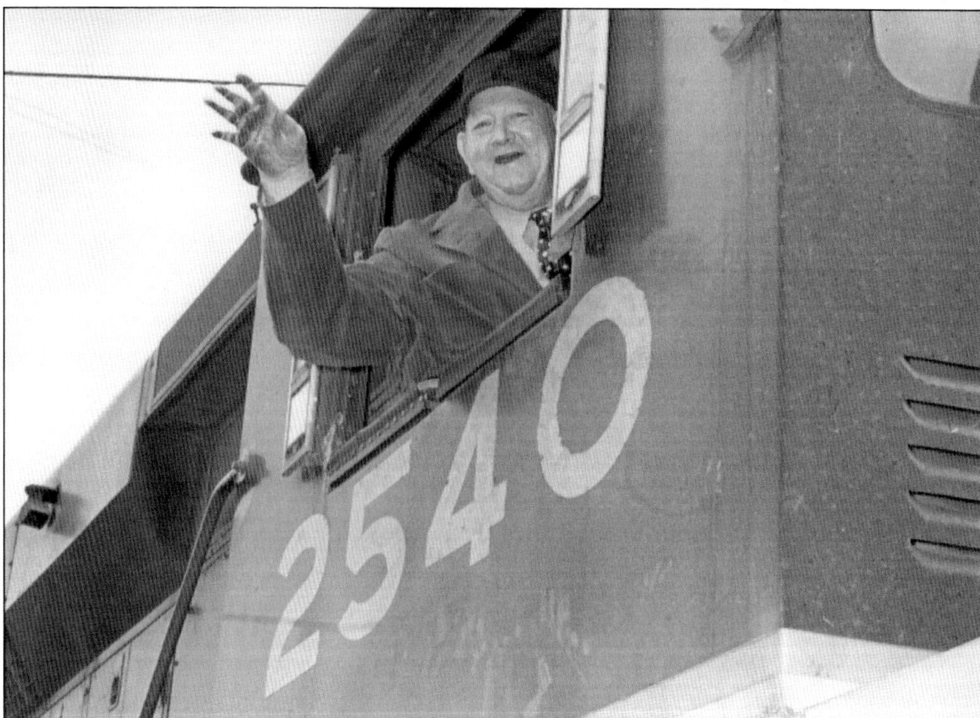

Five

The Final Years 1960–1979

The Southern Railway developed Spencer Shops into the main locomotive repair facility for diesels on the eastern lines through Virginia, North Carolina, South Carolina, and Georgia during the late 1940s and early 1950s. The railroad recognized Spencer employees through articles in *Ties* magazine and other railroad publications. The town of Spencer continued as a prosperous, viable community.

Everything changed in the mid-1950s, signaling the termination of Spencer Shops. The Southern Railway began to transfer or eliminate positions at Spencer and closed all buildings except the roundhouse and car repair shed by 1960. The company moved all remaining work to updated shops in Atlanta and Chattanooga. Reasons for the move included outdated steam-era buildings, an alleged dispute between the railroad and the State of North Carolina over oil and waste runoff into the Yadkin River, and the fact that D.W. Brosnan, the vice president of operations, wanted Spencer closed. The railroad started a process of razing unused buildings on the site by 1965, including the blacksmith shop, boiler shop (sold to Marion Machine Company), and woodworking shop, though the back shop was spared.

The railroad kept the roundhouse and nearby buildings to perform light repair and refueling on freight diesel locomotives still operating freight trains from Spencer Yard. By 1960, less than 100 worked at Spencer, with only a skeleton crew in the roundhouse by the 1970s.

The Southern replaced Spencer Shops by constructing a modern hump yard that opened in 1979 a few miles north in the community of Linwood. A hump yard uses gravity to sort cars into new freight trains, controlled by computers in the yard tower. The new facility included buildings for diesel and freight car repair and maintenance. All railroad operation at Spencer Shops ceased that year and moved into the new facility, known today as Linwood Terminal.

The Southern gave the remaining Spencer Shops buildings and land to the State of North Carolina in 1977 and 1979 to establish a state transportation museum. The first donation included the back shop, master mechanic's office, warehouse No. 3, and the flue shop, with the remainder two years later.

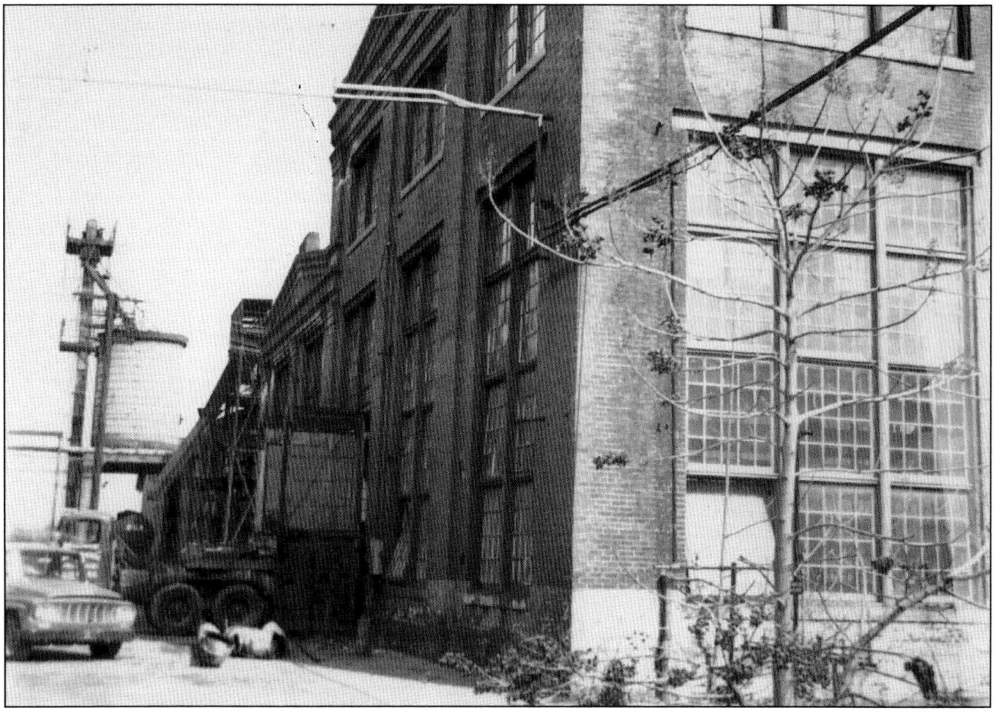

Spencer Shops changed drastically after the back shop closed in 1960. Once the employees were relocated to other Southern Railway shops, the buildings were left vacant and began to deteriorate rapidly. These images of the boiler shop and the blacksmith shop (on the next page), made on March 9, 1965, may have been the final ones before they were demolished. (Both, North Carolina State Archives.)

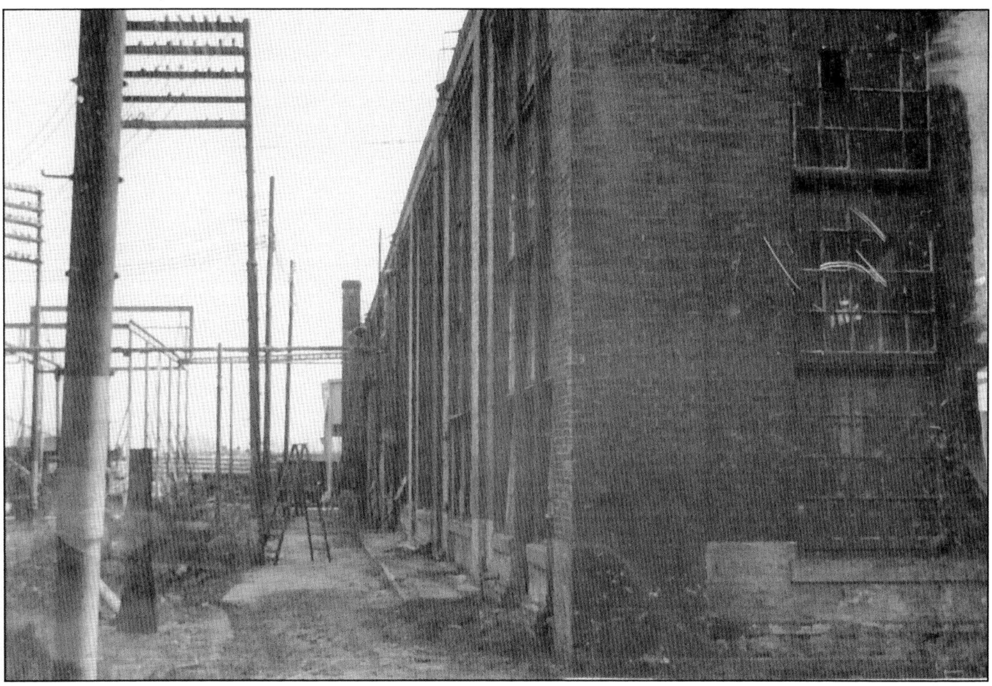

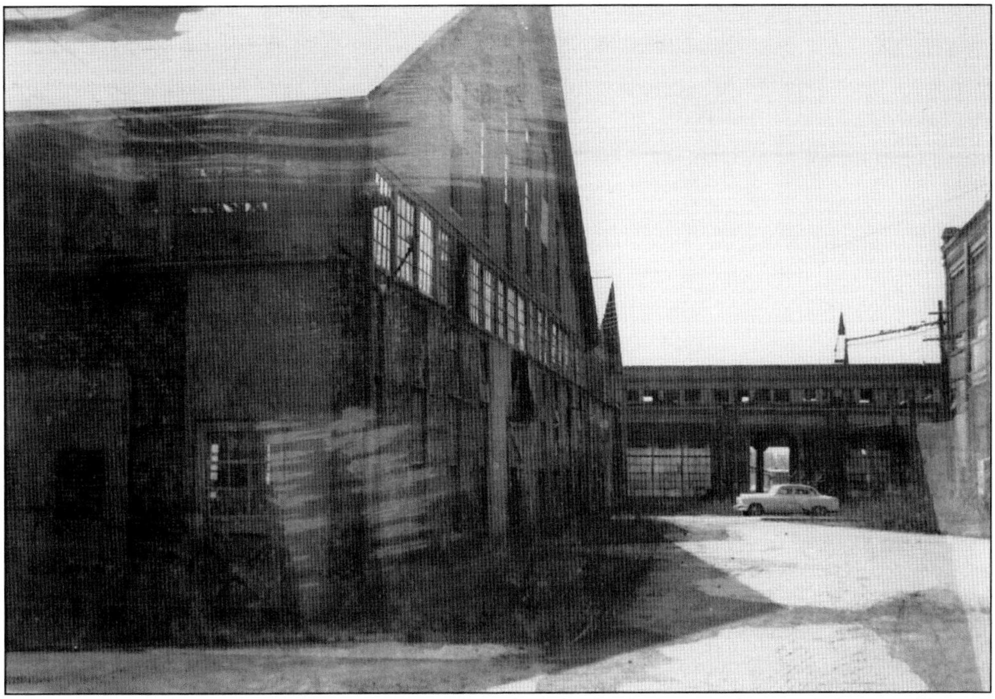

The blacksmith shop, above, shows the south end of the back shop and part of the roundhouse. The image below shows the building's profile looking east toward the rail yard. At the time of these photographs in 1965, the Spencer workforce was centered in the roundhouse and classification yard. (Both, North Carolina State Archives.)

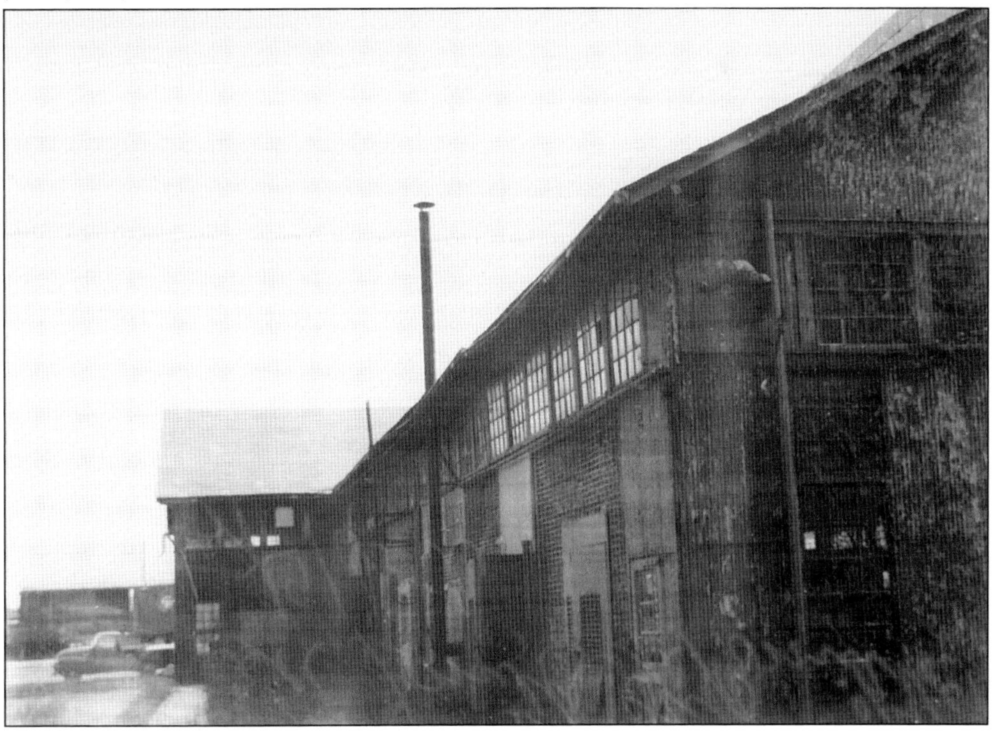

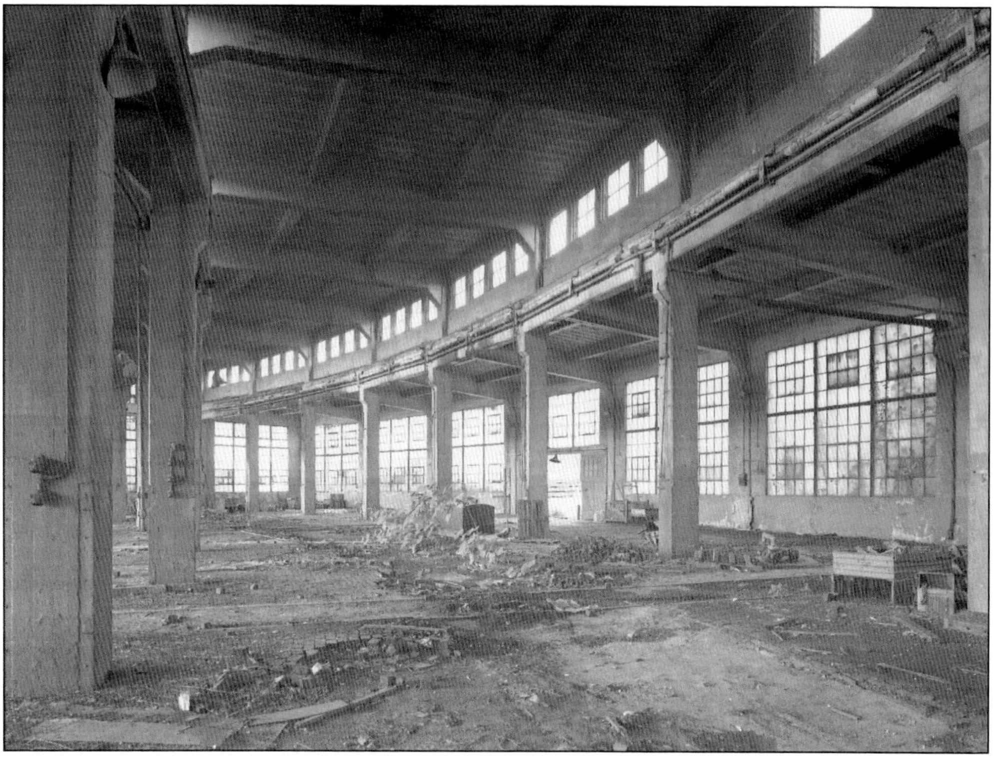

The roundhouse continued to operate through the 1970s, though far from the level of service of the 1930s and 1940s. The only stalls with operating tracks were the four that had metal roll-up doors installed during the late 1960s. Like several other buildings, plant growth and trash were taking over the structure. Workers even parked cars in the first 16 stalls, as well as the space around the turntable. (Both, North Carolina State Archives.)

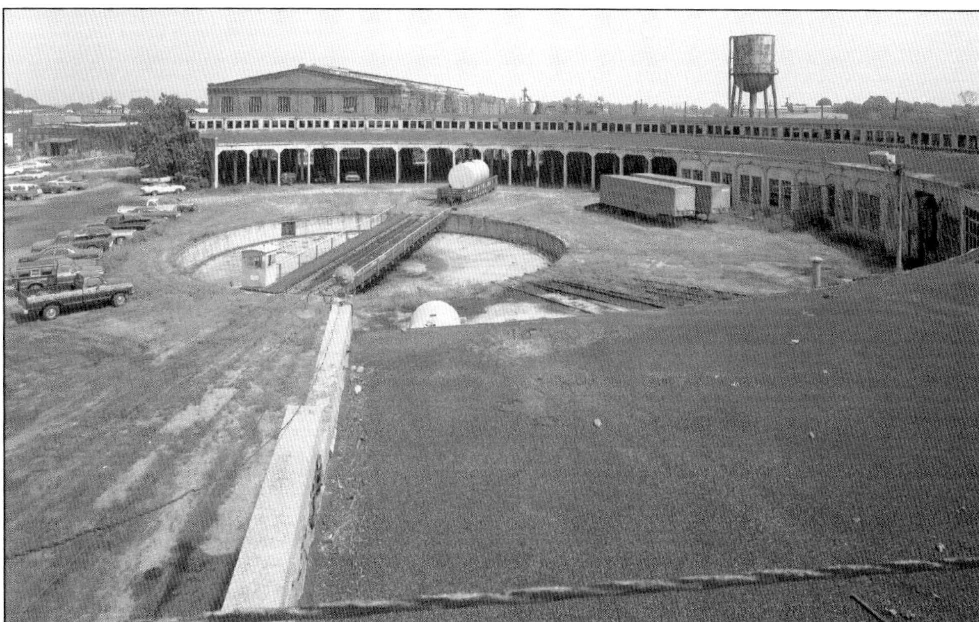

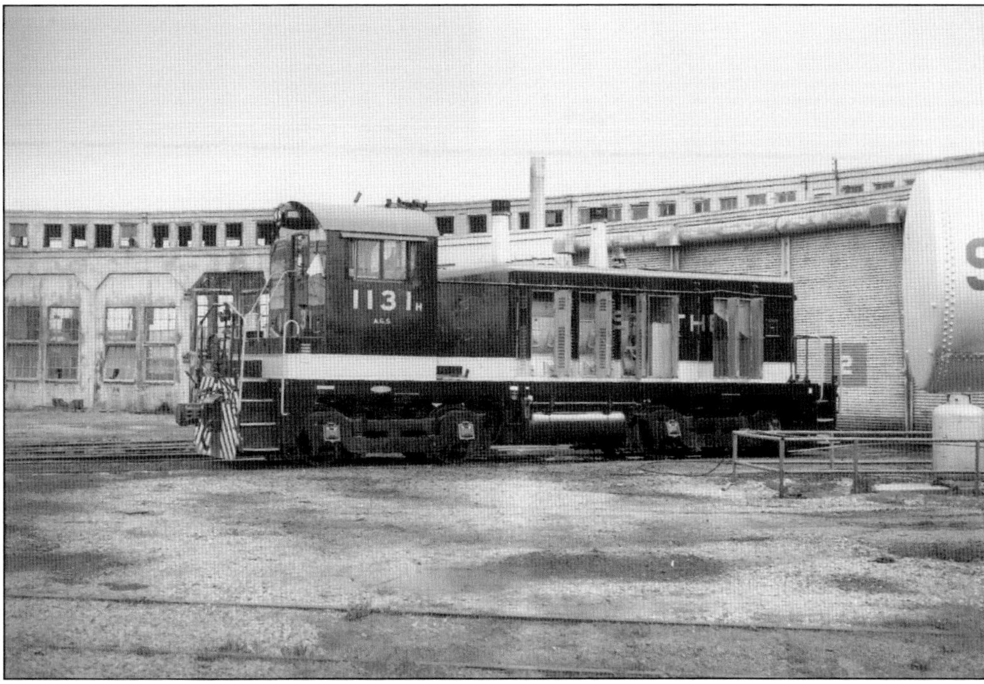

Locomotives at Spencer could receive 92-day inspections, replacement traction motors, or new filters at the roundhouse. Once finished, they would be serviced at the fuel tracks and wait their next call, just as locomotives had done for over 80 years. (Photographs by Marvin Rogers.)

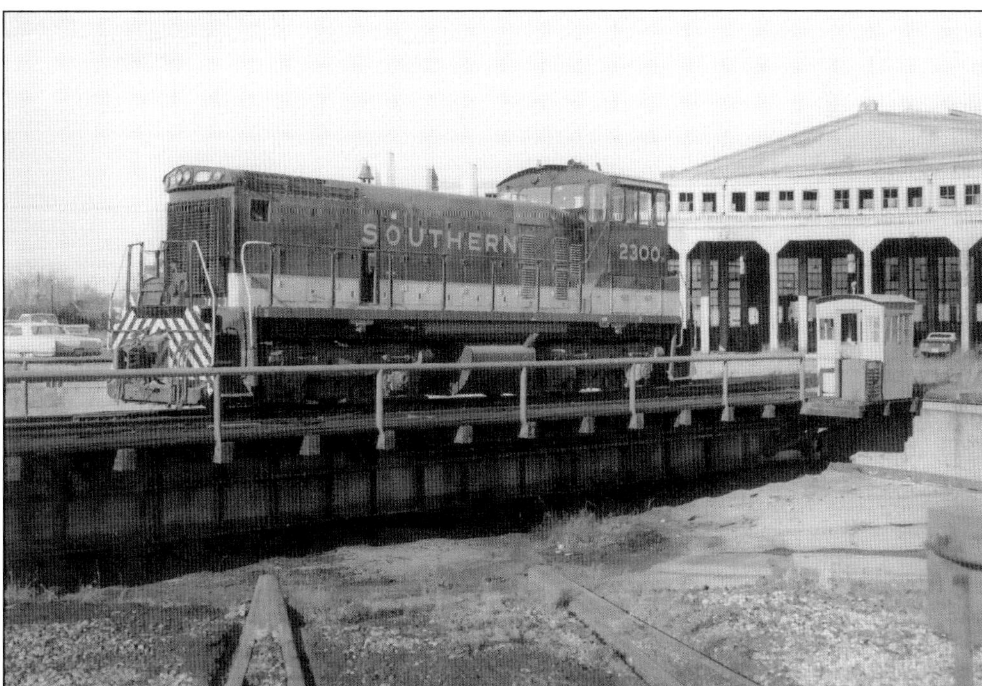

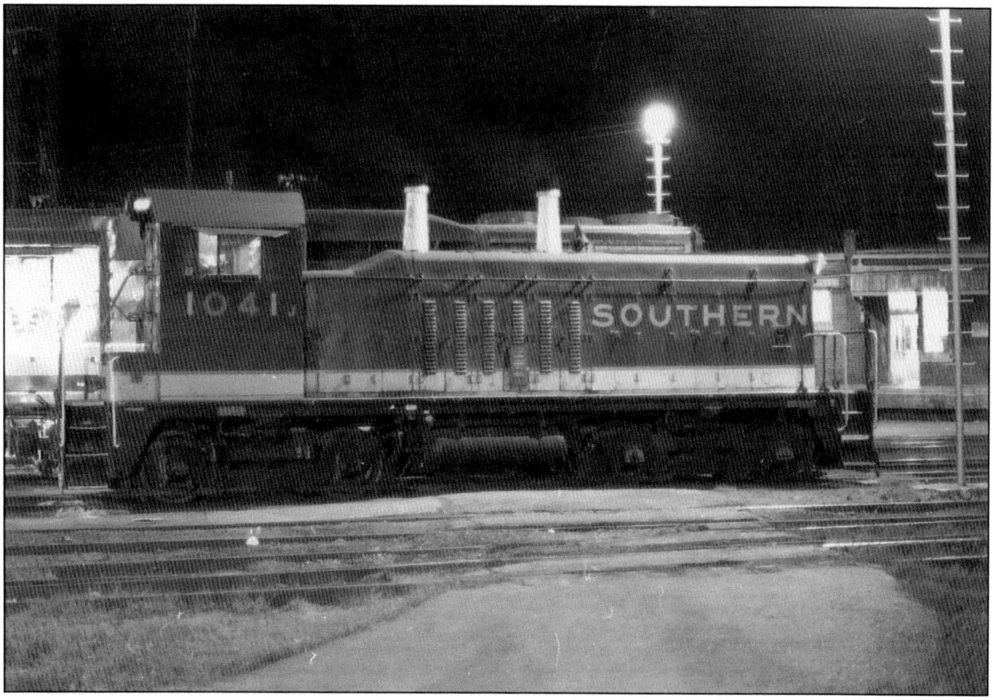

The roundhouse continued to service locomotives day and night as needed. NW-2 No. 1041 (above) and GP-7 No. 8266 (below) had both been in service over 20 years when these photographs were taken in the late 1970s. (Photographs by Marvin Rogers.)

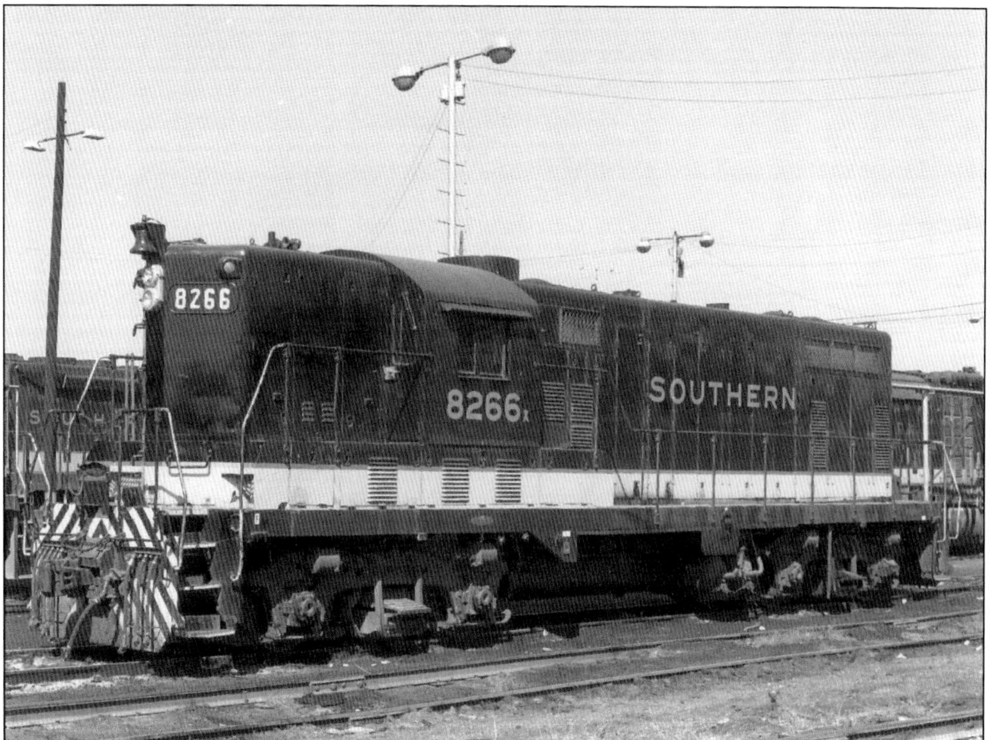

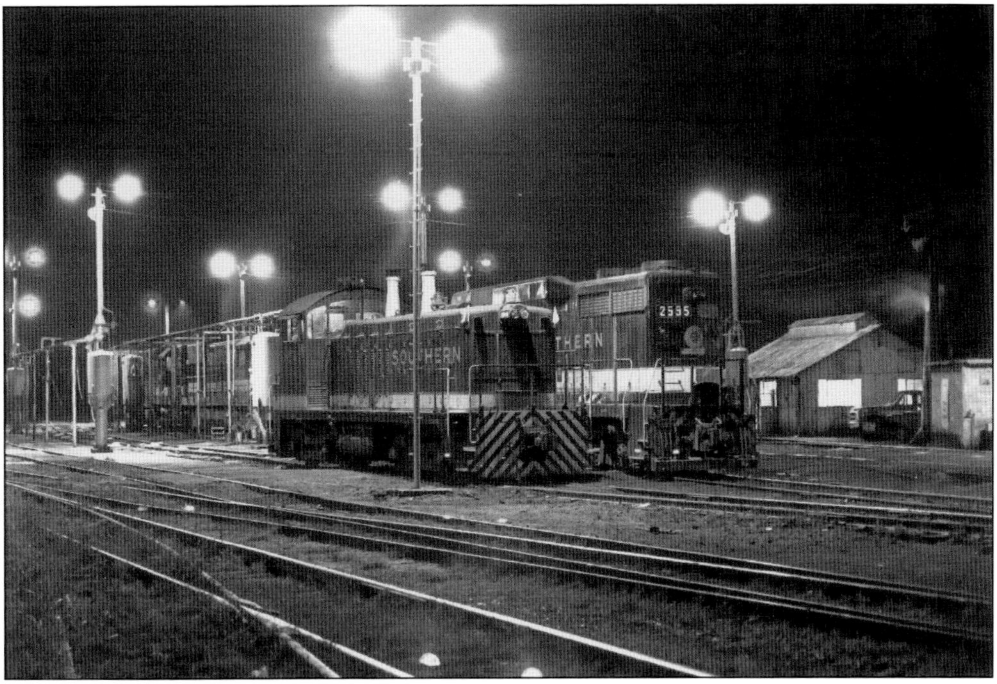

The 1970s were transitional years for the diesel locomotives on the Southern Railway. The fuel tracks at Spencer contained a mix of locomotives built in the 1950s, 1960s, and 1970s. (Photographs by Marvin Rogers.)

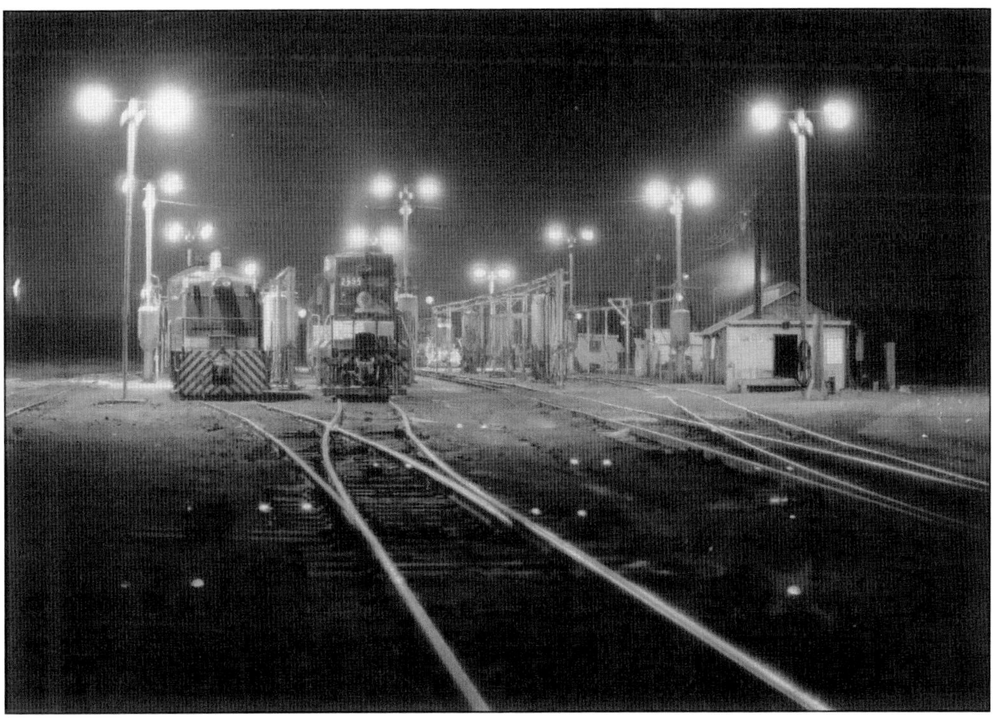

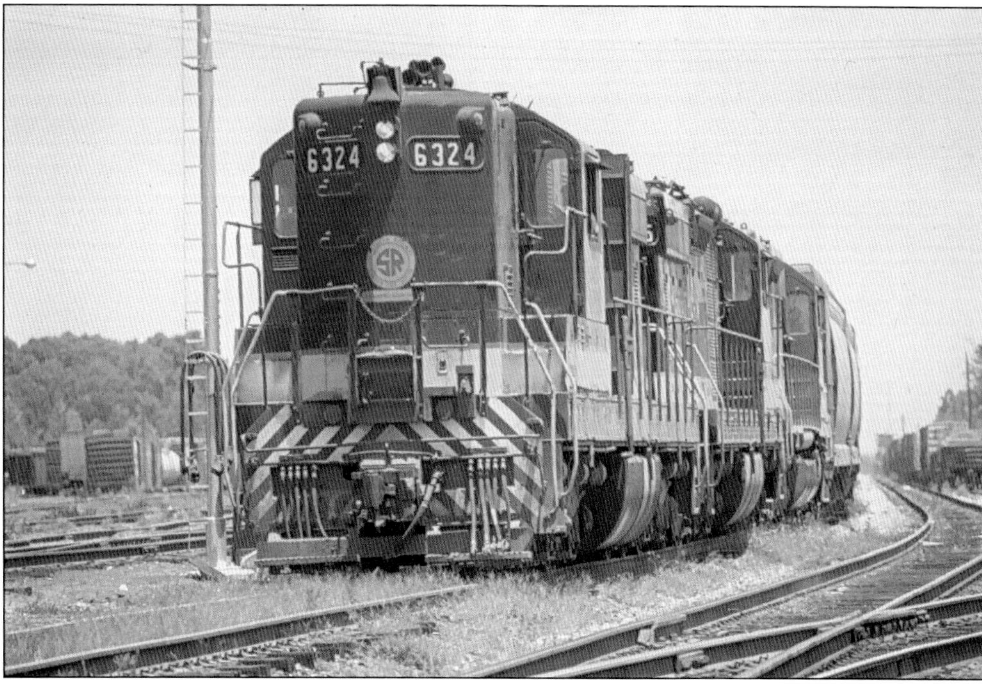

African Americans were allowed to become engineers during the 1970s and operated both passenger and freight trains between Washington, DC, and Atlanta. These photographs show SD-24 locomotives that were built in 1959. They were retired in 1978. (Photographs by Marvin Rogers.)

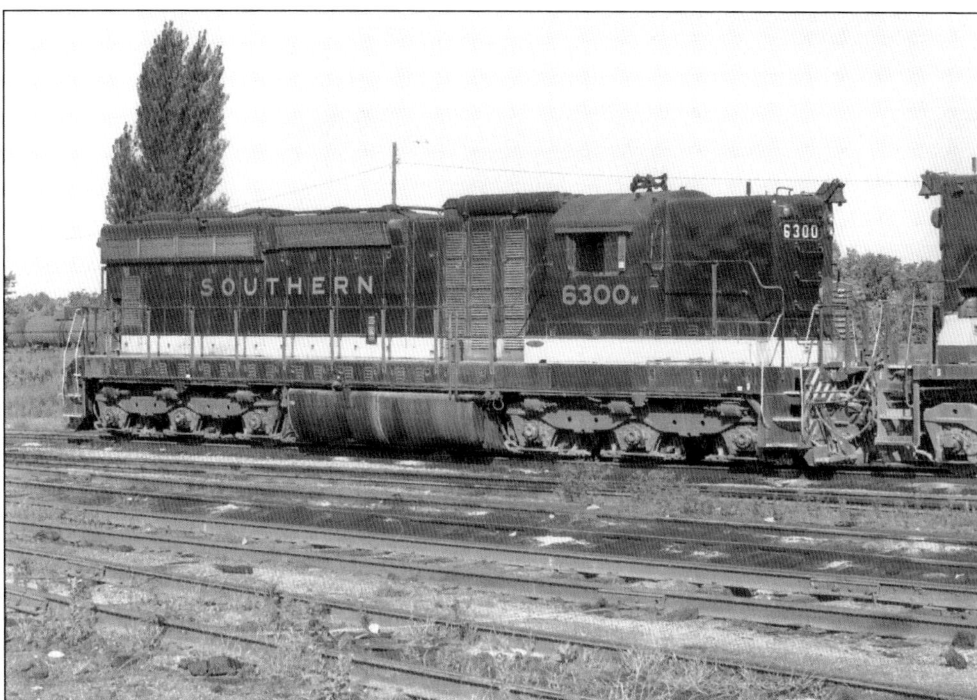

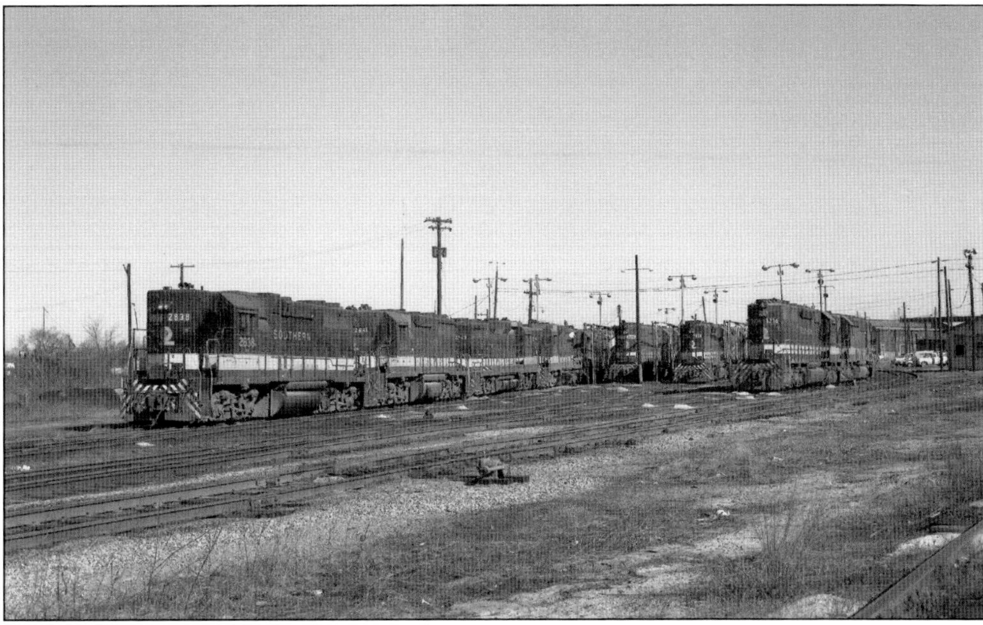

The fuel tracks at Spencer on January 28, 1978, illustrate the different EMD locomotives the Southern Railway used through North Carolina: GP-30s, GP-38-2s, SD-40-2s, and SD-45s. (Photograph by Robert Graham.)

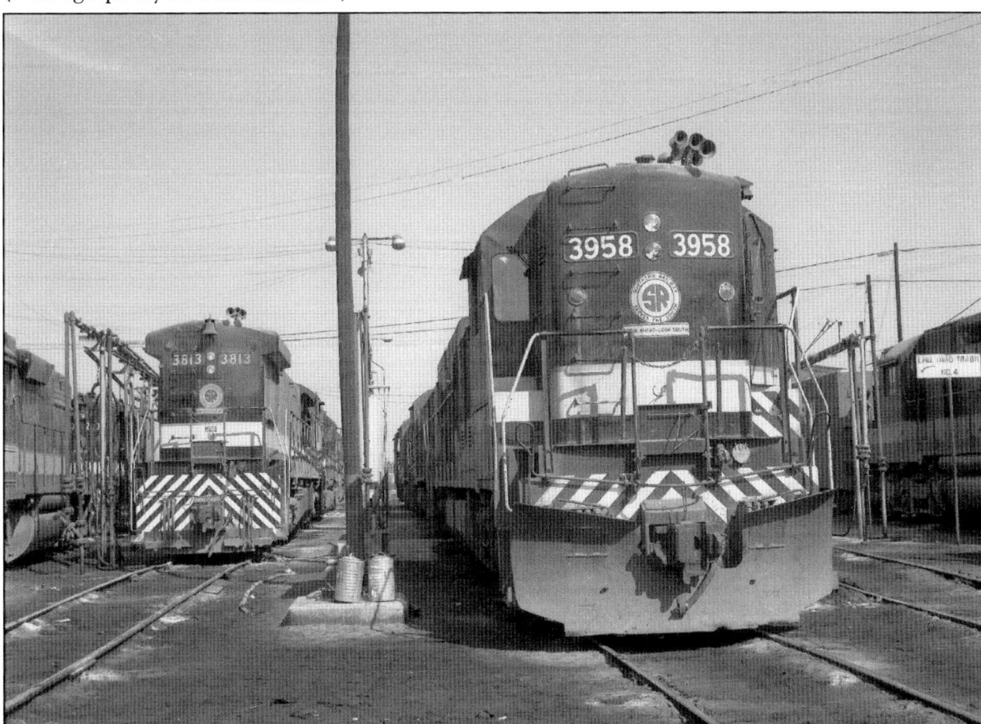

The Southern also operated General Electric locomotives through Spencer Yard, including U33C 3813 and U23B 3958. This photograph was taken on November 5, 1978. (Photograph by Robert Graham.)

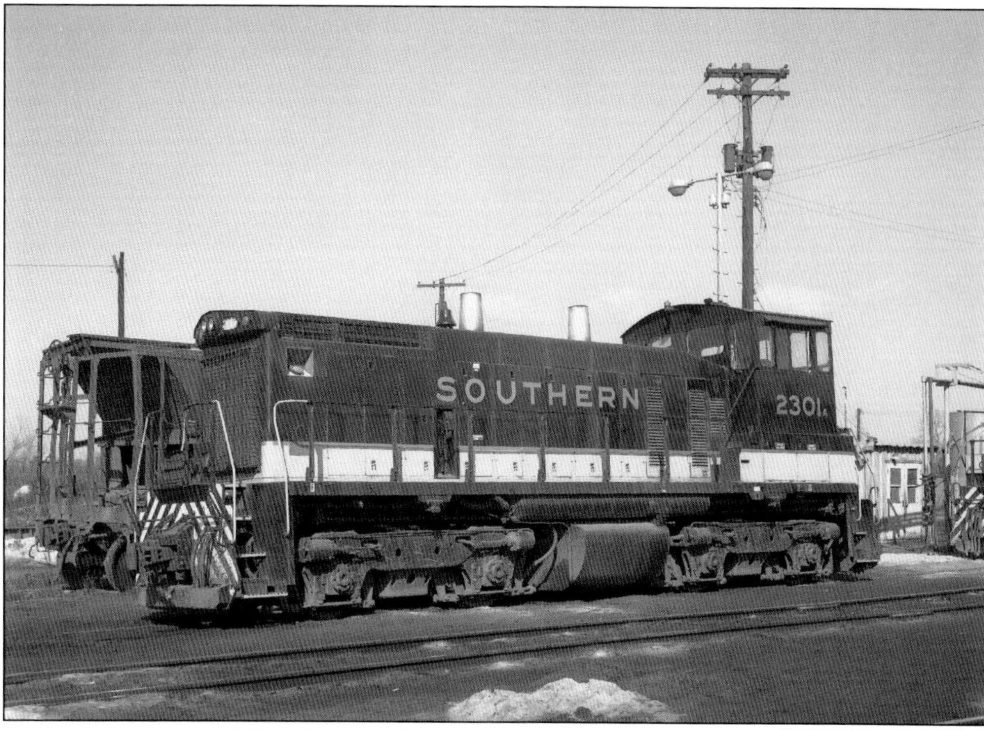

The Southern acquired SW-1500 switch locomotives from EMD in 1968 to replace older switch locomotives built in the 1940s. No. 2301 sits in the fuel tracks in Spencer on January 29, 1979, beside a hopper converted for sand service. These hoppers were used to transport sand to locomotive service facilities across the Southern Railway system. (Photograph by Robert Graham.)

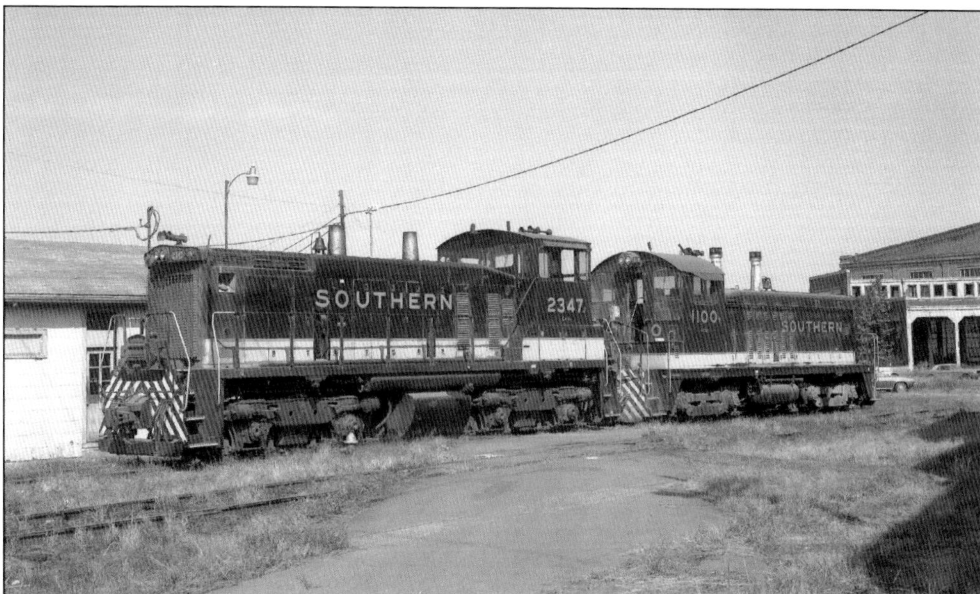

The last Southern SW-1500, No. 2347, is coupled to SW-7 No. 1100 beside the yard office at Spencer on February 4, 1979. These switch locomotives were used for yard service or to move locomotives to the roundhouse for servicing. (Photograph by Robert Graham.)

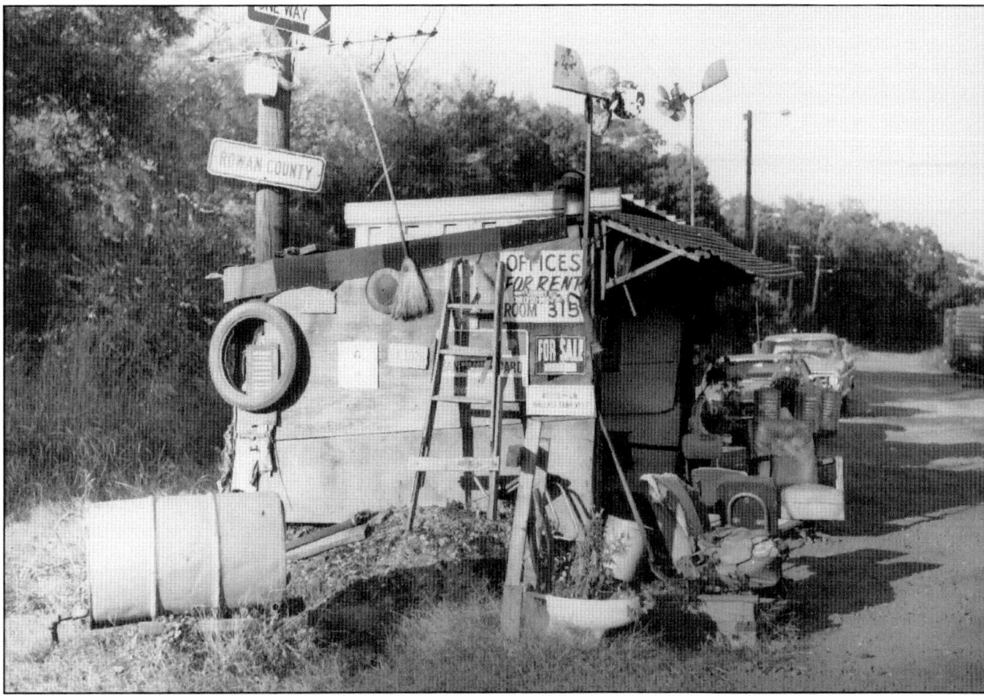

The crew's yard shanty, near Eleventh Street in Salisbury, definitely had plenty of character during the 1970s. Eleventh Street, at the south end of Spencer Yard, was the location used by the Southern to swap crews and locomotives on freight trains. Norfolk Southern still uses a modern building in this location today. (Photograph by Marvin Rogers.)

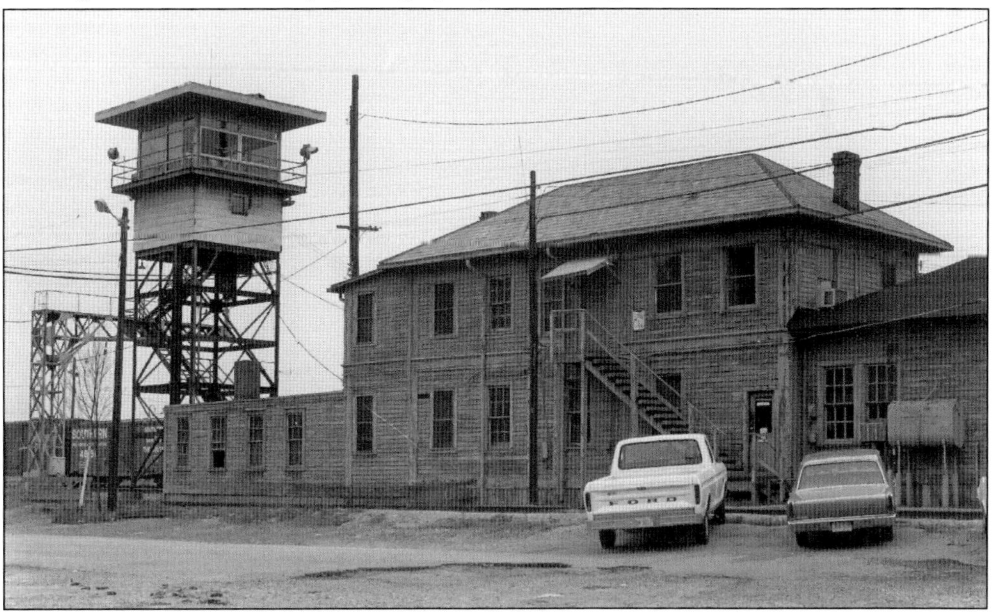

Spencer Yard still used the older two-story yard office in the mid-1970s, alongside the modern yard tower constructed for better visibility across the yard. The tower was located between the main freight classification yard and the smaller yard near the transfer sheds. (Photograph by Marvin Rogers.)

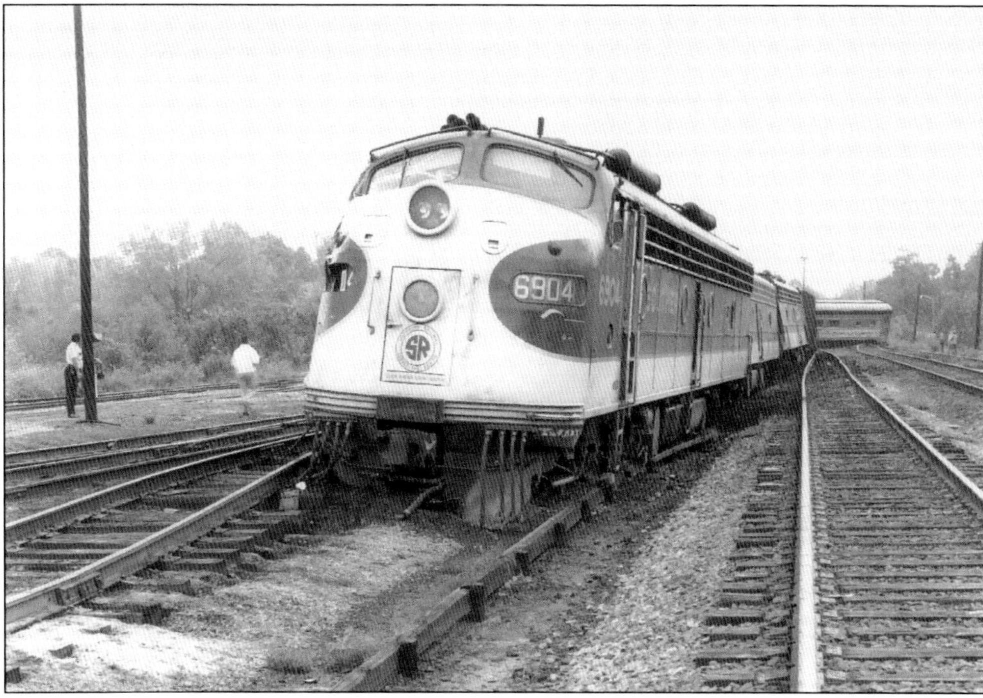

The *Southern Crescent* passenger train No. 1 derailed at Spencer Yard on October 8, 1977, and sideswiped several freight cars. All four E-8 locomotives, 6904, 6907, 6903, and 6900, were damaged, along with several passenger cars. (Photographs by Marvin Rogers.)

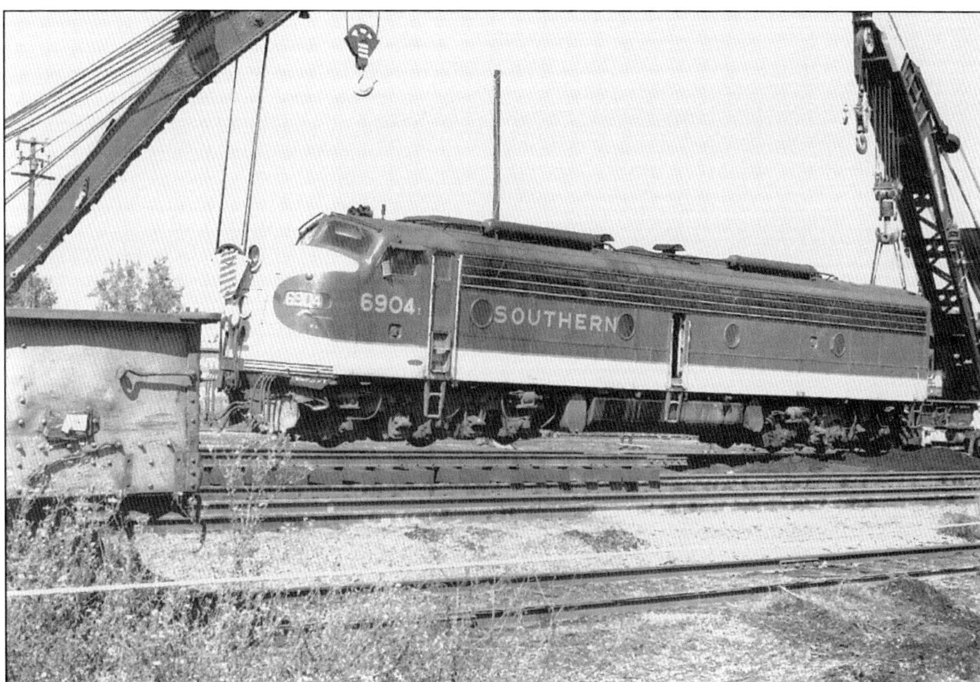

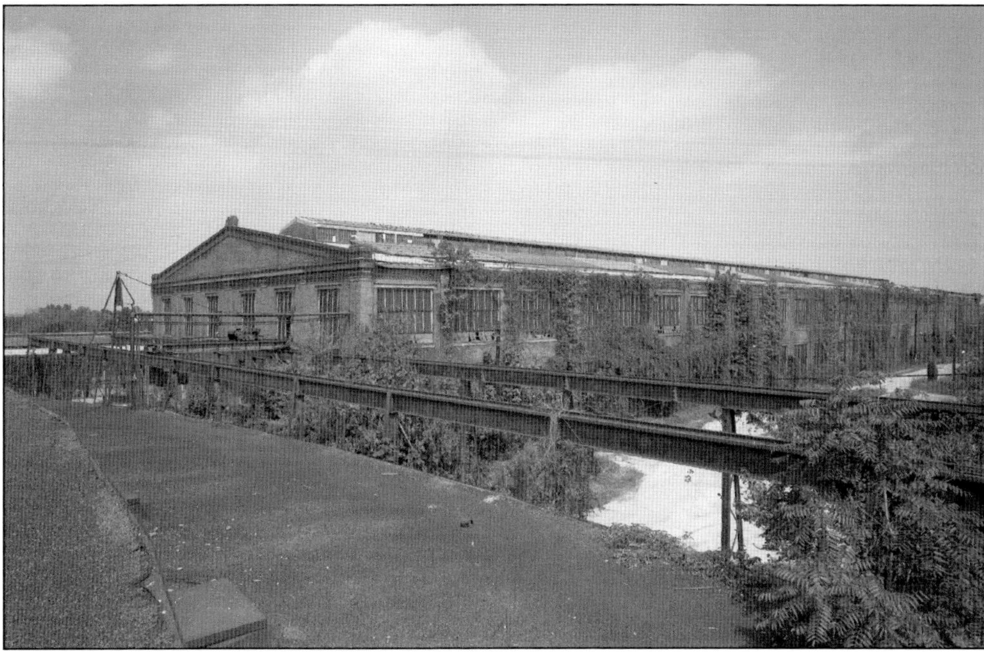

These photographs, which belongs to the State of North Carolina, document the remaining Spencer Shops buildings in 1977 during talks with the Southern Railway to preserve the facility as a historic site. The next few pages show the decayed state of the buildings after 17 years of inactivity. This page shows the back shop, as viewed from the roundhouse roof, and the north end beside the powerhouse and master mechanic's office. (Both, North Carolina State Archives.)

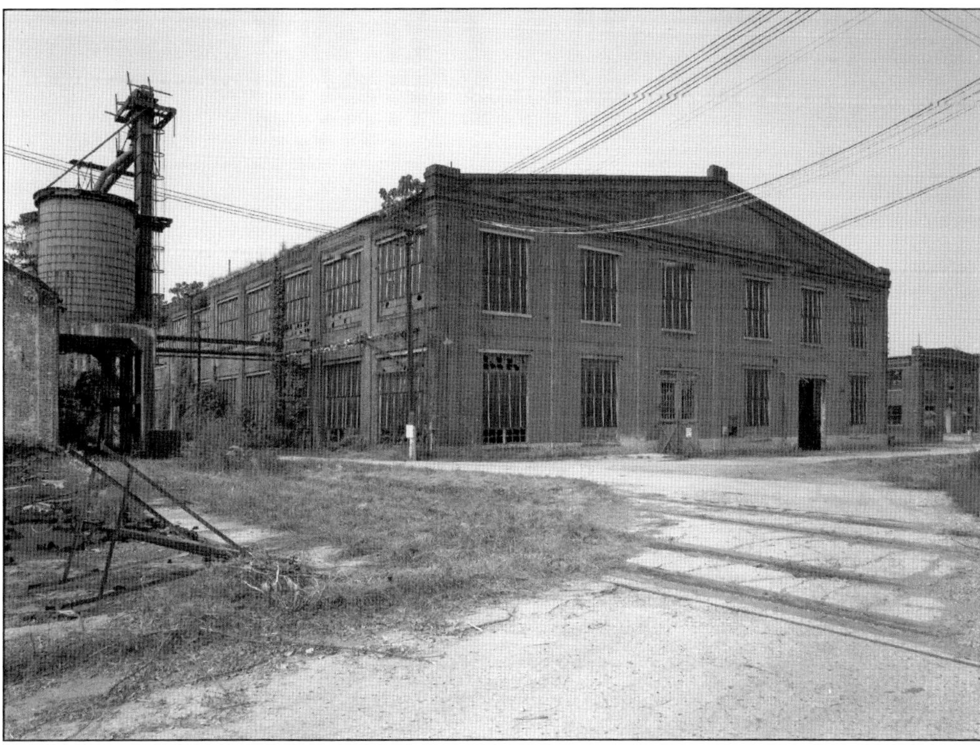

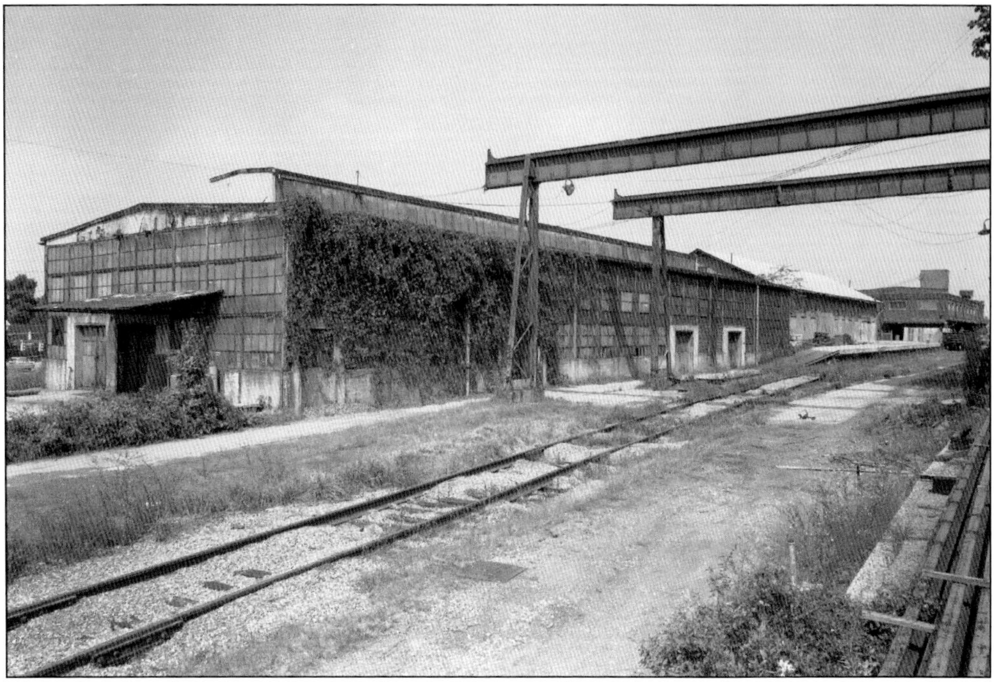

The photograph above shows the flue shop, gantry crane rails, warehouse No. 3, and the rear of the master mechanic's office. The photograph below shows the front of the master mechanic's office, which was receiving some window work on the lower level. This block of buildings was among the first donated to the State of North Carolina in 1977. (Both, North Carolina State Archives.)

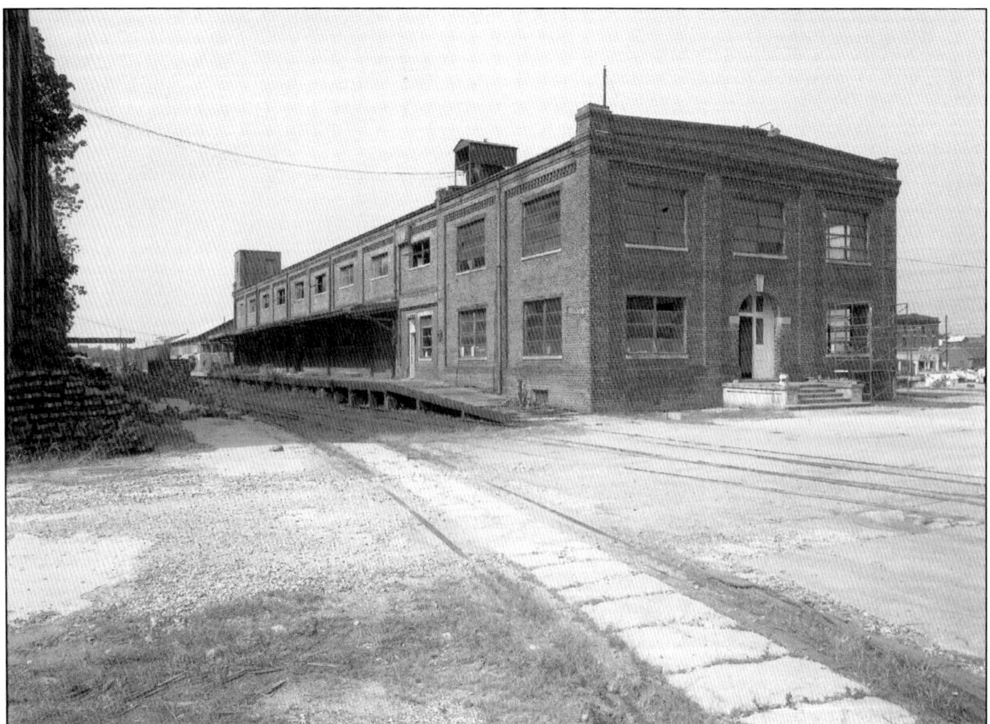

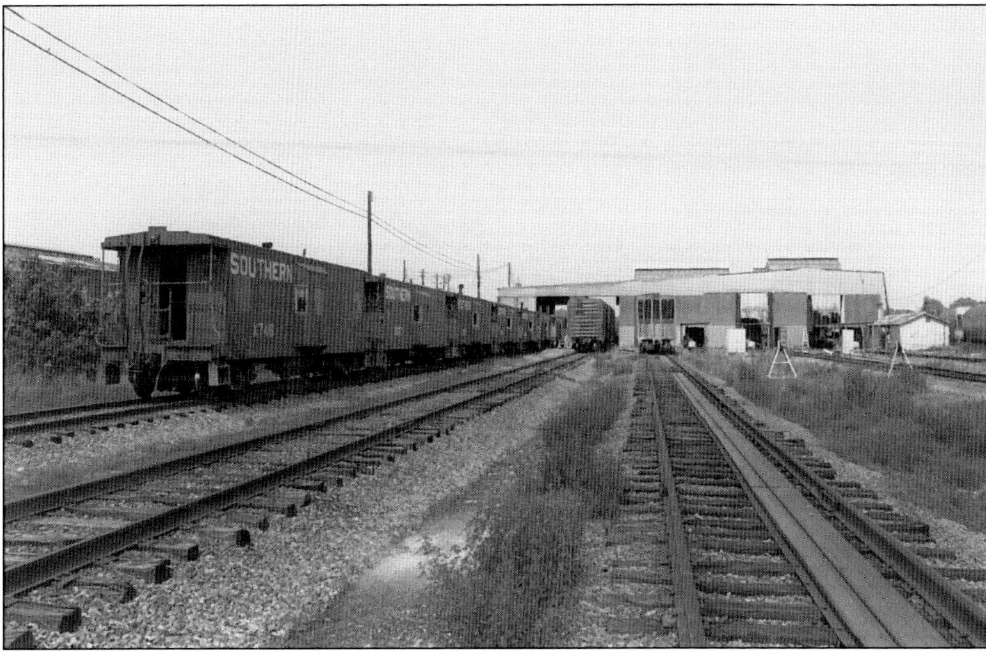

The Southern donated the remainder of the 57 acres for the North Carolina Transportation Museum in 1979 after the opening of Linwood Terminal. Buildings donated in 1979 included the car repair shed (above) and the oil house (below). Both of the photographs were taken in 1977, while the buildings were still used by the Southern. (Both, North Carolina State Archives.)

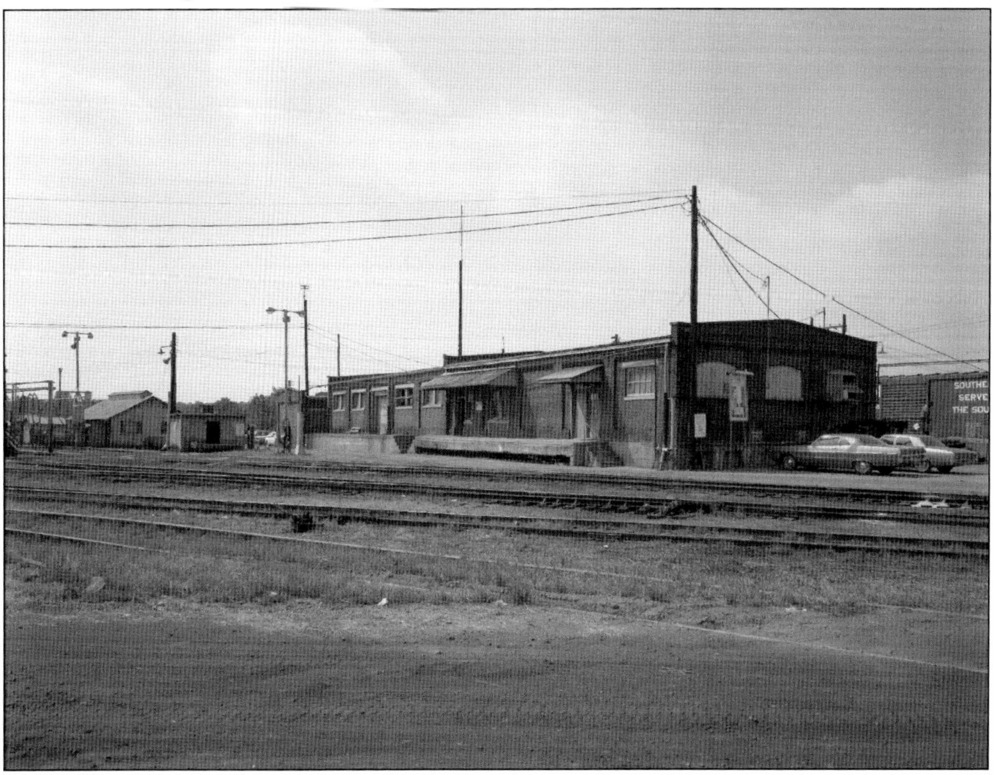

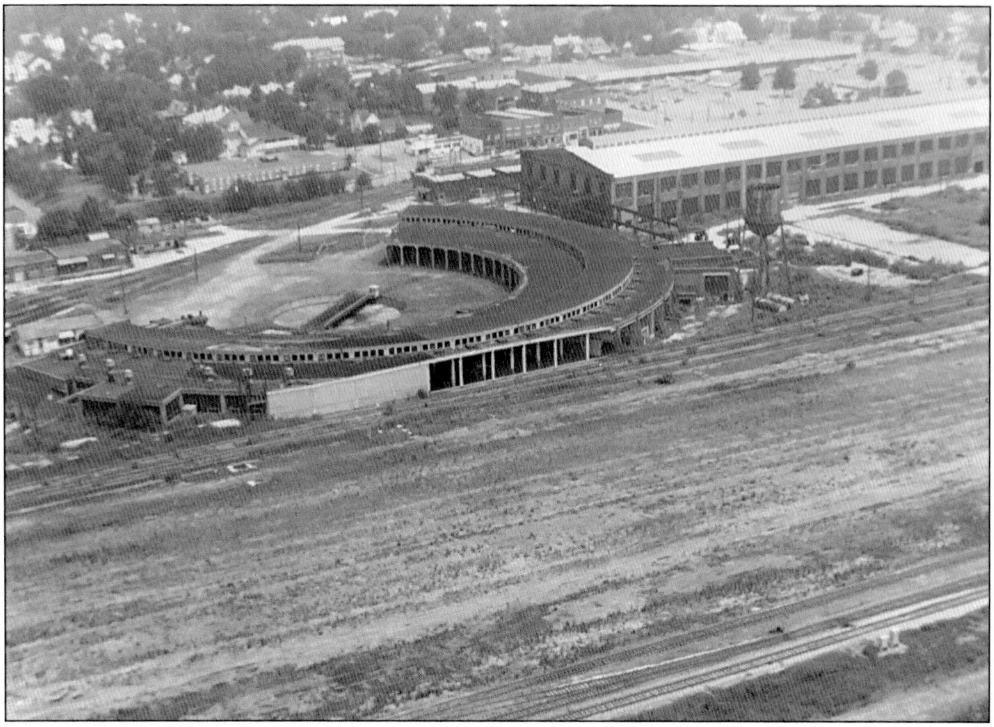

The State of North Carolina started removing vegetation and debris from the shop buildings after the donation in 1977 and opened the first public exhibit in 1983. These aerial images show the buildings around 1980, not long after the freight classification yard was removed. Some museum passenger equipment is being stored in front of the master mechanic's office. (Both, North Carolina Division of Archives and History.)

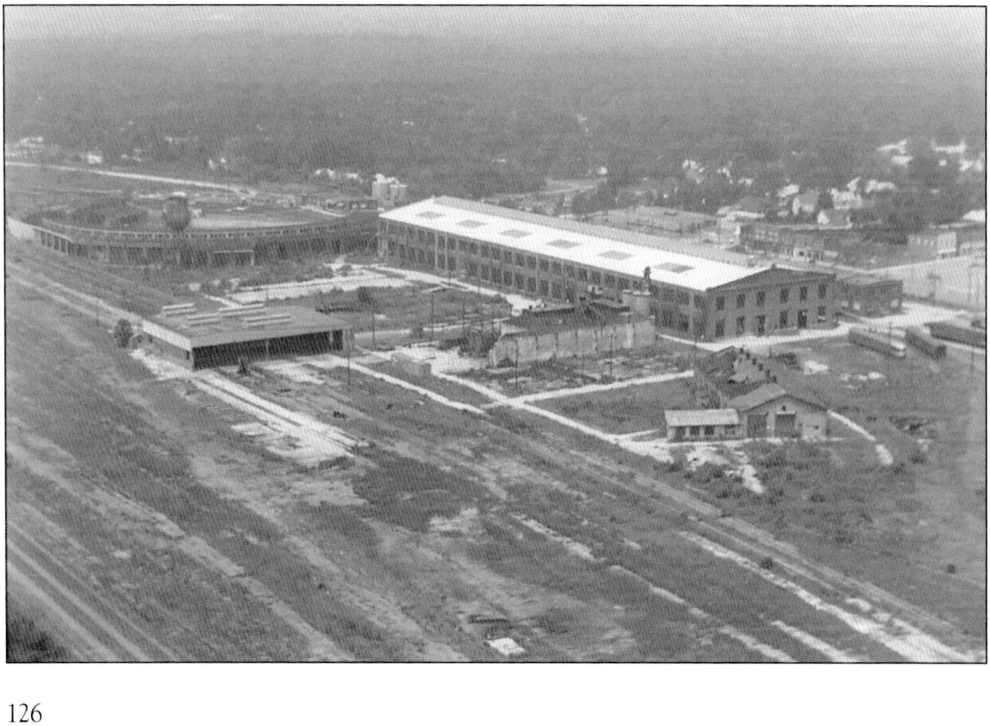

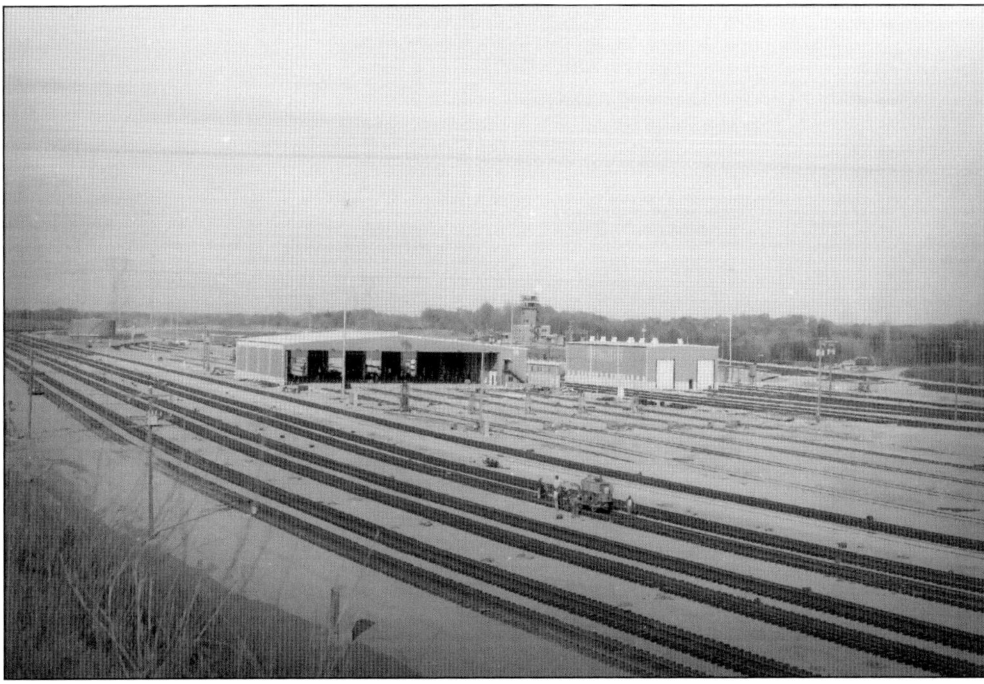

The new Spencer Yard, later called Linwood Terminal, opened in the fall of 1979. The facility was built from the ground up at a cost of $48 million. The small building with the white doors is used for locomotive servicing, and the large open building is used for freight car repair. This yard is the dividing point between the north and south operating districts of Norfolk Southern's Piedmont Division. (Photographs by Marvin Rogers.)

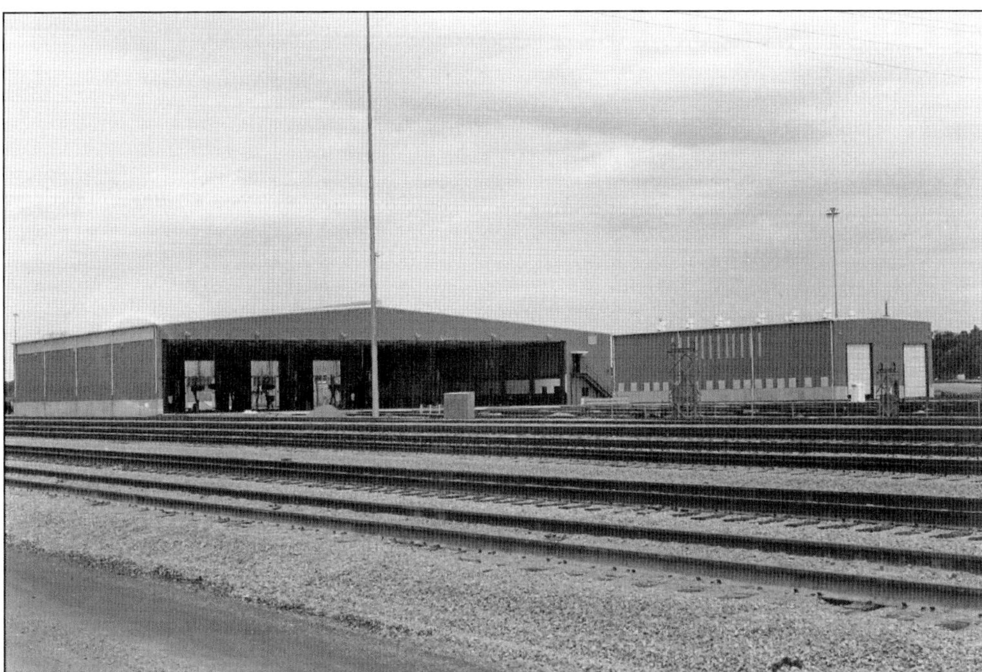

Discover Thousands of Local History Books Featuring Millions of Vintage Images

Arcadia Publishing, the leading local history publisher in the United States, is committed to making history accessible and meaningful through publishing books that celebrate and preserve the heritage of America's people and places.

Find more books like this at
www.arcadiapublishing.com

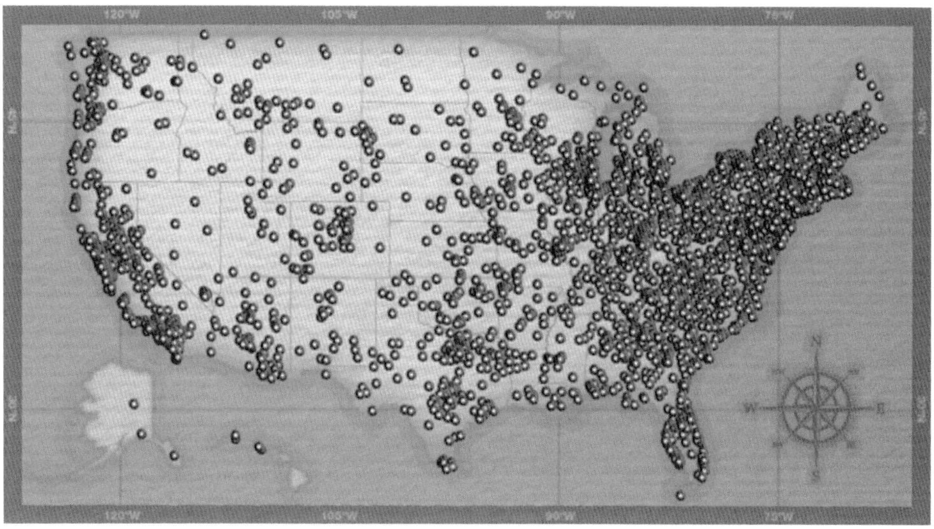

Search for your hometown history, your old stomping grounds, and even your favorite sports team.

Consistent with our mission to preserve history on a local level, this book was printed in South Carolina on American-made paper and manufactured entirely in the United States. Products carrying the accredited Forest Stewardship Council (FSC) label are printed on 100 percent FSC-certified paper.

MADE IN THE USA